D0090544

STEALING AMERICA

STEALING AMERICA

WHAT MY EXPERIENCE WITH CRIMINAL
GANGS TAUGHT ME ABOUT OBAMA,
HILLARY, AND THE DEMOCRATIC PARTY

DINESH D'SOUZA

BROADSIDE BOOKS
An Imprint of HarperCollinsPublishers

HarperCollins books may be purchased for educational, business, or sales promotional use. For information, please e-mail the Special Markets Department at SPsales@harpercollins.com.

Broadside Books™ and the Broadside logo are trademarks of HarperCollins Publishers.

FIRST EDITION

Library of Congress Cataloging-in-Publication Data has been applied for.

ISBN: 978-0-06-236671-9

15 16 17 18 19 DIX/RRD 10 9 8 7 6 5 4 3 2 1

FOR DEBBIE FANCHER,
Immigrant, patriot, and the woman I love

CONTENTS

STEALING AMERICA

A NOTE TO THE READER

The language spoken in a confinement center is extremely coarse. Hardly a sentence is uttered that does not contain obscenities. There is no way to convey the sense of place and even the meaning of what convicts are saying without using some of this language. Out of respect for the reader, I've scaled it way back and used asterisks to bowdlerize the most offensive words.

Chapter 1

CRIME AND PUNISHMENT:

How They Taught Me a Lesson

If a man wishes to be sure of the road he's traveling on, then he must close his eyes and travel in the dark.[1]

—John of the Cross, *Dark Night of the Soul*

The mood in the courtroom was tense and electric as I entered, accompanied by my superstar lawyer Benjamin Brafman and another attorney, Alex Spiro. We were in the Daniel Patrick Moynihan United States Courthouse in lower Manhattan, the offices of Judge Richard Berman. Brafman, with his elegant locks of hair brushed back, looked completely at home in this environment. I, on the other hand, was not.

I tried to look nonchalant, or at least expressionless. Inside, however, my heart was pounding with terror. In a very short time I'd know if I was headed to federal prison. My crime? I had exceeded the campaign finance laws by convincing two of my friends to contribute $10,000 apiece to a candidate for the U.S. Senate from New York; then

I reimbursed them for their contribution. For this—I subsequently discovered—I could be prosecuted as a felon and sent away for up to two years. I had already pleaded guilty to the charge. Now I was going to find out whether the judge would give me a prison sentence.

My greatest fear was not prison itself. At Brafman's suggestion, I had hired a criminologist with extensive experience in the various federal prison camps. "If you get prison," this fellow told me, "it's going to be a white-collar camp, most likely Taft or Lompoc in California. You're going to be surrounded by accountants, lawyers, dentists, bureaucrats. All the others in there have proven themselves through good behavior. These are nonviolent criminals, just like you."

That part—the "just like you"—jolted me. I almost didn't hear the rest. "You'll have to work part-time, but you'll have lots of free time. There is little contact with the outside world. No cell phones and no laptops. But you can send emails from a general computer that is monitored, and you can make three hundred minutes of phone calls per month, also monitored. That's not much, but you'll get used to it. Taft, the camp I'd recommend for you, has pretty good facilities, a gym, a running track, a tennis court. You're a writer, so do a lot of reading and writing. I'll help to prepare you for what to expect. If you stay busy, and use common sense, you'll be fine."

Fine? I took that as an exaggeration. Even if there was little danger of being stabbed or raped, how can someone who is locked up for two years, without a phone and a laptop, and such limited contact with the outside world, be fine? My deepest fears were over my nineteen-year-old daughter. She, I knew, would be devastated. I had recently gone through a difficult divorce and unfortunately my daughter's relationship with her mother had been, at least temporarily, severed. Even though my daughter was now in college, in terms of immediate family, I was all she had.

I was accompanied by a few close friends, and two sympathetic journalists, the seasoned veteran Jerome Corsi from WorldNetDaily, and a young reporter for Breitbart News, Adelle Nazarian. Nazarian said she was an immigrant from Iran and understood where I was coming from politically. Most of the crowd was hostile. The liberal press was there in force, from the staid *New York Times* to the rabid *Daily News*. The reporters are so young, I thought to myself, and how delighted they look at the prospect of me being sent away. These people hated me because I was a person of color who was also a conservative. They had regarded me as a race-traitor, an enemy of the people. Jonathan Capehart, a blogger for the *Washington Post*, opined that "Dinesh D'Souza is a disgusting man. . . . D'Souza should be in jail where he would no longer be able to assault the rest of us with his special brand of racist bile."[2] For guys like Capehart, I was about to get my comeuppance and they were about to get their schadenfreude.

In the back of the room, I even had a critic from the evangelical right: I noticed the sly reporter from *World* magazine there to continue that publication's long-standing vendetta against me. She avoided my gaze. Brafman told me the men walking around with badges were from the government's prosecution unit. I noticed their smug expressions, anticipating victory, as if my incarceration were a foregone conclusion. There were also a few ordinary folk who had read about my case and came out of curiosity.

My attention focused on the prosecutor, Carrie H. Cohen, a woman with an enduringly haggard and harassed expression, as if life has done her wrong. From two previous court hearings, I knew she was brash and abrasive. Carrie never shook my hand and she avoided eye contact with me; I got the impression she considered me, like all defendants, to be vermin. She also had an irritating habit of referring to herself as the Government. "The Government does not agree." "Your honor, the Government will prove . . ." "The Government takes objection." Meanwhile, I'm thinking, Who elected this woman? She reminded me of Inspector Javert from *Les Misérables*. Of course I kept these thoughts to myself. I asked Brafman's associate Alex Spiro, "How important a case is this for her?" He said, "For Carrie? Oh, this is a career case. This could make or break her career." Carrie, I realized, badly wanted me in prison so that her career could advance.

I knew that Carrie was a stooge, an enforcer for people higher up than her. The most important people—her boss, an Asian-Indian federal prosecutor named Preet Bharara, and his boss, the attorney general Eric Holder—were not in the courtroom. Also absent was the biggest boss of them all, the president of the United States, Barack Obama. That trio, I knew, would all take a considerable interest in the outcome of my sentencing.

My thoughts were interrupted by a loud voice in the courtroom. "United States versus Dinesh D'Souza." What a phrase! I winced. "Please stand for Judge Berman." The buzz quickly subsided. In sauntered Judge Berman, fully robed and looking solemn as usual, his head bobbing from side to side like an old family horse. Behind the judge came three of his clerks. Slowly, ceremoniously, the judge took his seat. The clerks planted themselves in chairs against the wall.

Then began what I am going to call my official castigation.[3] Normally sentencing is a perfunctory business, but not this day. The judge gave me a verbal flaying from the bench that lasted for the better part of an hour. During this time the clerks watched with evident bemusement; they seemed to enjoy watching their man carry out a ritual flogging.

The judge insisted I had "willfully and knowingly" violated the law. He added, "Mr. D'Souza's crime is serious." One of the purposes of punishment, he suggested, is to discourage others from committing similar violations. "The public certainly needs to be deterred . . . from making phony contributions and violating the election laws." I took this to mean I was going to be punished not just for what I did but also to send a message of discouragement to the general public.

The judge then rejected any suggestion—either by me or my lawyers—that I was being selectively prosecuted because of my public criticism of the Obama administration. That claim had been widely circulated in the media, especially the conservative media. For Berman, however, making an interesting deviation into Texas terminology, it was "all hat, no cattle." Referring to my public statement that "we don't want to live in a society where Lady Justice removes her blindfold and winks at her friends and targets her enemies," the judge opined that

"I'm totally confident that Lady Justice is doing her job and that she's not taking off her blindfold to target Dinesh D'Souza." There were mild titters from the audience. Leftist reporters, bloggers, and photographers were in a very good mood this morning.

Things did not improve from there; they actually got worse. At Brafman's suggestion, I had submitted to the judge some two dozen or so letters from family members and others, including some prominent liberals, testifying to my good character. Alluding to them, the judge sounded dismissive. "The court receives packages of letters of support not unlike those submitted in this case in virtually every criminal case, including one I received just the other day where a defendant had pled guilty to a conspiracy to commit a Hobbs act robbery of drugs involving fake police uniforms, badges, police car sirens, and the possession of two guns to be used in connection with the robbery conspiracy." The judge added that "someone wrote in his behalf to me, 'I have known the defendant'—who, by the way had five prior convictions—'for almost twenty years now. To be honest, throughout all the many years of knowing him, he's always been a loving, kind, well-mannered, dedicated, hard-working, respectful young man.' "

The judge seemed to be in a Freudian cast of mind, a psychological disposition I attributed partly to his former tenure as a family court judge. The letters I had submitted, the judge said, simply couldn't explain why I, "a successful, famous political commentator, author, lecturer and film-maker at the pinnacle of his success, would commit an election law felony." In other words, why would I do something so self-destructive? "That's taking a staggering, enormous risk."

The judge proceeded to play on the courtroom TV a recent interview I had done. I could see Brafman scratching his head, and even others in the courtroom seemed puzzled. This did not seem a normal thing for a judge to do. I found it strange to see myself on the screen in that bizarre setting. The sentencing was beginning to take on the character of a "show trial," which I knew would not be altogether displeasing to the leftists in the courtroom. I wondered if I was going to get prison time for something injudicious that I said in a TV interview.

But as I listened to myself, I didn't detect anything incriminating—no smoking gun. I had pointed out to the interviewer how liberal offenders who had done far worse things than I were not even investigated, much less prosecuted. I said I believed I was being selectively targeted and that I would not be intimidated into silence by the Obama administration. My host was entirely convinced, but not Judge Berman. In fact, the judge seemed annoyed to hear me speaking a lot. "He is a talker," he remarked. "In fact, he's almost a compulsive talker. I don't think he's a listener." Hm, I'm thinking, I am on a talk show! And as a writer and speaker, I do actually talk for a living! In this respect, my profession isn't so dissimilar from yours, Your Honor!

Once again, these thoughts stayed within the corridors of my mind. Judge Berman continued his critical commentary: "Mr. D'Souza, having every right to be interviewed, continues to defeat and minimize the significance of the crime and of his behavior by reference to other people, other issues, and other events, including by reference to President Obama." He added, "The campaign law offense and much of the inaccurate chatter and interviews surrounding this case do not promote respect for the law and need to be remedied." Finally he said, "I'm not sure, Mr. D'Souza, that you get it. And it's still hard for me to discern any personal acceptance of responsibility in this case."

Yes, acceptance of responsibility. Of course I accepted responsibility, but it seemed that the judge—and he wasn't the only one—was looking for something else. He wasn't satisfied with contrition over what I did; he wanted contrition for who I was. Moreover, he seemed eager for some sort of a display; he was looking for abject humiliation, for tearful confession, for recantation and apology. I wondered what would happen if I delivered what he wanted, and concluded my remarks by saying that I had now become a liberal. Would everyone applaud and allow me to go home, my earlier misdeeds forgotten and forgiven?

I would rather go to jail, I resolved, than participate in a show-trial "conversion." I would not apologize for my public criticism of the Obama administration. And if that's what you want, Judge Berman, then take a hike!

Listening to this judicial diatribe, which I found almost surreal, my mind flashed back to the scene of the crime. It was, in fact, my office at the King's College, in New York. My friend Wendy Long, whom I've known since my days at Dartmouth, was running for the U.S. Senate in New York. I had urged her not to run, because she had no experience in electoral politics. "It's a brutal business," I had told Wendy, "and I fear it will break your wings." But she was adamant—she didn't think raising money would be a big problem—so I told her that if she decided to go for it, I would help her.

In March 2012, I gave Wendy $10,000. This, she told me, was the campaign finance limit. I also agreed to let Wendy's campaign use my name on its fundraising literature. But as the months went on, Wendy urged me to do more for the campaign. Hey, Dinesh, can you speak at a fundraiser on the Upper East Side? Would you come to Westchester to talk to some donors? Can you have dinner with a group of Indian doctors who might donate to the campaign? I wanted to help, but I was frenetically promoting my film *2016: Obama's America*. As much as I adore Wendy, I found it virtually impossible to do any of those things.

I was walking by my assistant's desk one afternoon in August when he informed me, "Wendy called. She has something to ask you." Wanting to do more for her campaign, I got an idea. I asked my assistant, "Do you like Wendy? Do you support her candidacy?" He said, "Sure. You know I do." I said, "Would you be willing to give her ten thousand dollars if I then reimbursed you?" He agreed. And then I approached another friend of mine and made the same arrangement. It was done. I was relieved. I knew I was getting around the campaign finance limit, but not for a moment did I consider I was breaking the law.

Wendy lost the November 2012 election, as most people expected. Life goes on, and 2013 seemed to bring new challenges and opportunities: I started work on a new book and accompanying film, *America: Imagine a World Without Her*.

Then, one fine day, as I was walking through Central Park, I got a phone call from a friend saying that the FBI approached him and was asking questions about me. "Something about a campaign finance violation," he said. I was initially nonplused: what had I done? Then I remembered. Oh, that? Was that it?

I walked back to my apartment. Two FBI agents were waiting for me. I had always had the image of FBI agents as tall, intimidating guys wearing sunglasses. These two were puny kids, both in their late twenties or early thirties. And no sunglasses! Of course, I didn't speak to them. I told them I was going to get a lawyer. They gave me their business cards and left. They could not have been more polite.

I called a lawyer I knew in California. I told him about the FBI at my door. He said, "Wait. I'm not sure what you've done, but they are coming after you. So listen very carefully. Go out and rent a storage cabinet. Then collect your passport, your important files and papers, the books that you need for the next few months, and your laptop and other electronic devices. Get them out of your apartment and into the storage unit. You are likely to be arrested, probably soon, and when you do they may search your apartment and put everything they want into boxes, and you won't get those boxes back for several months. So whatever you need to get your work done, take it out of there now.

"You are going to need a criminal lawyer. Get Ben Brafman—he's one of the best criminal lawyers in the country. He's represented Michael Jackson, the rapper P. Diddy, bigwig CEOs and politicos. He just saved the head of the IMF, Dominique Strauss-Kahn. Do you know the case? The guy was staying in a New York hotel and the maid—Somali, I think—who cleaned his room accused him of raping her. Turns out the woman knew who he was, and was trying to get money out of him. It was an extortion deal, and Brafman exposed it. Yeah, Brafman's your man. He's a liberal Democrat—I feel I should tell you that—but don't let that deter you. He's the best you can get. I met him at a conference years ago, and when we hang up, I'm going to call him and tell him about you. So wait an hour and then contact his office for an appointment, okay?"

A few hours later, I was in Brafman's office, talking to the man himself. Right away I liked Brafman's straightforwardness. "Tell me what you did." And after I did, he asked me, "Did Wendy know about this?"

I said, "No." He said, "Good." Then he summed up my predicament: "What you did is illegal. That is unfortunate. What is more unfortunate is that you are a smart fellow, and you have committed one of the stupidest crimes in the history of American jurisprudence." What made it so stupid, Brafman explained, was that it was so unnecessary.

Brafman explained that there was a legal way for me to have given Wendy money. I could have given through a PAC, or political action committee—which is the way people give thousands, even millions, to benefit their favored candidates, Republican or Democrat. Heavy hitters like George Soros and the Koch brothers have figured out ways to contribute even larger sums, running into the tens of millions. And PACs are what liberal donors use when they sign up for those $25,000-a-plate fundraisers for Obama or Hillary. Brafman concluded that my problem wasn't that I gave too much; it was that I gave in the wrong way. As he said, and I couldn't help but agree, this was very dumb of me.

Brafman asked me how the U.S. government found out. I told him, "I have no idea. I don't see how they could have." At one point, Wendy confessed to me that she was having trouble with some of her campaign consultants. One in particular had become disgruntled and threatened to harm her and anyone close to her. I explained to Brafman how these things happen. Failed campaigns are often unable to settle their bills, and high-priced consultants who have been working for those campaigns don't like this. Of course they should realize this is a risk of doing business with a campaign—every campaign has a winner and a loser. Even so, vindictiveness and recriminations are not unheard-of, because political operators are not known for their *c'est la vie* sensibilities. I suggested to Brafman that perhaps one such operator told the authorities, to get back at Wendy.

I alerted Brafman to a second, more likely, possibility: the government was spying on me. This possibility could not be discounted, because the U.S. government was pretty much spying on everyone. What began as a surveillance of suspected terrorists had metastasized into a surveillance of American citizens who are not suspected of terrorism or any other crime. I told him that the chances that I might have appeared on the surveillance roster, however, were increased because of my public criticism of one particular individual.

Shortly after my film *2016* played in theaters, a vituperative attack on me appeared on the website barackobama.com. The article, unsigned, was strident and incoherent, in keeping with Obama's distinctive style. My film, it said, was a "deliberate distortion" produced by a guy with a "long history of attempting to add a veneer of intellectual respectability to fringe theories, conspiratorial fear-mongering and flat-out falsehoods."[4] Anyone reading this fulmination would have little doubt I had upset the thin-skinned narcissist.

Brafman's eyebrows shot up. "Are you saying that you were personally attacked by the president of the United States?" I said, "Yes." And opening up my computer, I showed him the article. "Amazing," he said. "I have never heard of anything like this." I told Brafman about how I had penetrated Obama's world, showing up at his family homestead in Kenya, interviewing his brother George in the Huruma slum of Nairobi. "One thing I found out about Obama since I began to study him," I said, "is that he's a petty, vindictive guy, cut from the same mold as his petty, vindictive father."

I confessed I had infuriated the most powerful man in the world, the man at the head of a formidable empire, and I guess this might be a case of the empire striking back. I felt no pride in telling Brafman any of this; on the contrary, I felt like an idiot. Here I was, a conspicuous public critic of the Obama administration, giving Obama and his minions in the Justice Department just what they needed: a pretext to go after me.

Brafman then gave me the silver lining. "You have come to the right place," he said. "I know those guys in the prosecution unit very well. Let me talk to them and help them to see the light." Brafman said that there were several facts in my favor. First, this wasn't a corruption case. I hadn't given the money to get something out of it; I had given purely out of friendship. Second, I wasn't even realistically trying to swing an election: as far as he could see, Wendy never had any chance to win, and lost by a landslide. Third, I was not a professional political fundraiser or campaign bundler. Fourth, I had no prior criminal record. Bottom line, Brafman said, "I think I can convince those guys to let you off with a warning and a fine. That's the normal solution for something like this."

I wanted Brafman so I asked him what his fee was. He told me, and I tried not to show my astonishment. There goes my retirement, I thought to myself. It was a bitter joke, one that I didn't share with Brafman. He must have read my mind. "It's a flat fee," he said. "There will be no other costs." I liked that part, the flat fee. "I'm good with it," I said. This was not a time for me to negotiate. Brafman said he would send me a contract. I left his office feeling very lighthearted. Perhaps this was something I could quickly put behind me.

Wishful thinking. Brafman returned from his meeting with the prosecutors, and he was visibly puzzled. "I told them that you admit making the contributions. I told them you are willing to take responsibility for that. They are still determined to prosecute you to the full extent of the law," he said. "They want a felony conviction. They may ask for prison time. I don't get it." I reminded Brafman that I was not on Obama's Christmas card list. No, Brafman said, that can't possibly be it. This had nothing to do with Obama. "This call was not made in Washington, it was made in New York. Preet Bharara is the one who made the call."

I had heard of Bharara. He was a *desi*—a fellow Asian Indian. A former staffer for Democratic senator Chuck Schumer, Bharara was known to be smart, ambitious, cautious, and ruthless. Based on recent news reports he seemed to take a particular relish in going after Asian Indians. He had arrested an Indian diplomat for bringing in a domestic servant from India and then not paying her the minimum wage. The woman said that since she was a diplomat and the maid wasn't a U.S. citizen, she was not covered by minimum wage laws. Bharara decided to show her who was boss. So he had her brought in and strip-searched. This wasn't the ordinary pat-down but the more extensive, and degrading, "cavity search." Even the Indian prime minister at the time, Manmohan Singh, spoke out against Bharara's "deplorable conduct." But Bharara shamelessly defended this action as standard security practice.[5]

Now, any Indian knows what it does to a woman's dignity to make her take off her clothes and to reach into the most private parts of her body. And what was Bharara's purpose? This was not a terrorism case; surely the woman didn't have weapons concealed in her private parts. This was about employing a maid. When I read this I understood Bharara. This is a man of a familiar Indian type, basically a thug who knows how to dress up his thuggery with the costume of bureaucratic routines and procedures. An Indian friend from New York summed up Bharara pretty succinctly: "This is a man with the soul of an East German border guard." I told Brafman, "It might be Bharara, but I suspect that Bharara is getting his instructions from higher up."

"I don't think so," Brafman responded. He speculated that maybe they were going after me because I was a "high-profile individual." But I pointed out to him that over the past several decades many high-profile individuals had done things far worse, and gotten away with them. Bill Ayers, for example, was involved in up to twenty terrorist bombings and yet he didn't get prison time. In fact, when I debated him, he joked with me that his slogan had become "Guilty as hell, free as a bird." I continued to insist that I was being selectively prosecuted, but Brafman remained unconvinced.

I was indicted on two charges: exceeding the campaign finance limit, and causing the government to record a false document. The second charge basically arose out of the same action as the first. By reimbursing two friends, I caused them to fill out their names, rather than my name, on the form they submitted. Since I was the actual donor, I had caused them to file, and the government to record, a false document. "They are using the second charge," Brafman said, "to pressure you to plead guilty to the first charge. But we have to take both of them seriously." Brafman explained that while the first charge carried a maximum of two years in prison, the second one carried a maximum five-year prison term. I could hardly believe I was hearing this. Was my offense so heinous as to require locking me up in federal prison for that long?

By mutual agreement with the prosecution, I showed up at the Moynihan U.S. Courthouse for my arrest. The two FBI agents who had showed up at my apartment were there. They handcuffed me behind my back. Then they put me into a car and took me to another building. There I was photographed—the infamous mug shot—and my prints were taken. I also had to give a urine sample. The whole process is tedious and humiliating. It is designed to demoralize you, to break your spirit. When I emerged from the building there were reporters barking questions and cameras flashing. My lawyers and I got into the car and drove away, just like I had seen in the movies. How unreal that this was now part of the script of my life.

Upon my arrest, a judge was assigned to my case: Richard Berman. He was a Clinton appointee to the bench, with a liberal Democratic background. "I haven't tried a case before him," Brafman said, "but I asked around. He has a reputation for being fair." What, I asked, are his politics? "Liberal," Brafman said. "But that's hardly unusual. Most of the judges in the city are liberal. Don't let that worry you." Actually, it did worry me.

Shortly after my arrest, Brafman asked me, "What have you written on the subject of campaign finance law?" I said, "Nothing." Brafman said, "Good. I hope your memory is good about this. The government has a whole bunch of FBI agents working on your case. They will read everything you've ever written. They would love to try and show that you broke the campaign finance law because you have contempt for such laws. Please let me know if you recall something you did write about the subject. I don't want to go into the courtroom unprepared.

"The FBI is all over this case," Brafman said, "and frankly I'm a little pissed." From the files the government was required to turn over to him, Brafman had just learned that the FBI had tried to convince my assistant at the King's College to wear a hidden wire. "Who do they think you are, John Gotti? We have admitted that you made the straw donations. This is totally over-the-top. Completely unprecedented, for a case like this." I could tell that Brafman, who doesn't normally live in the ideological arena, was beginning to entertain the idea that this case might have an ideological dimension. It reminded me of the moment in *All the President's Men* when Woodward and Bernstein realize that the principal malefactor may actually be the president of the United States.

There was more to come. A few weeks into the case, an FBI official was quoted in the media saying my case emerged as a result of a "routine review." Brafman admitted this was odd, because this routine review had apparently yielded a single offender. Later, several Republican senators wrote the FBI director asking for information about this review.[6] They never received a response. I contacted Harvard law professor Alan Dershowitz for his advice. "I know this territory extremely well," Dershowitz said. "What you did is very commonly done in politics, and on a much bigger scale. Have no doubt about it, they are targeting you for your views. I like Obama, and I respect Bharara, but I find what they are doing very troubling and detestable." I told Dershowitz that Brafman was skeptical about the selective prosecution and he said, "I'll talk to him."

By the time Dershowitz talked to him, Brafman was learning some new things on his own. Through his legal research he found out that most election law violations are referred to the Federal Election Commission. The FEC has an equal number of Republican and Democratic commissioners, to ensure that its judgments are nonpartisan. Typically, Brafman said, cases that do not involve corruption are handled as civil rather than criminal matters, and offenders are likely to face fines, not incarceration. "I don't know why your case is being handled so differently," Brafman confessed. "I'm not sure that the discovery of your violation was politically motivated, but I'm beginning to suspect that the decision to prosecute you may be."

Brafman filed a motion with Judge Berman asking for the government's files, so that we could look for evidence of selective prosecution. The judge, however, refused. He said that in order for us to have the files we would have to show evidence of selective prosecution. Our point, of course, was that the evidence was likely to be in those files. The judge was unmoved. At this point I basically had a decision to make: go to trial and take my chances in front of a jury, or plead guilty and rely on the judge to give me a fair sentence.

On the eve of trial, Brafman told me, "I've been talking to the government, and they have assured me that if you plead guilty to the first charge carrying a maximum of two years, they will drop the second charge carrying a maximum of five years."

I recognized the game. This is how prosecutors are able to win cases that they might otherwise lose. They pressure people into giving up a couple of fingers, under the threat that they might otherwise lose an arm and a leg. I pointed this out to Brafman and he said, "How do you think the feds have a conviction rate higher than ninety-five percent?" I knew: that's because they have stacked the odds in their favor.

Brafman said that because my case was so unusual, I had a chance that a jury would refuse to convict, but I should also remember that I was in liberal New York, and so my chances were fifty-fifty at best. Much would depend on the final instructions the judge gave to the jury. I realized that however decent his reputation, I could not risk placing five years of my life in the hands of a liberal Democratic judge. However crazy it may seem, he could imprison me for five years for doing what I did. In that case my supporters might scream, but I would still have to do the time. I decided to plead guilty to the first charge. This put me in the vulnerable position of risking two years in federal prison. But Brafman said that was an extremely remote possibility. "The government wants a conviction," he said. "They aren't trying to ruin your life."

When the government filed its sentencing memo to the judge, however, Brafman discovered that they were very much trying to ruin my life.

The government proposed a sentence of ten to sixteen months. In order to justify this, however, Bharara and his team had to show that other people who violated the law under conditions similar to mine had received comparable sentences. This was actually impossible to show since no person who had done what I did had even been prosecuted, let alone sentenced. So the government pulled a series of cases, all of them involving corruption, and then submitted them in summary form to the judge while leaving out all the facts that would have shown the corruption and thus distinguished those cases from mine.

In *United States v. Jenny Hou and Oliver Pan*, the government pointed out that Hou and Pan had used a straw-donor scheme to give $8,000; Hou got ten months and Pan three months. The government failed to mention that Hou was also convicted of wire fraud, obstruction of justice, and making false statements. Pan too was found guilty of multiple felonies. In *United States v. Joseph Bigica*, the government noted that Bigica had used nineteen straw donors to make $98,600 in illegal contributions and got five years in prison; the government left out that Bigica's contributions were part of an overall criminal scheme involving more than $2.5 million in tax fraud. In *United States v. Marybeth Feiss*, *United States v. Christopher Tigani*, and *United States v. George Tirado & Benjamin Hogan*, the government noted the amounts illegally given and the prison sentences handed down by the courts. The government, however, omitted to reveal that all these cases showed clear corruption: one involved trying to buy influence to secure government contracts, another sought legislative intervention to help a family liquor business, and a third pertained to tobacco company employees giving money for the purpose of influencing cigarette tax legislation.

Obviously these cases and the corresponding penalties handed down in them reflect why the campaign finance laws were passed: to prevent systematic abuse of the election process, and to prevent the corrupt use of money to buy the favor of holders of political office. None of this was involved in my case. What amazed Brafman, however, was the government's willingness to blatantly lie in court documents in order to secure a prison term.

I had my own theory about what was going on behind the scenes. The rumor was that Eric Holder planned to retire, and already there was speculation that Bharara was the leading candidate to succeed him. Pretty much every legal roster had Bharara on the short list. Now, I knew that Holder was Obama's attack dog. I mean this as a job description, not an insult; I suspect Holder would take it as a compliment. And Bharara is known to be unquenchable in his ambition, a man who will do anything to climb up the ladder. So how much ingenuity does it take to recognize the possibility of a deal between Holder and Bharara: get that Indian guy, D'Souza, and you can have my job when I'm out the door. Fail, and we're going with someone else. Having served in the White House, I understand how government works. At the top level, you don't even need to make explicit deals. There are implicit understandings in politics that operate to produce the same results that a written contract might have produced, while avoiding the problems that a written contract might cause, if it got out.

Everything fit this picture. "They want this very badly," Brafman told me, having no idea what nefarious schemes I had envisioned in my head. I didn't need to go down this road with Brafman. By this time, however, neither did I have to convince him that I was being selectively treated. Brafman said, "They don't just want to send you away, they want to put you out of business. They won't be satisfied with anything less than a substantial prison term." Brafman's sources in the U.S. attorney's office for the Southern District of New York said that the prosecutors there even had a betting pool going on how much prison time I was going to get. The betting range was from ten months to two years.

This betting stuff is apparently customary among federal prosecutors. Brafman alerted me to a remarkable book, *Three Felonies a Day*, written by a civil libertarian attorney, Harvey Silverglate. In that book I found the following passage: "At the federal prosecutor's office in the Southern District of New York, the staff, over beer and pretzels, used to play a darkly humorous game. Junior and senior prosecutors would sit around, and someone would name a random celebrity—say Mother Teresa or John Lennon. It would then be up to the junior prosecutors to figure out a plausible crime for which to indict him or her. The crimes were not usually rape, murder or other crimes you'd see on *Law & Order* but rather the incredibly broad and yet obscure crimes that populate the U.S. Code like a kind of jurisprudential minefield: crimes like 'false statements' (a felony, up to five years), 'obstructing the mails' (five years) or 'false pretenses on the high seas' (also five years). The trick and the skill lay in finding the more obscure offenses that fit the character of the celebrity and carried the toughest sentences. The result was inevitable: prison time, as one former prosecutor told me."[7]

I recognized right away how far this is from the ordinary American's civics-book conception of justice, or from anything the American founders might have contemplated. Here these government officials were betting they could get pretty much anyone; in my case, they were betting how long they could put me away for. What does it mean in a country when the agencies of government operate like this? Who is the greater danger to society: me or them? Brafman had more practical concerns on his mind. "At this point," he said, "my supreme challenge is to keep you out of prison."

By this point Brafman and I knew that the prosecution could not be trusted to act fairly in this case. But what about the liberals? I was most familiar with the blogs and chatter on left-wing sites like Gawker, Wonkette, and Salon. These people seemed positively jubilant about the idea of me going away for a long time. Among the liberal intelligentsia, however, there was a more cautious tone, perhaps stemming from the recognition that this stuff works both ways; what they do to us today, we can do to them tomorrow. Blogger Timothy Noah gently suggested that a stiff fine instead of prison would be an appropriate sentence. When Sam Tanenhaus interviewed me for the *New Republic*, he privately expressed his incredulity. "I hope you beat the prison thing, Dinesh. That's crazy." Publicly, however, Tanenhaus said nothing of the kind; indeed, he said nothing at all.

And what about the judge? The man seemed on an interminable soapbox. In fact, by this point even his clerks seemed to have lost interest. I could see bored, superior looks on their faces; they wore the expressions of twenty-somethings who had seen it all. I guess I understood: for defendants, it's our life; but for them, it's just an apprenticeship. Brafman, however, did not take things so lightly. As he heard

Judge Berman rail against me, as he listened to him go on and on and on, I could see his face darken. First he was troubled. Then he was dismayed. Then I saw him getting angry. His lip trembled slightly, and he wouldn't look at me; he just stared at Berman with a look of outraged disbelief.

Finally the judge finished. There was dead silence in the courtroom. At this point, I was completely convinced that I was going to prison. Brafman, I knew, shared this belief. And so did everyone else in the room. Everyone expected me to be sent to the slammer. The only issue was: for how long?

Brafman rapidly shook his head, as if he could hardly believe what he had heard. Rising ashen-faced to his feet, he asked for a short break, and went to the restroom to splash cold water on his face. When he returned his lips were tightly pressed. He was determined, almost pugnacious. He stood up and said, "I have been doing this for a long enough time to recognize that I am climbing a very steep hill, given the tenor of the court's remarks. But I intend to climb as hard as I possibly can."

Then he let the judge have it. He said Berman had it all wrong; he was misjudging the case and also my character. Brafman said that as a liberal Democrat, he too had initially viewed me to be some kind of political extremist. But in working with me over the period of a year, he had grown to see that I was a good and decent person, fighting for what I believed.

Brafman cited a letter from my assistant—the very person who had made the straw donation on my behalf—that informed the judge that, around the same time, I contributed $10,000 to an African American student whose family could not afford to pay for his last year of college. Brafman said he found this unbelievable. "I'm trying to imagine a president of Columbia or president of another school seeing a young student with hardship and taking out his personal checkbook and writing him a check for ten thousand dollars." More than anything else, Brafman said, this action showed that I was "basically a good person."

Then Brafman exposed the government's below-the-belt tactics.

Brafman's proof was contained in his written reply to the government's sentencing brief. This document, now available online, methodically exposed the prosecution's deception. It had two side-by-side columns, one listing the facts reported by the government in the cases it cited, and another listing the facts left out. These were not omissions by oversight, Brafman noted; the government had deliberately slanted its case summaries to deceive the judge into thinking that prison time was normal for this kind of offense. Moreover, the government had deliberately ignored cases that did not result in prison sentences.

Brafman said, "The zeal with which this case was brought from inception to the Southern District is uncharacteristic of any case that we have found." He added, "In this case things happened in this prosecution that are not ordinary." The government, for instance, refused to give me the normal two points of credit for pleading guilty. "Judge," Brafman said, "I have never had that happen in any case in thirty-seven years. I have never had a defendant who actually pled on the eve of trial lose his two points." Reluctantly, Brafman said he had come to the conclusion that I was being selectively prosecuted, not for what I did, but because of who I am. Brafman noted that I had long felt that way, and "in this case I think he's right."

Brafman concluded by making it clear to the judge that a prison sentence would be so out of the ordinary that it would cast suspicion on the judge's own fair-mindedness and place him squarely in the camp of the get-this-man-at-any-cost prosecution. He concluded, "There is not a single case anywhere in the United States of America that either I or the government with all of their resources have found where someone like Mr. D'Souza, who is a first offender, who is not an attorney, who is not a campaign official, who had no corrupt relationship with the candidate, who has given twenty thousand dollars through straw donors, has gone to prison." Indeed, "We cite in our memo a dozen cases far worse than the defendant's and all of the judges in all of those cases throughout the country imposed a nonprison sentence."

Brafman finally sat down. He had completed his tour de force; he was spent. Now it was out of his hands. I looked over at the clerks, who were staring, openmouthed, at Brafman. Their ennui was gone; they were totally riveted. The judge rubbed his chin, and then said something very strange. He made the observation that, from his point of view, there was no real disagreement; he and Brafman had basically said the same thing. "Everything that you have said and everything that I have said," the judge exclaimed, "has totally overlapped."

Brafman's face registered his amazement. Everyone in the court was incredulous. The two men were at opposite poles, the one impassioned in blasting me, the other impassioned in defending me, and yet here was Judge Berman professing his inability to tell the difference. Was he playing some sort of game? Was this the Twilight Zone?

The judge then turned to me. "Mr. D'Souza?" I had prepared a short statement to read, but decided on the spur of the moment to directly address the issue that seemed to have baffled the judge most about me. "Your Honor," I said, "I would like to try to answer the question you raised as something that has been disturbing and puzzling you about what's going on here, why would somebody like me do a thing like this." When I began to speak I saw Brafman's surprise—naturally he expected me to read my prepared statement—and the judge interrupted me. "Explain to me why you—you—are here and why you did what you did. Not somebody like me, some famous person, blah, blah blah."

I was not off to a good start. "Okay," I said, attempting to regroup. "I was seventeen years old when I set foot in America. I came as an exchange student from India. I grew up in a very settled community. Most of my relatives lived within a one-mile radius of where I lived. I didn't realize when I came here that I was actually never going home. In other words, I came here for a one-year program, after which I expected I would return home. But I stayed in America. America opened up doors of opportunity for me—I found myself a student at Dartmouth.

"The experience of leaving one's country is a little terrifying, because you leave everything that matters to you behind, your family, your friends, everybody you know. And you are insecure in many different ways, financially insecure, emotionally insecure. In some senses, you are insecure in your identity. Because you leave your old country, in some ways you are no longer Indian, and yet you begin to wonder if you'll ever be American. You are walking a tightrope between two buildings, and you feel in no-man's-land, somewhere caught in between.

"When I was at Dartmouth, I found a group of friends who welcomed me in. I became part of that group. You can say that they became my American surrogate family. I say that because at that time, in four years of college, I never went home. I had no money. So I basically earned my way here in America, and these became my close-knit friends who literally took me for the first time to a store to buy a navy-blue blazer, explained to me that that's part of the etiquette of being a Dartmouth student. And so the very basic assimilation to American life was accomplished by a group of close friends that I met basically between the time I was eighteen and twenty.

"Wendy Long was one member of that group of four or five people. So even though over the years we have lived in different places, different states, there is a certain kind of amalgam of hearts that occurs because of that. You feel very close to that person, and you care about them in a very fundamental way, not differently than you care about your family."

So that, I said, is why I went overboard in trying to help Wendy. I also wanted to address the judge's apparent concern that I was not contrite over my misdeeds. "I am not shy," I said. "I have not been reluctant to express my views in public. And I have done that for twenty-five years. It's not like I started doing that when this case began. I have been doing that for my whole career. There is no inconsistency in saying I disagree with the Obama administration. I think a lot of the things they are doing are wrong. There is no inconsistency with me saying that and saying at the same time I did something wrong, which I regret. I wish I never did it, and I will never do it again."

I urged the judge to give me a fair sentence, which I said was not a prison sentence. Then I sat down. I turned back to look at my friends in the audience. They had tears in their eyes, tears of concern for my fate. I also saw that Adelle Nazarian of Breitbart News was weeping. As an immigrant, she felt for me. I looked over at Judge Berman's clerks. Their catatonic boredom was long gone; they were completely mesmerized by what was happening in the courtroom. Judge Berman took a short recess, one of the most suspenseful intervals in my life.

When he returned he began by saying, "I don't think that it's necessary for Mr. D'Souza to go to jail." Just those words. A wave of relief came over me, although I tried to conceal it. I had steeled myself not to show expression even if I got two years. I didn't want to give my ill-wishers the relish of it. So I registered a blank expression, even though inwardly I was elated. Brafman, however, could not have been more delighted. His face darted from side to side, his eyes gleaming, as if to say, "Did you see me pull that off?"

Later, when I emailed Brafman to thank him for his stellar work on my behalf, he replied, "This was one of my finest moments in thirty-eight years of work and I am absolutely delighted that I was able to save you from prison. It is a badge of honor I will display proudly for the rest of my life." He added, "I will also have great joy in the outstanding success you will no doubt achieve in the years ahead. Indeed, having fought the government and prevailed will no doubt make you even more of a hero than you already are to so many, including me."

Having announced that he would not send me to prison, Judge Berman proceeded to hand down his sentence. I was given eight months of overnight confinement in a halfway house. I had to do one day a week of community service teaching English to new immigrants, as well as one hour of psychological counseling. I had to pay a $30,000 fine. I also got five years probation. Significantly, the judge said he could not require me to pay restitution since my offense had not harmed anybody.

What happened that day in the courtroom? I would spend many hours reflecting on that subject, as well as discussing it with Brafman, with others who were present in the courtroom, and with friends who are lawyers and political observers. One view is that Judge Berman never intended to give me prison time; he recognized how absurd that would be for what I did. He did want to make me sweat, however, and that accounts for the tongue-lashing he administered at the outset.

A second view, which I share, is that Judge Berman initially planned to give me prison time but was largely swayed by Ben Brafman. Either way, one thing was clear: the judge did not go along with the government's position. He refused to be the government's pawn and participate in its transparent public deception.

Therein lay my victory. Judge Berman had given me a harsh sentence, out of proportion to what I did. He was forcing me to sleep every night in a confinement facility for eight months. He was dispatching me to psychological counseling, which, while not onerous, is odd for a case like this. After all, I had not done something bizarre like store bodies in my refrigerator; was my offense really one that required me to have my head examined? When I figure my legal fees plus the court-imposed fine plus the confinement center assessment, the case has cost me over half a million dollars.

If you have any doubt that my sentence was severe, compare my case to that of Sant Singh Chatwal, hotelier, fellow Asian Indian, and Democratic fundraiser. In 2012, Chatwal pleaded guilty to making more than $180,000 in straw donations to several Democratic candidates, including Hillary Clinton. In fact, Chatwal was the founder of "Indian Americans for Hillary 2008." Chatwal also pleaded to witness tampering; the FBI recorded him instructing a government witness to lie under oath. Chatwal was clearly trying to buy influence; indeed, he had publicly stated of politicians, "When they are in need of money, the money you give, then they are always for you. That's the only way to buy them." Chatwal received a fine, community service, and three years probation. No prison time, no confinement. In sum, for doing something vastly worse than what I did, he got a vastly lesser penalty.[8]

I didn't know about the Chatwal case when I was sentenced. But even had I known, it would not have killed my enthusiasm. That day, I was jubilant. Why? Because I recognized that the government—by which I mean the Obama administration—had lost. Success for them meant discrediting me, destroying my career. This had already failed, since my supporters were savvy enough, even without knowing all the details, to know what was up. The government's only hope at this point was to send me to prison, to put me away, ideally for a long enough time that I could not make a movie in the 2016 election year. Had I received a year or more in prison, I would not in fact be able to do that. But now I could. Moreover, the left had intended my incarceration to be a propaganda victory, and now they could say goodbye to all that.

The prosecutor, Carrie Cohen, looked crushed as she left the courtroom. She avoided looking at me. Politically, she knew that I had won, and she also knew I knew. Pretty soon she would have to tell Bharara, who would probably recognize instantly that he was not going to succeed Eric Holder. And he would have to tell Holder, who would have to tell Obama. None of these thugs-in-power would be happy to hear the news! As I left the courtroom, my smile reflected the fact that all these scenarios were moving quickly through my mind.

That night, I could barely stop grinning as I discussed my sentence on the Fox News Channel's *The Kelly File*. I told Megyn Kelly that the government tried to put me away, but a federal judge refused to let them. "This is a big political win for me," I confessed. And the system worked; the sentence, albeit severe, had confirmed my faith in America. Megyn was incredulous. "Only you, Dinesh," she said, would use the occasion of a rather harsh sentence to reaffirm your love of country. After all, I was headed to a confinement center! I told Megyn not to worry; by the time I left, all those people would be Republicans! When the show was over, Megyn flung her arms around me and hugged me.

Shortly after my sentence, Eric Holder announced his resignation. I waited to see if Obama would appoint Preet Bharara to the job. He did not. Instead he appointed Loretta Lynch, U.S. attorney for the Eastern District of New York. I believe the message was: sorry, Preet, but you didn't come through for us, and now we're not going to come through for you. Our ambitious Indian water-carrier will have to wait a bit longer for someone to reward him for his henchman services.

I had won—for now. But I knew I still had an ordeal ahead. I had no way of knowing what was in store for me at the confinement center. Let me just say that it was not overpopulated with dentists, entrepreneurs, and CEOs. Rather, I was destined to spend every night for the next eight months sleeping in a dormitory with more than a hundred rapists, armed robbers, drug smugglers, and murderers. It would turn out to be one of the most eerie, and formative, experiences of my life.

Here, among the hoodlums, I learned how to see in the dark, and through this "night vision" I began to see politics very differently. I got to know the hoodlums and read some of their case files. I learned how they think and how they operate, how they organize themselves into gangs, how they rip people off and crush their enemies. I understood, for the first time, the psychology of crookedness. Suddenly I had an epiphany: this system of larceny, corruption, and terror that I encountered firsthand in the confinement center is exactly the same system that has been adopted and perfected by modern progressivism and the Democratic Party.

This book is an exposé of Obama, Hillary, and modern liberalism not as a defective movement of ideas, but as a crime syndicate. And I have to thank Obama, the liberals, and the judge for this learning opportunity. All of them are responsible for putting me in a situation that made this book possible. All of them wanted to teach me a lesson. And I can now say, with the benefit of hindsight, that their objective has been met. Little did they know what a valuable lesson it would be, even if not quite the lesson they intended.

Real Possibilities

All of this and more is yours.

Publications
- *AARP The Magazine* – helping you feel great, save money and have fun
- *AARP Bulletin* – your source for timely insight and news on health, Social Security, and more

Discounts
- Savings on dining, entertainment, and shopping
- Access to hundreds of grocery coupons
- Buy your car the AARP way - visit www.aarp.org/abp

Insurance
- Access to AARP-endorsed auto, homeowners, life insurance
- Access to Medicare Supplement Insurance

Travel
- Up to 25% off on car rentals
- 5% - 20% off at national hotel chains

Programs & Tools
- Driver Safety Program – refresh driving skills and possibly qualify for discounts
- Caregiving Resource Center – toolkit to plan for loved ones who need your help

Volunteer
- Volunteer opportunities through *Create the Good*
- Discover programs available through your local chapter

The AARP Membership Card
- Your AARP Membership Card makes it easy to take advantage of all the programs, services, and discounts AARP members value most

Call 1-877-902-6053,
visit www.aarp.org/mymemberbenefits or
www.aarp.org/espanol for more information.

Real Possibilities

Enjoy your free gift with many thanks from AARP.

And this gift is just the beginning...

===

Chapter 2

THE WORLD AS IT IS:

Inside the Confinement Center

===

I have thought it proper to represent things as they are in reality, rather than as they are imagined.[1]

—Machiavelli, *The Prince*

I checked into confinement on October 2, 2014, just ten days after my sentencing. My lawyers had given me the impression that I could start six weeks later, but to everyone's surprise, the judge issued a terse order insisting that I begin immediately. In fact, he expressed surprise that I was not already in confinement.

Before I checked in, my probation officer—an affable woman named Kathy Schwarte—informed me what I would have to pay for my confinement. I knew from the judge's ruling that I would be charged for my captivity. I found this odd: if they are forcing me to do this, how can they bill me for it? The short answer to this is that they are the bosses and they can do it because they have the power to do it. My monthly tab, Kathy informed me, would be $3,000. Great! I thought.

I'm paying $100 a day—basically Holiday Inn rates—to sleep with a bunch of criminals for eight months.

The center is located in a run-down Hispanic neighborhood of San Diego. The street itself is largely deserted. The confinement center has no signs to indicate what it is. It looks like a warehouse. There is a tall fence around it, laced with barbed wire. But there were no security guards that I could see from the outside, just uniformed staff behind the front desk. It could have been the reception desk of any drab government or commercial building. It was across the street from a waste processing plant. A mild stench from that plant filled the air the night I checked in. I arrived wearing black pants, a black T-shirt, black shoes, and a cheap watch. There is no uniform but I decided to dress inconspicuous and dress down. I also drove a rental car.

The staid Hispanic fellow behind the desk had my paperwork ready. He had me read it to make sure all the information was correct. According to the documents, I was to be confined overnight from October 2014 to May 2015. My release date had already been determined: May 31, 2015. I was also given my inmate number: 69851-054. "What do I do with this?" I asked. "Memorize it," the staff guy said. "You'll need it the whole time you are here."

My attention was directed to the Breathalyzer, and I realized I was being tested for alcohol. This, I was informed, would be part of my daily routine. I could check out at 6 a.m. each morning, and was required to be back by 9 p.m. each night. Every time I checked back in I had to blow into the machine. I was then ushered into another room for my urine test. This, I was told, was to make sure I was drug-free. The urine test was not part of the regular regimen but could be administered anytime upon request. Finally, a male staffer patted me down and ran a metal wand over my body, to make sure I was not carrying a weapon.

I was then escorted through the entrance area and into the facility. The main area is the dining room, which has a kitchen area in the back and two long tables, with plastic chairs piled on top of the other in one area. That, I said to myself, is where I will *not* be eating, at least if I can avoid it. If I'm here just nights, I plan to make my own food arrangements.

It wasn't mealtime just then, but sitting around one of the tables was a bunch of guys, and there were others walking around, and a few on the pay phones in one of the hallways. Apparently one of the pay phones didn't work, because I saw a guy bang the receiver, yell "Sh*t!" and kick the wall. Self-control, I thought, is probably in short supply among this cohort.

For the first time I got a glance at the population of the facility. I tensed up; I could see that they were pretty rough, the kind of guys that I had never previously encountered in normal life. The vast majority of them were Hispanic, and there was a sprinkling of whites and blacks. Everyone seemed to have tattoos on their heads and all over their bodies. From what I could hear, Spanish was spoken in here more than English.

What a group! Now I was destined to spend my nights for the better part of a year with them. These were my fellow inmates. I told myself to get used to it, yet I knew that this was going to require a mental adjustment on my part. I reminded myself of the line from Milton, "The mind is its own place." I resolved that I would use my mind to control my emotions, to regulate my anxiety. I may be a captive while I am here, I thought, but in my mind, I remain free.

I was led up the stairs and at the top I could see the entrance to the dormitory area where I had been assigned to sleep. Next to it was some kind of a TV room where a group of men were watching mixed martial arts and cheering. "Kick his ass!" "Show him how it's done, homie." I was directed to a conference room where I was handed a packet of materials, including a rulebook for the confinement center. "Read it," the staffer said to me. His name was Oscar; I could see it on his name badge.

Oscar seemed like an approachable fellow, so I said to him, "I'm really glad this is not prison."

He seemed surprised. "You're coming here from prison, right?"

"No," I said. "I've never been to prison. This confinement is my sentence."

"Hah!" He seemed puzzled by that.

"I'm glad I avoided prison," I said. "I've heard bad things about what goes on there."

"Hah!" said Oscar. "In prison," he added, "you get a much better class of people."

"What do you mean?" I asked. This did not sound good.

"Yours is a nonviolent offense, right?"

I nodded.

"White-collar prison," he said, "is full of doctors, dentists, business guys, even one or two mayors or city officials. These are people who didn't pay their taxes, or cheated Medicare, or did insider trading, stuff like that."

"Sounds pretty harmless," I said, not entirely convinced.

"Most of the camps have a library, church services, a gym, tennis court. And you can leave if you want to. No one is going to stop you."

"Really?"

"I know one warden who tells inmates, don't try and escape. Let me know if you want to leave and I'll call you a cab."

"Don't they have corrections officers to chase after you?"

"I guess you haven't seen the size of those corrections officers. If you had, you'd realize that they ain't gonna be doing a lot of chasing."

He smiled and then added, "You meet some really interesting people in prison. You know, Martha Stewart was in prison."

Yes, I knew. "And here?" I said. "What about here, in the confinement center?"

"This is different, man. These guys here have done it all. Murder, rape, armed robbery, drug smuggling across the border. You name it, we have it."

"You have murderers here?"

"Oh sure. Most of them are old m*therf*ckers, though. You see, they've already done their prison sentences. All these people have.

We are helping them transition back to society. Or at least that's the theory."

I knew the theory.

"Is it safe here?" I asked. My stomach was feeling knotted.

"For the most part. Remember, these people have all done time; they don't want to go back. So they behave themselves, as I said, for the most part. Mind your own business—you'll be fine."

Then he added, "Do you have any doubt that you can protect yourself if someone attempts to rape you?"

Uh-oh. "Is that a problem here?"

"Not really," he replied, "but I have to fill out this form. I need to put in your answer: yes or no."

I told him I didn't know how to answer the question.

He sized me up. "I'll put down no," he said. "But in any case, you're going to have to do the rape instruction class. It's mandatory. It's called PREA."

"PREA?"

"The prevention of rape something-something. It's a really good class. That's the first thing I want you to do after settling in."

The first thing? I found it odd that I was starting off my confinement by going to a rape class. I remembered what my Dartmouth pal the radio host Laura Ingraham had told me. "Don't trust anyone in there," she said, "not even the staff. If you have a cell, check around the place every night, because someone could plant drugs in there and blame it on you. Sleep with one eye open, because they can pay someone to knife you. Don't think it doesn't happen. It happens; just make sure it doesn't happen to you." I knew I would have to be careful, but I wanted to resist becoming paranoid.

Then Oscar took me to the upper-level dormitory where I'd be sleeping for the next eight months. The place was L-shaped, with around thirty bunk beds lined up in neat rows. Up against the walls were lockers, very much like the lockers you get in high school. Milling around, and reclined in a number of beds, were my fellow convicts. I surveyed them with interest, and noticed that they were studying me with equal curiosity. Their eyes said to me, "You are a stranger for us—we are not used to your kind." This was not news to me—I wasn't used to their kind, either.

"Here," said Oscar, "is where you'll be sleeping." I noticed I had been assigned a top bunk right near the entrance. The fellow sleeping below, who wasn't around at the time, had several pairs of his shoes under the bed and a towel hanging from the side of his bunk. My mattress, I noticed, was around two inches thick, and it came with two sheets, a thin covering, and a pillow. This is pretty Spartan, I said to myself. I shouldn't expect a Tempur-Pedic mattress, or a Westin Heavenly Bed. At the same time, I thought, this should not be a hardship for me. I grew up in India, where I slept on a mattress pretty similar to this one. Here I didn't have a blanket, but that didn't faze me, either. Hey, I'm in San Diego—I should be fine with what's here.

"There's another dorm downstairs," Oscar told me. "We got about sixty guys up here, and sixty down there. You stay in your dorm, okay? Don't go into the lower dorm." I nodded.

Oscar pointed me to my locker and gave me the combination, 4-34-8. It took me several times to get the combination to work; I hadn't used a locker like this since 1978, when I was in twelfth grade in public school in Arizona, having just arrived there as an exchange student from India. Wow, I said to myself, I am now in my fifties and I am back to using a locker. Life seems to have come full circle.

I checked out the bathrooms. There was a shower area with several showerheads, but Oscar told me that in this facility men don't shower together; rather, you call out to find out if someone is in the shower and, if there is, then you announce that you are next. One person showering at a time—I found this reassuring. As for the toilets, there were five of them in my dorm, and I noticed, with some relief, that they were pretty clean, not as clean as in a private home, but something like you'd find in a train or bus station. In any case, I planned to make minimal use of the bathrooms and take my showers during the days, at home.

I changed into sweatpants and a sweatshirt for the night and, when I returned to my bunk, I saw that there was a big guy below me—

a slovenly white fellow with his hair braided in strips. "Let's not get too cozy," he said, his voice almost a mumble. "When I get back to my wife, I don't want to wake up in the morning and whisper your name."

It took me a second to realize that he was totally joking! I smiled, but at the same time I felt my Adam's apple travel down my throat. Standing at my bunk, I could see the dozens of men in the dormitory, and I felt the same strangeness I felt when I first arrived in America, the feeling of being in a completely unfamiliar place. Moreover, every single man in here was a criminal. I had never seen so many criminals at such close quarters. Now I was to spend every single night with them for eight months. Be brave, I said to myself. Don't show fear; look people in the eye.

My main concern was safety. In particular, I had no intention of being raped, and so it was with some trepidation that I entered the little trailer behind the confinement building to attend my PREA class.

No sooner did I enter the little classroom than the instructor, a very bored-looking African American woman, announced to the dozen or so of us present, "You have a *right* not to be raped."

A right not to be raped! I cannot say I was super-encouraged. Moreover, she insisted, "Under the Obama administration, we have adopted a zero-tolerance policy toward prison rape." She gestured with her hands to indicate quotation marks.

A zero-tolerance policy. I abstained from raising the point, but I wondered what the policy had been *before*.

She handed us an informational pamphlet, which was evidently the limit of the protection we were to receive at the hands of the federal government.

Still, we were not entirely on our own. If I was raped, I learned from this class, the government was willing to offer me a number of services. For instance, I was entitled to a free pregnancy test! I was also entitled to a free AIDS test! And, if this were not enough, I was also entitled to free mental health counseling!

Man, are we lucky or what? Where else do people put you in an environment where you can get raped, and yet if that happens, give you all this stuff? And it's free! This isn't Mexico, homie, or India! Only in America!

I was trying to bolster my mood. I found myself coping with the situation through sarcasm. Over time I also found myself becoming more shameless. And in this respect I came to resemble the other inmates, who were also shameless. Their attitude was "Who gives a f*ck?" and I realized, with some surprise, that that was also becoming my attitude.

Already the forces that be, both inside and outside the facility, were screwing with me. First, the director of the facility, an oversize woman known by inmates alternately as "Miss Williams" or "the Bitch," informed me that any media appearances I did would have to be cleared with the Federal Bureau of Prisons. I would have to submit written requests to her. I pointed out that frequently I received media requests for interviews the same day. "Those will not be approved," she said.

Kathy, my probation officer, had assured me that since speeches were part of the way I made a living, she would allow me to travel two days a month. But the Bureau of Prisons rejected this request. The reason, Kathy conveyed to me, is they felt I would be undermining my sentence by having nights away from confinement. A few days later, the BOP decided I would not be allowed to travel outside San Diego County.

I protested: I could easily do meetings in Orange County or Los Angeles and return the same evening. By the BOP's own logic, I said, returning the same night to confinement would not undermine my sentence. Kathy agreed, but the BOP overruled her. Later, we took this up with the judge, but he sided with the BOP on this. No travel for me for eight months.

The BOP also decided to reduce my hours of freedom. Instead of being out of the facility from 6 a.m. to 9 p.m. seven days a week, I would be released from 6 a.m. to 7 p.m. six days a week. Sundays I would have to be in confinement the whole day, although I could apply to leave for four hours to go to church. "They're trying to torture me in small ways," I said to my case officer at the facility. He was a bespectacled Hispanic guy named Cazares. Although liberal in his politics, he was also a Christian, and he had seen some of my videos debating atheists such as Bart Ehrman and Christopher Hitchens. Cazares liked me, but he also knew that the system—which is to say, the government—did not. "They are watching you," he said. "You are not an ordinary inmate. Remember that."

I did, but far from producing in me the desired humility, this information only added to my shamelessness. And, as I mentioned, I was not alone.

During my first couple of weeks in confinement, I tried to keep to myself. I made only perfunctory conversation—"How's it going?" "What time is curfew?"—and mostly just read and worked out.

This changed one evening when I was sipping coffee in the dining hall. I was approached by an African American inmate who looked different from everyone else in the facility. He was well-dressed, in a brown suit, with shined shoes, and, of all things, a hat.

"I hear you're an educated man," he said, sitting down and moving his face very close to mine. "Written a bunch of books and sh*t."

I said nothing. In the background, I could hear 1970s music coming from the kitchen and a Korean guy behind the counter was singing along, "When the lights go down in the city."

"Prison sucks, doesn't it?" the man continued.

I didn't reply.

"All your friends desert you," he whispered, "like cockroaches in the rain."

Then he added, "I'd like to have lunch with you sometime."

"Here?" I asked. "In the dining hall?"

"Not here," he said, as if I had uttered the dumbest suggestion in the world. "Not with these m*therf*ckers."

I looked around, noting that there were quite a few m*therf*ckers milling about.

"Let's have lunch downtown," he said, pronouncing each syllable, "at the U.S. Grant Hotel."

I figured the guy was crazy. No way was I going to meet him anywhere outside the facility. In fact, this was explicitly forbidden by our rulebook. The government, understandably, doesn't want felons hanging with each other because who knows what criminal schemes that may lead to?

I learned that the guy's name was Bundy and, by coincidence, I saw him again a few days later in the restroom. He was perched on a chair, and a young black guy was giving him a haircut. Applying shaving cream to my face, I asked what his crime was, and he informed me that he was convicted of embezzlement.

"I hope you realize," he clarified, "that's a white-collar offense."

"That was news," he added, "to my judge. He did *not* expect that."

Bundy recalled that when he had entered the courtroom for his embezzlement trial, the judge had said, "I am very surprised to see a black man in my courtroom who is not here for drug dealing."

Mr. Bundy was not happy with this remark.

"Even though my lawyer tried to stop me," he said, "I got up and told him, 'Your Honor, you are an ignorant m*therf*cker.' "

I almost cut myself with my razor. "You told him that to his face?"

"Sure! And then I said to him, 'If you don't respect me, I will march right up your courtroom and kick your ass.' "

And for this Mr. Bundy got another six months added to his sentence. I was not surprised to learn this. Still, I couldn't help admire his attitude. He was not willing to be disrespected, and he was willing, at considerable risk to himself, to let the judge know how he felt.

Over time I saw that Bundy's attitude was actually quite normal for my fellow inmates. A few days into my confinement, I saw quite clearly that these people are all rebels. They are always talking back, breaking rules, tempting the system. The system plays a large role in their lives, and their attitudes about it are instructive.

Although there is a strict rule against drugs, and we all take a Breathalyzer test every time we check into the facility, I routinely smelled marijuana in the bathroom. Contraband is bought and sold, and I was always getting suggestions for how to beat the system.

"You want a drink?"

"We're not allowed to drink in here."

"I know. Who gives a f*ck?"

I was reminded of the attitude of many Americans during Prohibition days. They refused to follow laws they considered stupid or unrealistic. Indeed they took pride in flaunting them. This seemed to be the attitude here as well.

"Where," I asked, "do you get alcohol?"

"Ever heard of Vons? CVS? We buy that sh*t across the street."

I guess the pat-down system that we go through every time we enter the confinement center is not foolproof.

I said I wasn't happy about being assigned an upper bunk. (I hadn't slept so far off the ground since my freshman year at Dartmouth.)

"No problem," someone told me. "Go tell them you get dizzy. Say you walk in your sleep. Tell them you have some rare disease. They don't want to risk it—they'll move you right away."

I also discovered that there were ways to get extra hours of freedom on Sunday.

"You can get out of here on Sunday if you go to the DMV." This is a Filipino guy telling me this.

I'm definitely interested. My sentence allows me to get out six days a week to work, but on Sunday I'm supposed to be confined the whole day.

"How can I get out on Sunday?" I ask. "Can I go to the DMV to get my license?"

"No, I mean you can get out *every* Sunday. The first time you say you have to get a form. The second time you say you have to turn in the form. The third time you say you have to take a test. The next time you say you have to retake the test. We haven't even gotten to you taking your picture. And once you're done with the DMV, you tell them you are job-hunting and have to go to the public library to find job listings. You can get hygiene passes, church passes. It never ends, man."

"I didn't know the DMV and the public library were even open on Sunday."

"Who says they are? But they don't know that. You are dealing with complete dumb f*cks, remember that."

This contemptuous attitude—that the system is run by buffoons—is pervasive, and, I have to say, also shared by the some of the people who run the confinement center. Maybe even judges and lawyers take this view; before I went in, Ben Brafman told me, "You are going to be surrounded by people who have IQs of seventy."

I informed him that I had read somewhere—I think it was in Charles Murray's *The Bell Curve*—that criminals have very low IQs.

"I'm not talking about the criminals," Brafman said. "I'm talking about the people who run the facilities. Those are the ones you have to worry about."

"Why?"

"Because they are the ones who have the power. It's not like they have eighty percent of the power and you have twenty percent. They have one hundred percent and you have zero. And they are the stupidest people on the planet. Even dumber than the criminals."

My view has been to treat the staff with the utmost respect, recognizing how dangerous it is to treat them any other way. My fellow inmates, however, disagree. They cannot resist mocking and demeaning the staff whenever the opportunity arises.

Every day, for example, we go through a pat-down as we return to the facility from work furlough. I go through without a word, as a pair of burly hands makes its way along my shoulders and down my arms and across my stomach and over my pant pocket area and down my legs, right to my ankles. By contrast, other guys routinely say things like, "Juan, make sure you don't enjoy yourself too much."

And, "Cardenas, stop! Now I got a boner."

Another surprise is to see some of the criminals refer to the supervising staff using the N-word.

"Hey, n*gger." This is a white guy from my dorm addressing the Hispanic guy behind the desk.

And the term doesn't faze the Hispanic guy one bit. He responds as if being called by his actual name.

"Yeah?"

Later I ask the white guy, "Weren't you concerned about offending him?"

The guy said, "They're used to it. Besides, they know I have to be here and they don't. So f*ck 'em—if they don't like it they can get another job."

Why, I wonder, do these criminals have such contempt for the system? Is it because they don't believe in justice, or have a corrupted conscience? Is it because they consider themselves innocent—they don't recognize they broke the law? Is that why they are so hard to rehabilitate?

I had expected most of the inmates to make a point of protesting their innocence. In the movie *The Shawshank Redemption* all the convicts routinely insist, "I didn't do it." Morgan Freeman's character is virtually unique in admitting his guilt. This is the stereotypical image of what criminals are like.

Yet in eight months of living with these offenders, I am constantly struck by their willingness to acknowledge freely and frankly what they did, including admitting their own stupidity.

Consider Mfume, a black guy who told me I was free to use his real name. (I'm not doing that; I've changed the names of all the guys I write about.) Mfume is a big guy, between 230 and 250 pounds, elegantly dressed and soft-spoken, but not super-bright. I came to this conclusion based on the following conversation.

"What are you in for, man?"

"Armed robbery," he said.

"Really? You tried to rob a bank? Grocery store?"

"No," he replied. "I tried to rob Camp Pendleton."

"The military base?"

"Yes."

I must have given him quite a look.

"Yes," he agreed. "I was a stupid m*therf*cker."

"Why did you choose the base?"

"We'd been hitting up grocery stores and getting a thousand dollars, two thousand dollars. But we had heard that there was fifty to sixty grand in the commissaries at the base."

"How did you expect to pull it off?"

"It was an inside job," he said. "We had someone on the inside who had organized the whole thing."

"And you got caught?"

"Yeah, a Marine saw us and sounded the alarm."

Mfume said that when he tried to escape he saw that his getaway car had taken off. He was quickly subdued by a group of armed Marines.

"I almost got away," he said. "I used some of the moves that I've seen football players use on *Monday Night Football*. They had to chase me for almost half a mile before they got me."

I asked Mfume to tell me a little about his life. "I was raised by a white woman," he said, "but she took off on me. Now she runs an escort service in Vegas, but she's not doing that well. The recession was a big hit." Mfume himself has alternated between white and black women, although he's currently married to an African American. "I have six children from three moms," he says, as if this were the most natural thing in the world.

Mfume now is virtually philosophical about the whole thing. "I was desperate to feed my family, and my faith was at a low point, so I decided to become an armed robber. I tried to rob from the military and I am myself a vet. Can you believe that? How messed up is that? I carried a gun and I put people's lives, and my family's future, in danger. I got nothing out of it—well, what I got was a five-year sentence.

"I was preparing myself for fifteen years. I know I deserved at least ten, especially when I remember all the other crimes I've committed. But the judge was lenient. So I've got nothing to complain about, man."

Like Mfume, the other inmates here know they broke the law, and they often admit that they had been breaking the law for quite a while before they got caught. I don't hear too many excuses. These aren't professors or lawyers; they wouldn't know how to begin rationalizing what they did.

I am also struck by their deep sense of justice. For them justice and injustice are not abstractions. This is not the Harvard Law School case study approach. It is the street case study approach.

We can see how many criminals view justice through the eyes of Sam, a white guy in my dormitory with tattoos of skulls and women all over his arms and neck. Everyone knows him as the Hell's Angel since he is, or used to be, in that motorcycle gang. "Sam's a really nice guy," my bunk mate tells me. "Don't get me wrong, if you say the wrong thing to him on the street, he'll shoot you in the face. But otherwise he's an okay guy." I've gotten to know Sam since, and I can testify that this is an accurate assessment.

Sam told me he's been in and out of prison since the late 1970s.

"What was your most serious charge?" I asked him.

"Murder."

"Did you do it?"

"I killed the bastard, yes, but it was in self-defense."

"He was coming after you?"

"Well, he would have if I hadn't killed him first."

"So it wasn't really self-defense."

"Yes, it was. The guy was a known assassin. For me, it was kill or be killed."

What started the whole thing was that the guy insulted Sam's mother-in-law. Sam at the time was looking after the ninety-year-old woman. He explained that she was chronically ill, so he took her to the grocery store, cooked and cleaned for her, even drew her blood and gave her medications. I notice that, even now, Sam was moved when he spoke about his mother-in-law.

I'm not suggesting that Sam is a model citizen. He was a routine drug offender; he sold drugs in prison. He had not only stolen; he claimed to have stolen from the mob, and from the police. With relish, he described how he was arrested on a gun charge in the Midwest. The officer didn't know he had a rap sheet. Sam was able to convince him to let him go on $2,000 bail. Sam said he didn't have cash, so he paid with American Express Travelers Cheques.

"Then," Sam said, "I walked my ass out of there and drove to the nearest American Express office, where I reported my checks stolen. They gave me a hundred-dollar cash advance. When I reached the next town, they had nineteen hundred dollars in new Travelers Cheques waiting for me."

The boldness and ingenuity of this simple maneuver amazed me. I would never have thought of it, nor would I have the guts to attempt it. Yet criminals like Sam have learned to be Machiavellian, willing and able to exploit whatever opportunities or loopholes are created by the system.

Sam also shed light on how criminals view the relative merits of the American prison system. He had served time both in the United States and Mexico. "The Mexican prisons are different, man," he recalled. "They don't have cells—they just give you a corner, and that's your corner. Don't be surprised if you wake up and find rat bites all over your body. When it rains, the water comes right through the ceiling.

"No wonder the Mexicans love our prisons," he continued. "We have toilets, regular meals, jogging tracks. They can't believe it. They never want to leave."

Not that he found prison in Mexico unendurable. "It's not all bad in there, man. You've got hookers coming through the prison, people selling tacos and chile rellenos and sh*t. Don't ask me where the meat is from, it's probably dog meat, but I ate it and it tasted good."

In the same genial tone, Sam proceeded to tell us how he had beaten up or stabbed at least a dozen rapists and child molesters over the years. In one case, he said, he took the combination lock from his locker and used it to bash in the head of a child molester. In another case, he and a molester were being transported cross-country and, sitting in the back of the car, he beat the other guy so badly that the police officer told him, "Look, you have to stop. If he's dead when we get there I'm going to get in trouble." In another incident in Texas, one of Sam's buddies stole a knife from the kitchen and he used it to stab a man who had raped an underage girl.

"I got no tolerance for those sickos, you understand? I mean, let's leave the women and children out of it, okay? I mean, have some respect. I don't care if they know I did it. So extend my sentence—who gives a sh*t?"

The Mexicans call the pedophiles *chomos*. "It's like a badge of honor," one of them told me, "to stick a *chomo*. It's the prison version of the Congressional Medal of Honor."

This is how it is for rapists and child molesters in prisons across the country. They have to watch themselves, because the prisoners will beat or slash or kill them. In some cases they will be caught and punished; in others the guards will watch and let them.

How, I asked Sam, does one get a weapon into prison to stab or kill a rapist or child molester? "Guns are usually out," he said, "but you can sometimes get a zip gun, basically a pipe with a bullet. Mostly we do it with sharp objects that we buy from the outside."

Do the guards, I asked him, bring them in and sell them to you?

"Usually it's the plumbers and electricians and repair guys who are fixing stuff in the prison. There are always people around here, fixing sh*t. That's the best way to get stuff, from them. Because if we can't, then we have to make it ourselves."

Make what?

"You're a writer, eh? Well, give me a hardcover book and I'll rip the covers off. Then I'll wet it and fold it into thin strips. Then I'll rub soap over the strips and wet it again, so the water seals over it. If I keep doing this, within a short time I'll have a dangerous weapon in my hands. Those guys better watch out, because here comes Sam."

I was struck by the harsh moral code of the criminal underclass. Crime is crime, but apparently there are some crimes for which the criminals themselves deem conviction and imprisonment insufficient punishment.

This is another way of saying that even the people who consciously break the law have not entirely lost their sense of justice. On the contrary, they are willing to take more risks to impose justice than virtually anyone on the outside. Would you risk five years of additional prison time to stab to death a reprobate who molested a child? I wouldn't. But they do.

For several months I puzzled over the conundrum of why criminals who know they broke the law and have a keen sense of justice are nevertheless so incorrigible, so arrogant, so shameless.

Then a guy, while playing poker, said something that caught my attention. "I had to do it," he said, explaining why he had set another guy on fire. "It wouldn't be right to let that m*therf*cker get away with it." And then it hit me. The reason that criminals are so shameless is that the law, as it is applied, offends their sense of justice.

My conversations in confinement got me thinking about everything I had learned about "law" and "justice." We often think of them in abstract terms, and we think that the law is, at least in a democratic society, the mechanism to impose justice. In our school textbooks, we learn about how people are protected through "equal protection" and "due process of law." Criminals regard such talk as pure BS. And come to think of it, what do those terms actually mean? If you've even been through the criminal justice process, you know that there is nothing "due" or equitable about the way that people are treated or the way that punishments are proportioned to offenses.

Criminals see through BS because they live at a very elemental level. Prison, in this respect, resembles the state of nature. The inmates cannot stop cursing. When they feel like it, they belch and fart. Spitting is very common, especially into trash cans. I heard one inmate scolding another for not locking his bathroom stall while he was masturbating. Still, his only objection was not to the action itself but to the fact that the guy was making too much noise!

Hardly anyone in the confinement center ever talks about politics. Their main concerns are more basic: food, sleep, money, and sex. I have listened on my bunk bed to many conversations discussing one or several of these topics. One night, while I was trying to read, I heard a half-hour conversation about the breasts of the waitress who works at Del Taco down the street. She was, in the words of one voyeur, "a hot tamale." Apparently several of our guys were there, and each one took turns describing her endowments, their angle of vision, what they would do if given the opportunity, and so on.

This focus on the simple urges of the body became more comprehensible for me in a book I was reading at the time, Solzhenitsyn's *One
Day in the Life of Ivan Denisovich*. Denisovich is in the Soviet concen-
tration camp, and he spends the whole day trying to get a cigarette.
He doesn't even care if it's a cigarette that has already been smoked,
that a guard may have discarded. He runs into a filmmaker named
Tsezar giving an erudite analysis of the Russian film director Eisen-
stein. Denisovich listens politely, but he couldn't care less. All he cares
about is getting a cigarette. When he realizes he won't get one that day,
he leaves. Then he finds a spoon, which he hides in his felt boot, and a
piece of hacksaw blade, which he pockets. Those things are much more
useful to him than aesthetic analysis.[2] That's the same attitude these
guys in the confinement center display.

Criminals are not absorbed with the world as it ought to be. They are
more concerned with the world as it is. And this gives them a singular
focus, a realism, that is often lacking among members of the journalis-
tic and political class. We are used to "high talk," to dissecting without
end the way things ought to be. Taxes ought to be higher, or lower.
America ought to stop Iran from doing this or that. Murderers ought
to be put away for life. Blah, blah, blah.

This is a long way from the criminal angle of seeing things. For
criminals, no one "ought" to do anything. All that you need to do is
get through the day, and for that you need to know what is actually
going on.

This distinction—between the world as it is and the world as it
ought to be—has its roots in Machiavelli. Machiavelli faults the ancient philosophers for focusing on "imaginary republics and principal-
ities which have never in truth been known to exist."[3] In his view, they
wasted a whole lot of time debating how things should be. Machiavelli's emphasis was on how things really are. *The Prince* is an instruction manual drawn from practical lessons of what successful princes
actually do to maintain and expand their power. Machiavelli knew
that people care about morality, and so princes cannot ignore it. What
princes should do, Machiavelli says, is pretend to be moral. Morality,

in short, is a ruse. Machiavelli is the founder of con artistry as a political ideology. I doubt many of my fellow criminals know his work, but
I feel sure they would understand it.

Machiavelli's distinction between how things are and how they
ought to be has practical implications, even for the criminal justice
system. "Innocent until proven guilty." "Presumed innocent." "Better
that ten guilty people go free than that one innocent person be imprisoned." This is the way things ought to be. But it is not the way that
things actually are. In fact, that noble-sounding principle has very
little to do with our system of justice as it is actually practiced today.

If you know anything about the prison system, you know that most
defendants are brought into the court in prison clothes and handcuffs,
precisely so that they are "presumed guilty." Moreover, lots of people
are serving prison sentences even though they are innocent of the
crimes with which they are charged. What's more, prosecutors know
they are innocent, or that they have been entrapped, or selectively
targeted, or are being punished for not cooperating. And if you don't
know these things, you will before you finish this book. So to keep
repeating these mantras, or debating their nuances, is to show a deep
ignorance of what's actually going on.

In other words, criminals think that law sometimes undermines
justice, and I think they are right. These criminals are not as learned
as the justice-mongers who will no doubt sneer at them, but they have
one advantage: they have actual experience with the system; they have
confronted it, fought it, and lived it. And I, being one of them, have my
own actual experience of dealing with it.

"How'd they find out about you, man?" one Hispanic guy named
Ramon asked me, after we had concluded our game of chess.

"Don't know," I said. "They were probably spying on me."

"Of course they were spying on you," he said. "They spy on all the
rich m*therf*ckers."

"No," I said. "They spy on everyone."

"They don't care about everyone," he said. "They care about people
who have money. They want to know where that money is, so that they

can get it. My friends and I do that all the time when we are pulling a job."

My mind went to a passage I had recently read in Thomas Piketty's *Capital*. Piketty calls for laws that require people with money all over the world to report their assets, leaving nothing out, to a global authority. Piketty insists it is important for governments to have accurate tracking of the resources of all the people who have money.

"Casing the joint," Ramon said. "That's what we call it. We case the joint so we know where the stuff is. That's why the government is spying on you and every other rich millionaire in this country. They want to own you, man."

I thought about this. Terrorism is of course the official explanation for the mass surveillance of citizens. But does surveillance on this scale make any sense? Downloading people's contact lists, reading their emails, listening to their calls. What started as a plan to catch bad guys could easily have metamorphosed into a scheme for tracking everyone. Maybe the government is casing the joint—or, more accurate, casing the citizen—and terrorism is now merely a convenient excuse.

The cynicism of the criminals seems almost boundless, but it is grounded in facts that are hard to dispute.

"I met several politicians in prison," Ramon confided during another one of our games. "City councilman, deputy commissioner of housing development, even a couple of local mayors. Every single one of them was pissed about being caught. Not about what they did, but about getting slammed for it. They are pissed because they are doing the same thing other politicians are doing. But they got busted, and everyone else got away with it."

"Got away with what?"

"It goes all the way up," Ramon said, his eyes lighting up. "Look at all the politicians—congressmen, senators, presidents—who came into office with nothing and leave as multimillionaires. So how did this happen? It just happened?"

I thought of Obama, who came from nothing and had a relatively paltry net worth when he ran for the presidency. Or Hillary, who said she and Bill were dead broke when they left the White House. Hillary has been ridiculed for that statement, but it's true that the Clintons, like Obama, started with very little and had to make their way up the economic ladder. Still, look at them now! The Obamas and the Clintons all live lives of almost unimaginable extravagance. The Clintons have soared from zero to $100 million at warp speed. Obama is setting up to join them, so that he too can live like a king when he leaves office. Ramon raises a valid question: how did this happen?

I got more cynicism in a conversation I had with an African American drug dealer who described the FBI in rather unusual terms.

"Of all the gangs," he said, "the FBI is by far the scariest, man."

The scariest what? "That's what they are, man, a gang, just like the Crips and the Bloods. They got gang uniforms, they got passwords, and they got the best weapons of any gang in the world. They know it, and we know it, and we all relate to each other on that basis."

Another gang, he suggested, was the Drug Enforcement Agency. "Half the time they are fighting the drug gangs," he said, "and the rest of the time they are making friends with them."

At first, I found this hard to believe, but then I saw a detailed report in the *Washington Post* about how DEA agents had "sex parties" with prostitutes hired by local drug cartels. This had been going on in Colombia for several years, from 2009 to 2012. DEA agents also received cash, gifts, and weapons from cartel members. Significantly, when the higher-ups at the DEA learned about this, they didn't investigate it. Neither did the FBI or the U.S. Marshals Service.[4] I began to realize that gangs are a basic unit for building social ties and organizing human behavior. Throughout history, they have served as a surrogate form of family. I began to think about how gangs operate in the larger society. Were there gangs in politics? If so, surely they wouldn't describe themselves as such. How, then, can we recognize them?

"You have to realize, homie, that Obama's a gang leader, just like I used to be. We're two n*ggers in the same business, and we're both after the same thing, which is money and power. The difference is that I got caught and he's still doing it."

I remembered the story of a pirate who was robbing boats off the Aegean coast. When Alexander the Great heard about it he sent for him. "What is your idea," he asked, "in infesting the sea?"

The pirate replied, "The same as yours, in infesting the land and the water. But because I do it with a tiny craft, I'm called a pirate; because you have a mighty navy, you're called an emperor."

I checked and found this story in Augustine's *City of God*. Augustine concludes, "What are kingdoms but gangs of criminals on a large scale? What are criminal gangs but petty kingdoms?"[5]

This, then, is the idea I want to pursue in this book. It's the idea inspired by my criminal compatriots, that the biggest thieves are in the government, that they are still at large, and that what they are stealing is America itself, its wealth and power. My fellow criminals don't know this to be true, but they suspect it, and I intend to prove they are right.

I'm also writing for everyone else, you noncriminals out there, to show you what's really going on. "The guilt lies with the organization," Joseph K. blurts out in Kafka's *The Trial*. "It is the high officials who are guilty."[6] We will see that, in our situation, Joseph K. has it exactly right. I've lived through a Kafkaesque situation, but I have not returned from it empty-handed.

For the past several years I've written about how Obama and the left are motivated by anticolonialism and anti-Americanism, how they see America as the bad guy, and how they seek to diminish America's wealth and power. This is true as far as it goes, but I now think it doesn't go far enough. In the confinement center I've really had time to read, and observe, and think. In the process, I've had a chance to reflect on my life, its accomplishments, its mistakes, and where I want to go from here. I've also clarified my thinking about Obama, Hillary, and the progressives.

It's too simple to treat the progressives as if they were simply failures in intellectual or ideological reasoning. Anyone who thinks this should consult Nietzsche's *The Genealogy of Morals*, a book I'd read in college but one that came alive for me in captivity in a new way. In Nietzsche's terms, we as humans aren't just trying to discover truth or to "get it right"; we are also trying to improve our position in the world. Humans aren't driven by the intellect alone. They are also driven by powerful motives of selfishness, covetousness, and envy. Nietzsche calls this the will to power.

Now I see that the ideological convictions of Obama, Hillary, and the progressives largely spring out of those base motives and that irrepressible will to power. The progressives have unleashed a massive scheme for looting the national treasury and transferring wealth and power to themselves, and their ideology of fairness and equality is to a large degree a justification—a sales pitch—to facilitate that larceny. Previously I didn't see this very clearly; now I do.

The truth is that for too long, like many intellectual conservatives, I have lived in a world of ideological abstraction. The progressives love that. They encourage parlor-room discussion about justice and equality while they systematically feast off other people's savings and loot the taxpayer. This book goes to the heart of what really drives these people, what they are doing, and how they are doing it. I recognize this will upset progressives; they just don't want me talking about it, for the same reason that thieves don't like to hear the alarm go off.

My first night in confinement was tough. I was scared, so I kept my eyes open. Every little sound—a door opening, a guy going to the bathroom—startled me. I stared at the ceiling and realized that this was how I was going to be sleeping for a while. I was a criminal among criminals. Even though the dormitory was fairly spacious, I felt claustrophobic. I knew it had nothing to do with the room; it had everything to do with the recognition that I was not free to leave. Freedom, I realized, is best appreciated when one doesn't have it. I was tired the next morning, but I got out of bed determined that I wouldn't let this captivity bring me down. Rather, I would make the best of it.

In the subsequent weeks, I became even more resolved. Captivity is a learning opportunity. I never wanted to be in confinement, but having found myself there, I considered myself an anthropologist in a strange land. In a sense, I had a unique opportunity to "study the natives." I had to remind myself, however, that I was not an outsider looking in; I too was one of the natives. Still, from my special vantage point among the convicts, I found it possible to examine their way of speaking, their habits, their experience, most of all their way of seeing the world. By seeing the world through their eyes, I widened my own angle of vision. Their subculture gave me insights into the larger culture. And this book is an attempt to trace the contours of that wider moral and political landscape on which most people sleepily dwell.

If we learn to see afresh the people who are strange to us, we can also learn to understand in a fresh way the things that are right in front of us. There are real crooks in this country, and not all of them are in prisons and confinement centers. Once we comprehend them—who they are and how they operate—we can act together to stop them.

Chapter 3

HOW TO STEAL A COUNTRY:

A Heist to End All Heists

As far back as I can remember, I always wanted to be a gangster. To me, being a gangster was better than being president of the United States.

—Ray Liotta as Henry Hill, *Goodfellas*

What is the most valuable thing the world has ever produced? The automobile? The airplane? The computer? The answer is actually an obvious one. The most valuable thing the world has ever produced is America. Consequently, the wealth of America is the greatest accumulation of resources and power in history. Not surprisingly, thieves are very interested.

This book is about a remarkable scheme to steal America. The scheme I refer to is under way, and in fact is working extremely well. America is being stolen; a good bit of it has been stolen already. When I use the term "stealing America," I am talking about the theft of the wealth of America. I am not talking about some group of people living off the public weal, or taking control of this or that industry. I am not even talking about theft of resources of the federal government. Rather, I am referring to the entire wealth of the nation, the value of the homes and the lifelong savings of all the people, the sum total of the assets of every industry from banking to electronics to oil drilling, all the funds allocated to health and education and every other service, both private and public; in sum, the entire wealth of America, built over more than two centuries. The thieves I am speaking about want all of it.

In fact, they want more. They want to own your businesses and your savings, how you work and whom you associate with, but they also want to control your education, your faith, your family, and what you watch on TV. They seek to regulate how you feel and what you think and how you love. They want to control your dreams and ambitions, your personal aspirations, your "pursuit of happiness." They want to own you, and to a considerable degree, they already do.

Machiavelli says there are two ways to steal a country. The first is external theft, which usually means conquest. A nation or group from the outside invades the country and rules it for its own benefit, or loots it and then leaves. The other is internal theft, which usually means tyranny. A dictator comes to power, typically through a coup, and then places himself in charge of the wealth of the nation, appropriating it at will for himself and his gang of associates and enforcers. The theft that I am referring to is internal theft, but it is not carried out dictatorially, but democratically. In other words, this is theft of the nation's wealth carried out through the normal political process.

The concept of democratic theft may seem puzzling, even paradoxical. How can the people of a country steal from themselves? We can gain some initial insight into the issue if we consider how democracy works among convicts, and how it is often the preferred mechanism for carrying out crimes and executions.

"Prison," said a young Hispanic guy, Roc, as we both stood in line to check back into the confinement center one evening, "is a democracy. Everything is settled by a vote."

I looked quizzically at Roc; I was surprised to hear this. Roc and I had played cards with a few other guys a couple of times. We had talked a little, and he knew what I was in for, but that was about it.

Roc had his hair closely cropped on the side, and the hair on top was greased and brushed back. He had tattoos covering his neck, shoulders, and arms. Actually pretty much everyone in the center had tattoos, and that's including inmates and staff. I may have been the only guy there who abstained from using my body as a billboard. Roc wore a tracksuit, but the pants were pulled way down to reveal an ample display of underpants. This, I could tell, was in keeping with the latest fashion among the criminal class. Again, I was a nonconformist in this respect.

"A vote?" I said.

"The gangs," Roc explained, "put everything to the members. Say a guy wants to leave the gang. Should we let him: yes or no? We have to vote on that. Let's say he leaves without getting permission. Should we kill him: yes or no? Let's take another vote. If he snitches to the police, should we also kill his family? Big questions, man. Even the gang leader cannot decide by himself. He has to take opinions into account. Usually there has to be a vote, and sometimes majority rule is not enough; the whole group has to agree."

Lowering his voice he added, "If it's the Black Muslims, they first vote and then they pray about it. They have to consult Allah. Allah also has to agree."

Across the counter a comatose staffer was reclined in a chair, his face slumped to the side. He looked like he had been shot, but obviously he was just taking a nap. I felt free to continue.

"How do you decide whether or not to take someone's life? What's that based on?"

"Before we vote we have to remember that we hold another man's future in our hands. Our decision affects not just him, but also his family. If we eliminate him, his whole family is f*cked. Still, in the end it's not based on the person, whether we like them or not. It's based on what's good for the gang, the bottom line."

"Bottom line?"

"What's good for business. A gang is a business. It needs loyalty and it needs fear. People have to be scared of us, and lots of times the murders are for that purpose."

What about a riot or a prison fight, I asked. Are those decided by the ballot? "A prison fight," he said, "is basically a free-for-all. If your friends are in it, you get in it. You don't have to know the reason. You do it just because you are in the gang."

Roc drew me back so that the comatose guy behind the counter couldn't hear anything, even if he was inclined to.

"Riots are different. Sometimes we vote on a riot; sometimes the leaders decide and we sign up. A riot has to be organized, man. They're hard to pull off. Looting doesn't just happen, contrary to what you hear on TV."

"The Ferguson riots," I said, referring to the looting and mayhem that followed the killing of black teenager Michael Brown by a police officer in August 2014, "are supposed to have occurred spontaneously."

"Spontaneously, my ass," Roc said. "It's hard to get any group to do something spontaneously. It's the job of the gang leader to plan the riot and to organize the looting. Looting requires a lot of tough m*ther-f*ckers to carry it out. But the toughest guy, who is the gang leader, is never directly involved. He's not stupid enough to be carrying sh*t out of stores. He's in a safe place, talking on his cell phone."

"It's all about the stealing, man," Roc continued. "Crime is basically stealing."

I thought about this, and it made sense to me. Murders usually occur because the criminal is trying to steal something and someone behind the counter, or the security guy, goes for his gun. Even rape is a form of stealing. The rapist takes something that doesn't belong to him, and does it by force.

"Rape," I said, "is not something that occurs democratically. It's not something that a group decides on based on the will of the majority."

"Who told you that?" he replied. "N*gger, were you born yesterday? Gangs make decisions like that all the time. We even have a term for it—it's called gang rape."

No, I wasn't born yesterday. But I was new to this environment. I was trying to learn as fast as I could.

By this time I had had my first confrontation with the Bureau of Prisons. The BOP had insisted I clear all media appearances through them. I decided to test this policy. I asked Megyn Kelly's producer to send me an invitation to appear on *The Kelly File*. I then submitted it to the head of the confinement center, Miss Williams, to forward to the BOP.

What happened next played out in my imagination. I could see some petty Obama official at the BOP scratching his head. I could see him calling a meeting. I could see a group of bureaucrats around a desk, wondering if there were First Amendment implications to silencing a guy like me. I could feel their fear as they considered whether they would be called on to answer for this.

All this was pure speculation, but speculation informed by my previous service in government. I know how these cowards operate.

My suspicions were vindicated when the decision came down. Williams informed me that the BOP had decided it no longer needed to approve my media appearances. I felt pleased. I had had a mini-skirmish with the BOP, and the score was Dinesh 1, BOP nil.

I was also learning the routines of confinement. Meals were served at bizarre times. Breakfast, for instance, was from 5 a.m. to 6:30 a.m. After that, there was no food until 11 a.m., which was lunchtime. I had no plans to eat there so I didn't really care. But on Sundays I liked to have coffee in the morning, since I was confined until 10 a.m. Sundays were my day to sleep in. If I wanted coffee, however, I had to get up before 6:30, because the coffee dispenser would be emptied at 6:29 a.m. sharp.

Tuesday was the day we got clean sheets. The only time to get those sheets was early in the morning, from 6 to 7 a.m. Roc was the one who told me about that the first week I was confined. I'm glad he did, because otherwise I'd have missed sheet-changing day and there is no other way to get clean sheets until the following Tuesday. Each week we'd strip our bunks and take the sheets, pillowcase, and towel to the laundry room and turn them in for a new set. The guy handing out the sheets made sure we all initialed our names on his sheet, I guess to make sure we took responsibility for all this government property that was being bestowed on us.

Every few hours, the staff at the confinement center called "Count." We had to return to our bunks and stand in front of them. A staffer would then walk through and make sure everyone was accounted for. Count was three or four times a day. Sometimes they would count in the middle of the night. Half-asleep, I'd see a female staffer wandering through the dormitory, checking names on her sheet. The inmates frequently commented on how long it took to do a simple count of 120 people. The process could take as long as an hour. During that time no one is permitted to leave their bunk area. When count is complete, an announcement is made: "Clear." Then we are free to go watch TV or go into the yard.

I had to do a mandatory class on hazmat training. Here I was taught about the use of hazardous materials. Since I didn't deal with any hazardous materials, the class did me no good. I knew there was no point to it. But I also knew there was no point pointing this out. Logic is completely useless in a place like this. There are rules, and you learn to follow the rules. To say that something doesn't "make sense" draws blank looks from the staff. They don't say anything, because there is nothing to say. It may not make sense to them, either, but they have a job to do.

Fortunately I didn't have to take any of the other classes: Anger Management Class, Depression Class, Parenting Class, Job Readiness Class, Transitional Skills Class. (I thought it was fascinating that the one class not offered was English Class. Apparently there was no need for Spanish-speaking convicts to learn English.) Roc had taken every class, not to learn anything, he said, but "just to pass time." Roc said the real purpose of the classes was so the confinement center could bill the government for conducting all these classes.

No cell phones in the facility—so I left mine in the console of my car. I could turn my cell in to them, to store in a box, but I wasn't about to do that; I didn't want them attempting to go through my phone. They had already inspected my car, searching it and making sure that my brake lights, turn signals, and horn all worked. The car inspection would be every month. There were also periodic locker inspections, when the inmates would be asked to stand outside, in the yard, while they went through everyone's locker looking for drugs, alcohol, and contraband items, notably cell phones.

The staff was determined that none of us keep a phone inside the facility. This, Roc said, was so that none of us could take pictures of the crappy food, the broken toilets, the cheap plastic chairs. I could see it. Roc was probably right that the confinement center was billing the government for all this crap at minibar prices.

Listening to Roc's account of crime and corruption operating through the democratic process, I thought, where have I seen this before? Then it hit me. I grew up in the world's largest democracy, India, where crime and corruption reach into the highest echelons of government, and are pretty much a way of life, at least for a substantial segment of the population. And, truth be told, the rest of the population is pretty much implicated, because it's hard to get by without participating in at least some types of illicit and corrupt activity.

From the time I was a wide-eyed kid, I learned how the system in India actually worked. It started when I was around fourteen, and a guy in my class died from drowning in a well.

"I feel so bad," I told my older friend Subash at the funeral. "What made him do it?"

"Do what?"

"I hear he committed suicide. He drowned himself."

"That's the official story," Subash said. "Actually he was killed by the Railway Station gang. Muslims."

"What did he do to them?"

"He insulted a Muslim kid, and the kid told his older brother, so they stabbed him and threw him into the well."

"But in that case the people who found him would see the stab wounds. The police would know about this. Why would they call this a suicide?"

"Because the police are in on it. They have been paid off."

"Why doesn't his family object?"

"There is only one way for them to get anywhere. They have to pay the police even more. Or they need influence that goes very high up. The problem is that this is a poor family; they have no influence. They know this, so they keep quiet."

A couple of years later there were reports in the paper about a fellow who was elected to be a governmental minister; he had a long criminal record, and had in fact conducted his election campaign from prison. I was so shocked that I called my uncle, a high-ranking political figure in India who has worked closely with the Indian police force, to explain what was going on.

"You realize, don't you Dinesh, that politicians are the richest people in India."

"I did not realize that."

"Every politician in India is corrupt, and there are close connections between politicians and gangsters," he added. "In this country, most people go into politics for one purpose—to loot the people. They consider this to be their election prerogative. Many of them are dirt-poor before they come into office. They leave richer than any businessman except maybe Tata, Birla, or Ambani. Politics is a business—I think you know this. What you may not know is that politics is part of the crime business. Don't forget, these men are thieves and we the people of India are the victims of their thievery. They are robbing us blind, and we know it, but there seems to be nothing we can do about it."

I nodded.

"The other thing about the politicians is that they are above the law. Did you read about the minister who was involved in the hit-and-run? No? Well, he was drunk, and he drove onto the footpath and killed four people. Slum dwellers."

"What happened?"

"*Tchah!* Nothing happened."

"Didn't anyone see?"

"Probably a hundred people saw him do it. But none of those people will testify. If they testify they are finished. Their families are finished. They are simply gone, *phut-a-phut!* Slum people are survivors; they are not going to take that risk."

"So the case is dropped?"

"The case is dropped. And the minister is still in office, giving speeches about the plight of the poor and sharing the wealth and social injustice. He is very shameless. They all are. Being a minister is a very good career choice.

"In fact," he continued, "let's talk about your career. Either you should study," he said, listing off a series of respectable occupations that I could enter, "or you should learn to shoot straight. There is no other future in India.

"I was thinking that you could be a politician or a police officer," he continued solemnly. "Both are excellent ways to make money. The public sector is a much safer way to be successful and rise to the top."

It was several years later that I understood what he meant. This was when, in my teens, I learned the ways of the cops and the Mumbai gangs. I got the stories from two guys in my school who were in the gangs, and my uncle—who was in a position to know—confirmed them. If you want to read all about it, pick up Suketu Mehta's book *Maximum City*. What he describes makes everything in here look tame.

Mehta points out that in recent years, the Indian police have become notorious for what is locally known as "encounter killings." An encounter killing is where the police show up at the hangouts of suspected criminals and open fire on them, killing as many as they can.

There is no attempt to arrest or try the criminals. The police know that process can take years, with uncertain results. It is a point of pride among the Indian police that they have figured out a way to short-circuit the process by simply gunning down the bad guys without wasting time or money on processing or trials or prison confinement.

My uncle would know about encounter killings. He isn't against them, but he thinks they should be carefully monitored by higher-ups like himself. The reason for the oversight, he says, is that there is too much potential for abuse. After all, many policemen really enjoy encounter killings. "This is where they get to act like the people in the movies," my uncle says, "except with real guns and real bad guys."

In my youth, I would think of Indian policemen as stupid, illiterate types. But in my later teens I learned to revise this assessment. These poorly paid government workers had figured out many ingenious ways to make money—more money than I could even conceive of at that stage in life.

In a typical case, the police would arrest some members of a particular gang. They would then begin negotiations with the gang's boss. "What will you pay us," they would ask, "to spare the lives of your members?" The gang boss would make an offer. If the offer came in insultingly low, the police would torture the gang members, informing the gang leadership that they were doing so. Mehta describes these torture techniques, which involve tying people to chairs, beating the inside of their legs with truncheons, keeping their eyelids open all night with matchsticks, and attaching their fingers, ears, and genitals to a portable generator so that electric shocks can be administered, causing the body to twist and jump.[1]

Then, to improve their negotiating position, the cops would call the boss of the rival gang. They would tell him that they had arrested several of his enemies, giving names and descriptions to establish the value of what they had, and ask what he was willing to pay to have those guys killed. The rival gang boss would make his offer. The police would then weigh their options.

Let's assume that the rival gang came up with a bigger number. A police van would then take the captured gang members to a remote part of the city, where they would be released. As they attempted their escape, the police from the van would open fire, killing all of them.

The next day the headlines in the newspaper would read, MUMBAI POLICE FOIL ESCAPE ATTEMPT BY DEADLY GANG. Articles and radio and TV reports would commend the cops for their outstanding bravery.

The public would heave a collective sigh of relief. Of course the police were too smart to use the same gambit every time. On other occasions they would engineer things differently. MUMBAI POLICE PREVAIL IN DEADLY SHOOT-OUT WITH GANG. In this case the police had lined up the gang members and ordered them at gunpoint to run toward the van. As this occurred the police mowed them down. Then they planted guns in the hands of the corpses. The reading public would marvel at the fact that seventeen gang members had been shot dead, and not a single policeman was even hurt. What incredible marksmanship! No wonder the Mumbai cops have long had the reputation of being the best police force outside of Scotland Yard.

I'm sure India is not alone: similar things happen in Thailand and Mexico and South Africa and just about every developing country. Corrupt politicians, corrupt cops; the typical third-world reaction is, "So what's new? Just make sure that you don't get caught in the net." Still, everyone knows there is no way to completely escape the net. Staying completely clean is not an option. Everywhere you have to pay bribes, pay "black" money, go around the law, figure out ways to finagle the system. If an Indian tells you he is an honest man, you can be sure you are talking to a liar. Everyone is crooked and scamming the system, not only the designated criminals and scammers but also the people designated to protect society from the criminals and scammers. In sum, the whole country is like one great big detention center.

It's a suffocating, depressing way to live, and I left India and came to America in part to get away from all that. From the beginning, America seemed to me a place radically different from where I came from. It offered me a new way to dream and a new type of life. And I've spent much of my career in conservative circles, praising and in a sense idealizing America. Several of my book titles—*The End of Racism*, *The Virtue of Prosperity*, *What's So Great About America*, and *America: Imagine a World Without Her*—convey this idealistic enthusiasm. My film *America* is essentially a vindication of Burke's criterion for intelligent patriotism: "To make us love our country, our country ought to be lovely."

Now, for the first time, facing political targeting and selective prosecution, plus my exposure to the world of the confinement center, a world utterly different than anything I had previously experienced, I am forced to ask whether I have missed the real America, the America that people actually live in. How lovely is that America, compared to the India I grew up in?

I'm not suggesting for a moment that India and America are the same. Life in the two countries is very different. As I had experienced it, the American way was the virtual opposite of the Indian way. But now India aspires to become more like America, and America seems to be moving in the direction of India. This is the scary thing. We are a long way from the third world, where crime and politics are pretty much the same thing. We haven't reached the point in America where the police will shoot you in order to collect a ransom.

But India is progressing and America is regressing. There are now powerful anticorruption movements in India, while the party in America that now controls the presidency is the corrupt party. And I will prove in this book that my confinement center inmates are right. There is, as they allege, a criminal syndicate that is stealing America in the same way that the corrupt politicians and gangsters have stolen India.

This book tells a new story of American politics, very different from the one you normally hear. The tale you normally hear is that American politics is a contest of ideas. There are two groups or parties, and they both share a vision of America as a free and prosperous nation. But they differ on means, on how to get there. Conservatives and Republicans, in particular, hold that liberal Democrats are horribly misguided people. The latter espouse the wrong set of ideas.

Obama, from this point of view, doesn't "get it." He thinks that higher taxes actually promote economic growth. He mistakenly believes that government will do a better job than the private sector in ensuring health care for people. He worries that hydraulic fracking to generate oil and natural gas might be harmful to the environment. He fails to realize that government control of banks and financial institutions will impede economic efficiency. He seems to miss the fact that "free" education is not free at all, because someone is going to bear the cost. In the conservative view, this isn't just one man's blindness; it is the blindness of a whole party, a whole movement. Consequently the conservative mission is to educate and correct Obama and the progressives, by implanting in them the right set of ideas.

The conservative view seems to be based on the classical idea, with its roots in Plato and Aristotle, that bad actions are the result of ignorance or folly. According to this tradition, virtue is knowledge, and sound actions result from sound understanding. Conservatives are often wringing their hands about liberals: "If only they knew the facts." Years ago, my American Enterprise Institute colleague Charles Murray said to me, "These liberal Democrats exasperate me. If only they could see the data!" A brilliant and principled man, Murray simply could not accept that they might be as familiar with the data as he was, and have other motives for believing as they did.

In my view, the classical idea that virtue is knowledge was completely capsized by the apostle Paul, who said, "The good that I would, I do not; the evil that I would not, that I do." [2] Paul here introduces the idea of a corrupted will that knows deep down what is right and wrong but nevertheless chooses to do wrong. Now, why would someone do that? Behind Paul's statement is a whole worldview, that human nature has a dark side, that people are not entirely rational, that we seek gratifications and rewards that are not rightly due to us, and that evil—not just folly—is an ineradicable part of human nature. Any politics that fails to take this into account is, I think, superficial and destined to fail.

Interestingly the classical view—that one's opponents do not have bad motives but are captive to well-meaning error—is not espoused by today's liberals and progressives. They are not shy to attack the motives of conservatives and Republicans. In the liberal view, the right is motivated by selfishness, materialism, greed, racism, sexism, homophobia, and bloodthirsty warmongering. So while liberals attack us as being wicked and immoral, we fault them for being good people who have simply gotten their policies wrong. We consider liberals to be proprietors of what the late Saul Bellow termed the Good Intentions Paving Company.

The conservative view of liberals certainly seems more magnanimous and more charitable. I would be all in favor of it, if it had any bearing on the truth. I would champion it myself, if it could show any results. But consider: as of this writing, conservatives have for seven years been lecturing Obama and the progressives. We have been educating them on the precise location of the Crimea. We have reminded them that Vladimir Putin used to be a KGB officer. We have notified them that the Iranian mullahs are not our friends. We have offered documentary evidence that they intend to do as they say and build a nuclear bomb. We have traced the bloody history of the Muslim Brotherhood. We have elucidated the dangers of government-run health care. We have made the case, both theoretical and empirical, for private enterprise. We have shown the danger of confiscatory tax rates. Yet these efforts seem to have come to nil. Obama and the progressives continue on their path. Evidently our educational schemes never work. We can't get through to them.

I'd like to suggest that this is because our basic approach is inadequate. In fact, the liberal approach is a better one, because it takes motives into account. Liberals may be wrong about our motives, but they are not wrong to look for what drives us, where we're coming from. Think of conversations you've had with a spouse or child in which you rebutted everything they said, only to realize that your rebuttals don't matter. Their stated anxieties are not what's really bothering them. Their loud complaints camouflage an unstated complaint that is hidden but propelling everything they say. Only when you figure that out can you actually solve the problem. The broad liberal framework for understanding us, by going to the issue of motive, goes deeper. For this reason it's a better one than our narrow framework for understanding them.

Probing people's motives is not easy and is always somewhat speculative. We see only what people do, not their inner thoughts. Still, we can infer from actions what people are thinking. And we can then match our inferences against other things they do, to check whether our inference is right or not. In this book I offer a theory that is derived from experience and close observation. It is a hypothesis, but I mean that term in a scientific sense. The hypothesis or theory posits motivations that we do not see, but it can be tested by matching it up against the facts we do see. If the theory is right, then like a good scientific theory it should also have predictive power. It should enable you to make sense of future behavior that arises out of the same basic drives and motives.

I begin with an irony. Whenever I hear liberals and progressives, they talk about unfairness—about how the ordinary American is being cheated and ripped off. The culprits are banks, pharmaceutical companies, insurance companies, greedy CEOs, Wall Street types, the capitalist system, the criminal justice system, the oppressive legacy of American history.

The general conservative impulse—one that I used to share—is to deny the premise, to reject the idea that there is any injustice or theft going on. Conservatives strenuously labor to show that the system is fair. For instance, when liberals point out that more than 95 percent of government prosecutions end with a guilty verdict—either through jury verdict or plea bargain—conservatives assume that nearly everyone who is accused must be guilty, so the 95 percent figure is proof that the criminal justice system is working well.

I used to be one of those conservatives, but now I've changed my mind. Not everyone who is prosecuted and convicted deserves what they get. Nor does America today reflect the fairness, equal opportunity, and social mobility celebrated in conservative tracts. On the contrary, many people don't have a real chance to succeed. Ordinary Americans are being systematically ripped off by a conniving, self-interested system. Even some businesses are complicit in this exploitation. So something very unfair is going on: here the liberals are onto something, even though they are wrong about what it is.

Now, we face a real whodunit: who are the culprits that are stealing

America? Moreover, what are they stealing—where is the evidence of theft? Finally, what is their modus operandi? In other words, how are they pulling off the job? In this book I'll answer all these questions; here I lay out my general framework and give you a preview of where the chapters are going.

I want to begin by showing what is involved in stealing America. This can be measured not only in terms of dollars but also in terms of what America has meant to the lives of its citizens. America's affluence, but also the American dream, is at stake. Today America has an $18 trillion economy and accumulated private wealth totaling approximately $75 trillion. America is also the world's sole superpower, what some have called a "hyperpower." This position gives America an influence that reaches beyond merely economic matters. The ordinary American is a beneficiary of all this, because it enables him or her to live not only an abundant but also a consequential life. These outcomes are the product of two centuries of hard-earned effort, not only by us but also by our forefathers. They are the birthright of all living Americans. Even I, as an immigrant, claim this birthright.

There are those, however, who insist that America's wealth is made up of stolen goods. This is a familiar litany: America stole the country from the Native Americans, the labor of the African Americans, and half of Mexico from the Mexicans in the Mexican War. Even today we hear, America's foreign policy and free market system are forms of theft, because they take what belongs to others and illicitly appropriate it. These contentions come from some of the wiliest figures in the progressive camp: Senator Elizabeth Warren, Nobel laureate and columnist Paul Krugman, investment guru Warren Buffett, and Nobel laureate and economist Joseph Stiglitz. Behind these figures are the great thinkers of modern progressivism, such as John Rawls and Karl Marx.

The contentions and proposals of this group demand careful consideration, and I do carefully consider them. But in the past, as in my book and film *America*, I treated them as philosophical and historical arguments being advanced in a disinterested way. Now, however, I recognize that they are not just academic and policy arguments. They are hardly disinterested; rather, they are intended to advance the interests of a powerful and grasping class of people. Even more, they are con men's pitches, pitches that are camouflaged as proposals to advance the common good.

Consider the most powerful of the theft allegations, the one about slavery. Certainly slavery was a form of theft: theft of life and labor. Abraham Lincoln expressed the essence of slavery when he said it expressed the maxim, "You work, I eat." And of course slavery in America began in the early seventeenth century and lasted until the second half of the nineteenth century. So the progressive appears here to be on very strong ground.

But now we raise the question: how did this theft end? Normally thefts are stopped by the police. Normally there is a force, typically acting on behalf of the victims of theft, that proves to be stronger than the thieves, and not only stops the theft but also brings the perpetrators to justice. Now, in this particular case, the theft was ended by America itself. The thief itself turned out to play the role of policeman.

In the Civil War, which was largely a white man's war, several hundred thousand whites died to secure for the slaves a freedom that the slaves were in no position to secure for themselves. Moreover, the wealth accumulated by the South in large part due to slavery was destroyed in that war. This was a fate that America could have avoided, in the manner that thieves, prior to being caught, have always and everywhere avoided answering for their crimes.

Yet America took upon herself the responsibility to end the theft of slavery. "Other revolutions have been the insurrection of the oppressed," Emerson wrote. "This was the repentance of the tyrant."[3] Now, a tyrant who repents is no longer a tyrant. The progressive charge, if true at one time, is no longer true and hasn't been for a century and a half. Yet it continues at full force, not because it has any intellectual validity anymore, but because it has become politically useful. In short, it is now part of the progressive con men's pitch.

How do we know that these progressives are con men? I will present a great deal of evidence in this book, but here, for starters, is a revealing clue. The progressives pose as the champions not only of fairness and social justice but also of compassion. They are the ones who insist on our obligation to those from whom we have allegedly stolen.

Let's leave aside for the moment whether they are right about the theft. What we do know for sure is that progressives assert there has been a theft. They further acknowledge that they are among the beneficiaries of it. Based on this, they would seem to have a clear obligation to return the stolen goods that they are currently enjoying. We might expect, from this analysis, to discover that progressives are the most generous people in America. We can anticipate that they contribute the highest portion of their incomes and time to help their wronged and less fortunate fellow men and women.

The truth, however, is that progressives are the least generous people in America. I saw this personally with Obama, who unceasingly declares that "we are our brother's keeper" even as he refuses to help his own half brother, George, who lives in a hut in the Huruma slum of Nairobi.

I met George in early 2012 when I interviewed him for my film *2016: Obama's America.* A few months after that, when I was back in America, George called me from Kenya to ask me to give him $1,000 because his baby son was sick. Surprised, I asked him, "Why are you calling me? Isn't there someone else you can call?" He said, "No."

So I sent him the money. I guess on that occasion it was I, not Obama, who proved to be his brother's keeper. And besides George, the president has other relatives in dire need—his aunt Hawa Auma, for example, sells charcoal on the roadside in rural Kenya, and desperately needs money to get her rotting teeth fixed. Although Obama is aware of their plight, he refuses to help them.

In this respect, Obama is fairly typical of progressives more generally. The evidence for this claim is in Arthur Brooks's study, *Who Really Cares.* Brooks bases his conclusions on data drawn from a wide range of sources that keep track of philanthropy. Brooks divides America into four groups: religious conservatives, religious liberals, secular

conservatives, and secular liberals. He finds that religious conservatives are the most generous people in America, and secular liberals are
the least generous. (Secular conservatives and religious liberals fall in
the middle.)

Now, this is a remarkable fact. And what makes it especially biting
is that secular liberals are much better off, both in terms of income
and accumulated savings, than religious conservatives. If the wealth of
America is made up of stolen goods, they are the ones who are holding
on to more stolen goods than anyone else. Yet the ones who have more,
and bloviate the loudest about compassion, turn out to be the least
compassionate; while those who have less, and are constantly accused
of being selfish and uncompassionate, actually give the most.[4] I think
we can reasonably conclude that progressive motives are suspect, and
that something else is going on here.

I will show in this book that progressives are the real thieves. Their
objective, well under way, is to steal the wealth of the country. Progressives aren't just after the federal purse—the $3 trillion federal budget—
or even the annual gross national product—some $18 trillion. They are
after the entire wealth of the nation: the full $75 trillion. Progressives
want to take over all the major industries, from education to health
care to energy to automobiles to investment banking to real estate.
From Wall Street to Silicon Valley, they want, as my fellow inmates
like to say, "the whole enchilada."

This is not to say that progressives intend to *seize* all that wealth, but
they do want to *control* it. Progressives generally can't create wealth, so
they seek to take it over once it has been created by someone else. They
do this through the various agencies of government, such as the IRS,
the FBI, the EPA, the FCC, the FDA, the BLM, and HHS.

Certainly progressive leaders intend to become fantastically rich
while pretending to serve the public good—look at the way the Obamas
and the Clintons live—but their ultimate goal isn't just money: it is also
power. Progressives like Obama and Hillary want to wrest control of
the levers of society so that they can run things for their own benefit,
and do what they want without restraint, above the law.

The progressive leaders' modus operandi is to achieve this summit by stealing from the productive and distributing to their political allies. They do this while siphoning off enough to live in extreme luxury and keeping control of the entire process for themselves. Why distribute at all? Because this is democratic theft, theft that operates through the democratic process. So the little thieves need to be compensated, even if their compensation turns out to be relatively meager. Democratic theft relies on creating a Manichean division of society between the rich and the rest of us, and then giving the rest of us a license to loot the so-called one percent.

The looters I'm speaking about aren't like the Ferguson looters, or the Baltimore looters, because that kind of looting, although reprehensible, at least requires work. You have to go out and take stuff. My fellow inmates in the confinement center would recognize that type of looting; they are frequently reminding me that criminal activity takes work. As one thief put it to me, "Stealing is hard, man. When you steal for a living, you can't just steal a little here, a little there. You have to be stealing every day. Stealing is a job, just like being a plumber or a business executive." But the looting that I'm referring to does not require daily activity. In fact, it requires little more than casting a vote every two or four years. Otherwise you can sit around, watch TV, and collect your free stuff.

As I said earlier, democratic theft seems paradoxical. How can the people rob themselves? Of course the people are not robbing themselves; rather, one segment of the people is robbing another. A large group, perhaps a majority, is through its elected leaders forcibly confiscating the resources of another group, perhaps a minority. This seems to be a fairly clinical description of what progressive politicians do— they extract and distribute money, minus of course their administrative fee. But hasn't that been going on for a long time? Isn't this how the system was set up? Doesn't democracy *sanction* this kind of redistribution?

I will say more about this in the next chapter, but the short answer is no. We live in a constitutional republic. Certainly this involves majority rule, but the scope of that rule is carefully delineated. Majorities have certain legitimate powers—such as the power to protect our lives, liberty, and property, and the power to make rules for the general welfare or common good—but these powers are deliberately restricted. Majorities are constitutionally empowered to do certain things but not others. In particular, they are constitutionally prohibited from confiscating the resources of minorities for their own benefit.

Imagine a situation in which 51 percent of the citizens gets the benefit of most government redistribution programs and pays no federal income taxes. This is not hard to imagine; it is actually our situation right now. This 51 percent then proceeds, through the democratic process, to confiscate an ever-increasing share of the income and wealth of the other 49 percent for its own benefit. Such actions may be considered democratic, but they are flatly unconstitutional. They are also an obvious form of stealing. Citizens have no obligation to go along with such theft. Democratic theft is still theft.

The main obstacle to democratic theft is the Constitution, our supreme law, devised by the founders. The founders recognized that every system of government is vulnerable to theft. In monarchies, the king has the power to steal from the people. In aristocracies, the aristocrats have the power to steal from the people. And in democracies, the majority has the power to steal from the rest of the people. Yet majority theft is no more defensible than minority theft, just as gang rape is no more defensible than individual rape.

The founders, as we will see, wanted to create an anti-theft society. They realized that to do this they must limit majority rule. So they approved a Constitution specifically enumerating what the government could do, and giving it no authority to do anything else. The Constitution specifically permits the government to raise money to pay the nation's debts and to promote the "general welfare," but it does not permit the government to extract money from you solely to benefit me.

In general, this system of theft prohibition worked well for the better part of two centuries, until progressives began to dismantle it. Progressive hostility to the founding puzzles many people, but actually it is very easy to understand. They dislike the American founding for the same reason that criminals dislike anti-theft statutes.

The methodology of theft is very simple and involves five distinct steps. First, plan the theft. Second, recruit allies. Third, pitch or justify the theft. Fourth, carry out the theft. And finally, cover up the theft. In this book, we explore this methodology, generally in the order that it is experienced by the victims. So we begin with the various pitches that progressive thieves use, along with actual thefts that those pitches made possible. This takes up four chapters. Then we move to the organizers and planners, the thieves' personnel roster. I devote one chapter to the progressive godfather, Saul Alinsky, and to his background among the mafia and various gangs. I also show how Alinsky is the man behind the crash of 2008—a largely untold story.

Then I devote a chapter to the education of Alinsky's two most capable disciples, Barack Obama and Hillary Clinton. Obama began with a different mentor—his own scheming father—but then "graduated" and got his first apprenticeship in the Alinsky network. In the quotation at the beginning of this chapter, Henry Hill says he'd rather be a gangster than president of the United States; Obama and Hillary have come to the realization that the best way to be a gangster is to become the president of the United States. In this chapter we see some of the scams these two have pulled off, from Obamacare to Hillary's "pay for policy" program, administered by the Clinton Foundation.

Theft on this scale takes a lot of work, including disciplined and painstaking recruitment of allies. The subsequent chapter shows how the thieves-in-charge recruit their co-conspirators, allies, and accessories. I show how envy—the lowest of all human emotions—is the hidden motive that draws together this coalition of aspiring thugs and burglars known as the American left. Then we find out how progressive thieves take over the government and then get their hands on the goods.

Throughout this book, I'll show how progressives use the agencies of government to cover up the theft. This, as we will see, involves the state hiring thugs and *caporegimes*, who are then given the latitude to engage in certain types of intimidation and violence. Henry Hill, the young gangster in *Goodfellas*, clearly understood how the system works. "If we wanted something, we took it," he says. "If anyone complained twice they got hit so bad, believe me, they never complained again." Hill and his buddies had to club their victims in an alley and quietly bury the bodies. By contrast, it is beneficial to progressive thieves that government intimidation be publicized. Progressive theft relies on keeping the citizens in constant fear.

As an immigrant and a patriot, I don't want to see America become a nation run by thieves and gangsters. Nor do I want to be a victim of this corrupt cabal of progressive Democrats. I am happy to see India move in the direction of America; I don't want to see America move in the direction of India. I may be a *vox clamantis in deserto*—a voice in the wilderness—but I want people to see what is going on, because in a democratic society, they are the ones who have the power to stop it.

The thieves have one vulnerability: they have to be elected. Their vulnerability, then, is our opportunity. This theft has to be halted, and I conclude with four specific ways to do that.

Chapter 4

CREATING NEW WEALTH:

America, the Anti-Theft Society

The businessman's tool is values. The bureaucrat's tool is fear.[1]

—Ayn Rand, *Capitalism: The Unknown Ideal*

From the dawn of mankind to the present, theft has been the way of the world. The great empires were established through large-scale theft. From ancient history alone, we can recall the Assyrians, the Babylonians, the Greeks, Alexander the Great, and the Romans. From antiquity to the present, tyrannies have stolen the wealth of the people. One of the greatest malefactors was Louis XIV of France, the Sun King, with all his regalia, looting the wealth of his country and distributing it among his sycophantic nobles. Entire social structures, from feudalism to the caste system, have been put in place to confiscate people's earnings and possessions, and thus institutionalize theft. Thievery is also one of the oldest professions, and the most ancient written works

in every culture speak of people making off with the goods and possessions of others.

For centuries, large-scale theft required no defenders because it had
no critics. In Ibn Khaldun's *Muqaddimah*, the Islamic historian describes without embarrassment one looting upon another. He speaks
of the Bedouins and later the Muslims taking booty—including slaves.
Of the Bedouins he writes, "It is their nature to plunder whatever other
people possess. They recognize no limit in taking the possessions of
other people." Of the Muslim fleets in the Middle Ages, he writes,
"The Christian nations could do nothing against the Muslim fleets,
anywhere in the Mediterranean. All the time, the Muslims rode the
wave of conquest. There occurred then many well-known episodes of
conquest and plunder. The Muslims returned victorious with booty."
Although Khaldun is a humane scholar, we detect no moral condem-
nation whatever of any of this behavior; on the contrary, his accounts
move between purely descriptive and frankly adulatory.[2]

When the ancients did stoop to justify theft, it was with the simple
maxim that might makes right. The classic expression of this is in Thucydides's *Peloponnesian War*. The Athenians approach the tiny island
of Melos and inform the Melians that they must ally themselves with
Athens and pay tribute, or else they will be destroyed. The Melians
appeal to justice but the Athenians will have none of it. It is the law
of nature, they say, for the strong to rule over and take advantage of
the weak. In the words of the Athenian delegation, "The strong do
what they have the power to do and the weak accept what they have
to accept."

The Melians admit they are weak, but say so for the very reason that
they don't want to interfere in the conflict of great empires; rather, they
wish to stay neutral, and since they are a small island, they will bother
no one. The Athenians emphasize that precisely because the Melians
are small, they must not escape. If the Melians escape, then larger territories may refuse to pay tribute. The Melians refuse to succumb, and
the island is besieged and then wiped out. All the able-bodied men are
killed, the women and children enslaved, and Athens resettles Melos

with its own citizens.[3] We see here not merely how strong nations have historically had no qualms about looting or leveling weaker ones, but also how terror is a standard mechanism used to bring the vulnerable to heel.

Even today, theft is a common way that private individuals and governments obtain wealth and possessions. Broadly speaking, we can say there are two types of theft: private theft and public theft. Private theft is perpetrated by individuals or crime syndicates. Public theft is perpetrated by public institutions or governments. Here at the confinement center, you can find both.

Steve is a white guy I met who has served time in prison both in Mexico and in the United States. I met Steve in the confinement center's indoor workout room. A short, slim fellow who wears army pants and a baseball cap back to front—to show the adjusto-strap to advantage—Steve wiped off the weights with his towel. "Wanna use these?" he asked. Ordinarily I would have been surprised to see such courtesy. But I had been in confinement for a little while: I knew that most people here are extremely courteous. When I watch TV no one will change the channel without asking me. Big black guys who walk in front of me will duck, so as not to obscure my view.

It all makes sense, I guess. When violence lies just below the surface, it's important for people to develop a code of good manners. Besides, fights carry a heavy penalty for these guys. It's called "Go back to prison. Do not pass go. Do not collect two hundred dollars."

Steve was arrested, he told me, when the cops found twenty kilograms of cocaine hidden in the back of his car. He had purchased the stash in Mexico from a guy named Angel with the intention of bringing it across the border and selling it to a dealer in America. Steve said he had gotten the drugs past the border control, and thought he was home free. He was now on the American side, driving in the Arizona desert.

Then, out of nowhere, a group of police cars appeared and surrounded his car. The cops pulled out their weapons and made him lie flat on the ground. They searched the car and found the drugs. Then,

Steve recalled, a car pulled up and a familiar figure emerged: Angel. The cops and Angel exchanged greetings. The cops then returned Angel's drugs to him, and Angel split the money he got from Steve with the cops. Then Angel drove away, and the cops took Steve to jail.

I find Steve's story revealing because it is a story about theft, and yet the one guy who ended up in prison was not a thief, while the real thieves all got away. Steve broke the law because he was trafficking in illegal drugs, but he didn't steal from anyone. He actually paid for the drugs. Angel, by contrast, sold the drugs to Steve but then got them back from the police. So Angel was actually stealing from Steve. And the police, by splitting Steve's money with Angel, proved that they were also thieves, and Steve—far from being a thief—was actually the victim of their theft.

This case may seem anomalous, but it is fairly common. Cartels routinely bribe U.S. government employees of the Border Patrol and the Department of Homeland Security to enable alien and drug smuggling across the border. Cash bribes and even sexual favors are sometimes doled out in exchange for sensitive information, necessary documents such as immigration papers, or simply to allow contraband or illegal aliens through inspection lanes. Even terrorists can make their way across the border if they pay off the right people.[4]

As this example shows, there are different kinds of thieves; some of them wear uniforms, and thievery is sometimes perpetrated under the guise of stopping injustice and upholding the law. I guess I can see where some of these inmates get the idea that all of America is a racket and that everyone is somehow in on it. Once I found this way of thinking to be borderline crazy; now I see there's an element of truth in it.

Part of people's confusion over my presence in the confinement center was that I hadn't stolen anything. In fact, in my early days at the confinement center, I had trouble explaining to the staff what my offense actually was. "So, you were allowed to give ten thousand dollars and you gave thirty thousand?"

"Yes," I said. "I used two straw donors to give ten thousand dollars each."

"Of their money?"

"No, of my money."

"So you gave too much money."

"Exactly."

"That's why you're here?"

"Yes. For exceeding the campaign finance limit."

"Oh, man, that is such bullsh*t."

Once I began to converse with fellow inmates, things went pretty much the same way. Initially guys started calling me "doctor" in the apparent belief that since I was Indian I must be a doctor. I explained that I was actually a writer and filmmaker, inspiring one guy to ask, "So why are you here?"

I said, "I was raising money for a friend of mine who was running for office."

He got pretty excited.

"Really?" he said. "Can you raise money for me?"

"No," I said.

He asked me to tell him about my offense, and I tried to, but he seemed uncomprehending.

"You gave too much money?"

"I did."

"Then—you did what?"

"Nothing."

"Come on, man. You shot someone, you paid someone off?"

"Absolutely not."

"You must have pissed off some very important m*therf*ckers."

"Yes," I agreed, thinking of one in particular.

"Holy sh*t! I'm really sorry, n*gger. And I thought you were a doctor who stole money from Medicare or something!"

Thievery is pretty common in prison and in the confinement center, although on a very petty scale. An African American, Shiloh, told me how he essentially ran a private store in prison. "I sold raw eggs, fruit, pies, and candy bars," he said. "I was a regular Costco." Mostly the provisions were pilfered from the kitchen. Then he sold them to other inmates. "People would pay me in cash, or sometimes they would pay me with sweatpants or sneakers."

The white supremacists, in particular, loved his fruit bags. "I would make a couple dozen fruit bags every day with apple slices, maybe an orange, sometimes even peaches and kiwi. The racists loved it! I was their favorite black guy in the prison. I didn't mind selling to them. It was good business, man. It kept me afloat with cash for the whole time I was there."

In confinement, most of the thievery I observed occurred at the poker table. One time the Filipino guy came out raging, "I'm never playing again! This is bullsh*t!" He seemed inconsolable, until an older white guy got it out of him that "I was cheated out of ten dollars." The white guy reminded him, "You are playing with m*therf*cking crimi-nals. *Of course* they're going to cheat you."

The Filipino guy persisted. "I know exactly who cheated me. I know exactly where that money is." To which the white guy said, "That's not the hard part. The hard part is getting that m*therf*cker to actually give you the money. Good luck with that, n*gger." The Filipino said, "I'm not going to be cheated. I'm going to go kick his ass." The white guy dissuaded him. "Don't be stupid. You want to get into a fight and go back to prison over ten bucks?"

Happily the Filipino saw the good sense of that observation and got into his bunk, still sputtering with rage. The next morning the first words out of his mouth were "I still want my money."

One may naïvely expect the authorities at the confinement center to make efforts to restrict theft. I call this "naïve" because the whole structure of the corrections system appears designed to engage in theft. It's not obvious, however, how this theft might occur or who its targets might be, so let's look more closely at how the system engages in its own distinctive brand of rip-off.

For the first couple of months I used to play chess with a white guy, Edgar, who was one of the few white-collar guys in the confinement center. Edgar looked out of place in confinement; he wore jeans, long-sleeve shirts that were never tucked in, and had windblown hair and a perpetual tan that suggested he had just returned from the beach. Edgar was just in for sixty days, having served eighteen months at the Taft prison camp. Right when he checked into camp, he recalled, the warden called him in for a meeting.

"Edgar," the warden said, "I notice that you haven't completed your GED."

Edgar told him, "I don't need my GED. I am an investment banker. I've worked at Lehman Brothers. I ran my own company for several years. I got caught up in the insider trading thing."

"Yes," the warden said, "but why didn't you ever finish high school?"

"It's a long story," Edgar said. "The short version is that I dropped out in the eleventh grade, moved to Seattle, and went to work and never looked back."

"Here at Taft," the warden said, "we will make sure you finish your GED."

"Again," insisted Edgar, "I am an educated man. I read several books a week about history, politics, finance, and taxation. I am way past the high school thing."

"Even so," the warden said, "I am going to make sure you get your GED."

At first, Edgar told me, "I thought I was dealing with a retard. But something caused me to press this guy, and finally he admitted that for every prisoner who gets his GED, the prison gets an additional twenty-five hundred dollars. Now, this guy knew that for some of the prisoners they might never make it—they might take the test and fail—but I was already an educated man, and so I was a surefire bet for him to get that twenty-five hundred."

"All that," I said, "for a couple of thousand bucks?"

"There are two million prisoners in the United States," Edgar said. "The whole system is designed to keep this number high, and going up if possible. Each prisoner brings the system around fifty grand a year. You do the math. It works out to one hundred billion dollars a year.

"That's just the starting point. The next challenge is how to use the system and the inmates to get more money out of the government. So they throw out furniture that's perfectly usable and put in for new furniture. They have classes where people show up, sign in, and then leave. They charge for the class, even though no one actually takes the class. They offer services that no one wants, and that produce no results, but for which they can bill the government. My GED—which I did get, thank you very much—is just a small part of this very big racket.

"This is the key to understanding the justice system in America. It is based on how to extract the most money."

Edgar alerted me to two government programs I'd never heard of that corroborated his cynical perspective. The first is the U.S. government's use of tens of thousands of illegal immigrants each year as slave labor. These illegals are captured and placed in detention centers, where they then do full-time labor in exchange for wages of approximately one dollar a day.

"That's less than people make in India!" I said incredulously.

"Look it up," Edgar said, and so I did. I found a *New York Times* article on the subject. Edgar was right.

The article said that roughly half the illegals that appear before U.S. immigration courts are, for one reason or another, not deported. Currently there are around 60,000 of them in detention facilities around the country. The government has them at its mercy. So it makes them an offer they find hard to refuse: work for us and for virtually no money. Since illegals in captivity aren't covered by labor laws, this exploitation of their condition is perfectly legal. And there are takers, mainly because the illegals don't have any other way of earning money.

One fellow, Pedro Guzmán, a native of Guatemala who was held at the Stewart Detention Center in Lumpkin, Georgia, told the *Times*, "I went from making $15 a day as a chef to $1 a day in the kitchen in lockup."

Of course, if someone in the private sector hires illegals for a dollar a day they can get in big trouble on multiple fronts. These rules, however, do not apply to the U.S. government. According to Carl Takei, a lawyer with the American Civil Liberties Union's prison project, "This in essence makes the government, which forbids everyone else from hiring people without documents, the single largest employer of undocumented immigrants in the country."[5]

A second government scheme Edgar alerted me to is called civil forfeiture or, more colloquially, "stop and seize." In April 2015, twenty-two-year-old Joseph Rivers boarded a train to Los Angeles to pursue his dream career as a music video producer. On him he had his life savings, $16,000.

At a train stop in Albuquerque, an officer from the Drug Enforcement Administration (DEA) approached Rivers and questioned him about his travel plans. Then he demanded to search Rivers's bag. Rivers consented, and the officer found an envelope with the cash.

The officer then seized Rivers's money through civil asset forfeiture laws. Rivers has never been charged with a crime, yet, as of this writing, the DEA has yet to return his money.

How, you might ask, can the government do this? Doesn't Rivers have constitutional rights? Yes, he does. But the government in forfeiting his money is exploiting an ambiguity in the law. Technically the government isn't doing anything to Rivers. Rather, the government is *accusing the cash itself of being part of a crime.* And since cash by itself doesn't have constitutional rights, the government simply takes it. The person carrying the cash then has the obligation to prove ownership and to prove that the money is not being used for any criminal purpose. Only then is the money returned.

Sound crazy? Originally civil forfeiture laws were passed to help the government deal with drug dealers and money launderers. But now the system is routinely used to target law-abiding citizens.

As the *Washington Post* revealed in an investigative report on the stop-and-seize program, the amounts of money confiscated each year are enormous. In 2012, the government seized $2.5 billion in cash alone from 62,000 Americans without warrants or indictments. In addition, the government confiscated another $4.3 billion in property: cars, boats, electronics, jewelry, and even homes.

Federal and local law enforcement authorities typically work together to acquire the cash and possessions of citizens. Then they split the money under a program that the government calls, without irony, Equitable Sharing. If local law enforcement pulls off the seizure, it usually keeps 80 percent of the money and sends 20 percent to the federal government, which deposits it in the U.S. Department of Justice's Asset Forfeiture Fund. The DOJ can then spend the money on various law enforcement activities. This sharing of the loot also enables local law enforcement to evade state and local prohibitions against civil forfeiture.

The Internal Revenue Service has also gotten into the act. In 2012, the IRS made 639 civil forfeitures, almost five times as many as it had in 2005. Only about 20 percent of IRS confiscations led to a criminal case, which means that lots of innocent Americans had their lives and businesses wrecked by civil forfeiture.[6]

For years I had thought of these shenanigans in terms of government waste. I was accustomed to reading about "pork barrel" projects. Republican senator Tom Coburn publishes an annual *Wastebook* listing outrageous examples of how the federal government spends money. The Government Accountability Office (GAO) publishes its own reports on the topic. Here are a few examples.[7]

Each year the federal government hands out more than $500 billion in farm subsidies. Once advocated as a measure to save the "family farm," currently these payment benefits go to a small number of politically well-connected recipients, some of whom live in cities like Chicago and New York, where there are no farms. Only 10,000 recipients get farm subsidies, each receiving an average of $417,000. Some of the recipients are billionaires like Paul Allen, David Rockefeller, and Penny Pritzker.

According to the GAO, each year the government makes approximately $125 billion in improper payments. This means that the government is handing out taxpayer money to people who are not entitled to receive it. In addition, sheer duplication of federal programs and services costs $45 billion annually. While this has been known for years, no serious efforts are made to eliminate this duplication.

The inspector general for the U.S. Office of Personnel Management reports the federal government pays $150 million in retirement and disability benefits each year to people who have died. These checks are then cashed by the dead person's family. Again, this problem can be corrected through more effective data collection, but the government seems unwilling or uninterested in correcting the problem.

Each year Congress allocates money for defense programs that the Pentagon doesn't want. In 2014, the government designated $90 million to upgrade the M-1 tank. The Pentagon says it has enough tanks, and Army Chief of Staff General Ray Odierno testified against the appropriation.

The Defense Department spent $500 million to purchase military planes for the Afghan Air Force that have since been scrapped because that air force could not afford to maintain them.

The Department of Homeland Security has one of the largest fleets of vehicles of any federal agency, but according to an inspector general report, 60 percent of its vehicles are scarcely used at all; in 2012 alone, these vehicles cost between $35 million and $50 million.

The IRS spent $11.6 million to buy computer software that remains unused. This is because the IRS doesn't have the space for it and does not have an effective inventory system for keeping track of its computer software.

Ninety members of Congress—mostly Democrats, but some Republicans as well—receive federal pensions in addition to their congressional salaries. Democratic congresswoman Joyce Beatty of Ohio, for example, gets $253,323 from her government pension in addition to her annual $174,000 congressional salary. This practice is commonly known as "double dipping."

Federal agencies paid nearly $50 million to the National Technical Information Service, a division of the Department of Commerce, for information that is available for free online.

Cabinet and federal agencies routinely spend tens of thousands of dollars commissioning portraits of senior government officials who like seeing their own image on the wall when they come to work every day. Commerce Secretary Gary Locke paid $19,500 to have an artist paint his portrait; Energy Secretary Steven Chu had his official portrait made for $21,100, and EPA administrator Lisa Jackson had her portrait done for nearly $40,000.

The DEA pays informants working at Amtrak to disclose passenger names. One Amtrak employee was paid $854,000 over twenty years. The DEA could have received this information free since the Amtrak police are part of a national law enforcement network that shares information among its partners.

Congress assigned $652,000 to build a new visitor center on the highway from Talihina, Oklahoma, to Mena, Arkansas, even though this particular highway already has three visitor centers.

NASA allocated $3 million to study how Congress works.

The National Institutes of Health currently has a $500,000 research project to figure out why obese girls are asked on fewer dates. The agency also spent $330,000 to study the sex and drug habits of gay and transgender men in Peru. Another $371,000 was given to study if mothers love their dogs as much as their kids by examining the way their brains respond to pictures of both.

The National Science Foundation (NSF) awarded $200,000 to a Yale University research project to figure out whether Wikipedia has a gender bias. The NSF also allocated $5.2 million for Columbia University to develop a video game called "Future Coast," where rising seas cause weather calamities, in order to "spur climate change activism."

The Department of Agriculture paid one coffee plantation in Hawaii $45,000 to use solar power to dry coffee beans, even though bean farmers all over the world have used the sun to dry their beans for centuries.

The National Endowment for the Humanities awarded Hope College a $300,000 grant to develop a game that connects Civil War reenactors online.

Waste is when you spend money on something you don't need, because you wrongly think you need it. Or you do need it, but you spend too much on it. None of Coburn's examples involve waste. Rather, the government is quite deliberately spending the taxpayer's money on projects that benefit the bureaucrats and their cronies. In many cases, members of Congress are buying votes with taxpayer money. So it's corruption. And it's theft. The money is not being stolen from the government; it's being stolen *by* the government. The victims are the everyday folks who work and pay taxes to fund this corruption and theft.

Returning to that prison warden who wanted an additional $2,500— he was a government agent filching from some guy who had to work hard to earn that money. I now saw not just the excesses of the prison system, but all government programs that went beyond their legitimate purpose, as elaborate schemes to rip off American taxpayers and workers. I realized right away that these were the thieves who would surely prove hard to police, because, after all, they were the police.

Government theft is now widespread in America, and yet America was intended to be an alternative to all this. This country was founded as an anti-theft society. We don't normally see it this way. We usually hear about grand principles: liberty, equality, and so on. But at the core, America is a country established in order to let you keep your stuff. Let's call this wealth protection. America is also a country designed in such a way that you can get stuff in the first place. Let's call this wealth creation.

Before America, the world was defined by two characteristics: theft and material poverty. By and large, it was a world of scarcity and very limited horizons. Americans have no idea what it is to live in such a world; it is, to use the title of Peter Laslett's famous book about pre-modern European society, "the world we have lost." Today we have to go to the poorest quarters of Africa or India to see it.

In her remarkable book, *Behind the Beautiful Forevers*, Katherine Boo describes life in an Indian slum. Describing the Annawadi district on the outskirts of Mumbai—just miles from where I grew up as a child—Boo tells us the story of a teenager, Abdul Hakim, who lives in a dilapidated hut and supports his family by sorting garbage and selling it to recycling plants. Abdul, she tells us, lives with and in garbage: empty water and whiskey bottles, mildewed newspapers, used tampon applicators, pieces of aluminum foil, old shoes, broken umbrellas, yellowed Q-tips, snarled cassette tape, and torn plastic casings that once held imitation Barbies, occasionally even maimed throwaway toys. Abdul is an expert at sorting this garbage. He knows garbage and feels comfortable around garbage. When he is scared, he goes and hides in the garbage.

Abdul is a very cautious boy. He works hard, yet he makes barely enough to survive, and there is no margin for error. "It's so much tension out there, the mind cannot wander," he says. "Every second you have to be alert." His aspirations are modest. He saves money to construct a thin barrier so that his family's hut can be separated from the hut right next to it. This will give his mother a modicum of privacy. He is hoping one day to reach the lower middle class. He has no other goals. A girlfriend is for him a complete extravagance; he believes that love is too much of a luxury for a poor boy like him. Besides, who can be expected to fall in love with a boy who smells of garbage?

Abdul focuses on his practical problems. He worries about such catastrophes as monsoon flooding, which can destroy the family hut; or disease, which can put him out of work or inflict upon him impossibly high medical bills; or even the risk of being struck by a car in Mumbai's chaotic streets. Most of all, Abdul watches out for others who want to steal from him the little he has. It is thieves, rather than fate, that threaten to ruin Abdul's fragile existence.

In order to survive, Abdul must avoid other scavengers who not only steal his merchandise but also sometimes seek to harm him so that he is disabled from working. This then opens up fields of opportunity for them. He must also elude the machinations of envious neighbors—also residents of the Annawadi slum—who don't want Abdul's family to get ahead and so do what they can to pull them down. There are gangs in the slums that extort money from young entrepreneurs like Abdul, seeking to obtain for free what Abdul makes through laborious effort.

Finally there are police extortionists and corrupt government officials who know that they can use their power to force or intimidate poor slum dwellers into lining their pockets. Boo describes one especially sly investigator, named Poornima Paikrao, who accumulates false but incriminating evidence against Abdul, knowing that she can blackmail the family into paying her to avoid the risk of a police prosecution. None of these people have the slightest concern about destroying Abdul's life.[8] In the words of an Indian proverb, to them the tears of a stranger are only water.

This is the way the world is for about half the existing population, and it is also the way the world used to be before America came along. There are no Abdul Hakims in America, and that's because America solved the problem of grinding scarcity that Abdul's life so poignantly represents. Between 1776 and 1789, the American founders devised a new system of government, what they called a *Novus Ordo Seclorum*, a new order of the ages, to enable the ordinary person to flourish and have an abundant, fulfilling life.

The founders were in a unique position; while previous societies were founded on "accident and force," as Alexander Hamilton put it, America was founded on "reflection and choice."[9] In other words, the American founders actually had a chance to start afresh, to think through in terms of first principles why people establish governments at all. To do this, the founders relied on the philosopher John Locke's idea of a "social contract." The social contract is a hypothetical or imaginary contract, but it helps to understand why people living without government—in what Locke termed a state of nature—might come together to form a society with ruling powers.

In his famous *Second Treatise*, Locke argued that in the state of nature we possess three things: life, liberty, and property. Each person is the owner of his or her own life. Each person also has liberty of action and thought. Finally, each person can through labor and exchange acquire possessions, however primitive or basic, such as tools, or a dwelling, or domesticated animals. These things—life, liberty, and property—are ours by right. No one can justly take them from us. Nor do we have the right to take away the possessions of others.

The problem, Locke understood, is that in the state of nature there is no justice, which is to say, no adequate protection for life, liberty, and property. The state of nature is the law of the jungle, where might makes right. Locke argued that to reduce their vulnerability, people contract with each other and enter into a pact of mutual self-protection. They establish governments for the protection of their life, liberty, and property. In short, the core purpose of government is a police function. Government exists to protect us from foreign and domestic thugs. In this way might is mobilized on behalf of right.

The founders agreed with this analysis. As James Madison put it, "The primary objects of civil society are the security of property and public safety." In the same vein, Hamilton stressed that the "great object of government is personal protection and the security of property." In *The Federalist*, Hamilton wrote that "a prosperous commerce is now perceived and acknowledged by all enlightened statesmen to be the most useful, as well as the most productive, source of national wealth, and has accordingly become a primary object of their political cares." Through business and trade, Hamilton stressed, "The assiduous merchant, the laborious husbandman, the active mechanic and the industrious manufacturer . . . all orders of men look forward with eager expectation, and growing alacrity, to the pleasing reward of their toils." [10] In other words, America was a country structured in a way that encouraged people to earn, and to keep what they earn, the anti-theft society par excellence.

For the founders, the most obvious form of thievery involved the taxes and duties imposed by the British. Viewed in hindsight, the actual taxes and duties seem insignificant, but for the founders there was a principle involved. In the Declaratory Act, passed in 1766 by the British Parliament, the British insisted upon a right to bind the colonies "in all cases whatsoever." Why should a foreign government have such complete authority over their life, liberty, and possessions? For this the founders had a simple name: tyranny.

Why should the king and the British Parliament, from thousands of miles away, be permitted to take from Americans what was made and earned from the sweat of their brows? The founders considered this to be straight-out theft. That's why they threw all that tea into the bay, launching the American Revolution and, much later, inspiring the Tea Party movement. The American Revolution was intended to end foreign tyranny and halt this illicit transfer of wealth—this international theft—being perpetrated by the British upon us.

But even when foreign thievery has been stopped, the founders realized, we need a government strong enough to resist domestic thievery. Consequently the founders established a government dedicated to the protection of property rights. In No. 10 of *The Federalist*, Madison writes that "the first object of government" is "the protection of different and unequal faculties of acquiring property." [11]

Notice that this is not an incidental function of government; it is the main one. Madison recognizes at the outset that accumulations will be uneven or unequal. It is precisely to facilitate these inequalities that governments exist. The police are here to protect not only our lives but also our possessions. No one has a right to steal from someone else, and no group is entitled to appropriate the wealth or possessions of another group.

The founders realized that obviously there would be disagreements about how governments should go about exercising these basic functions. These disagreements spring from the diversity of human nature. So, for example, various people in a society may disagree over the nature of a foreign threat and whether going to war is necessary to protect the nation's security. Similarly, people may disagree over whether to impose taxes, or how much taxes to impose, or on whom, to pay for the war.

It would be nice not to have these disagreements, and to decide questions based on unanimous agreement. Yet unanimous agreement can almost never be found—it is a chimera—and thus if unanimity were required for governments to act, obviously there would be anarchy. Consequently the founders created a system based on majority rule, to be decided by free elections.

Majority rule—let's call it the rule of 51 percent or more—is the best practical surrogate for unanimity. It is an imperfect surrogate, because even under majority rule there are dissenters who can number as many as 49 percent. But the only alternative to majority rule is minority rule, whether that minority be just one or a few or the full 49 percent.

Clearly it is unjust for a minority to rule over the majority; this would simply be another form of tyranny. So majority rule is the best way for a society to decide disputed questions about how government should go about achieving its legitimate aims. A minority may be frustrated by decisions made in this way, but that frustration is always temporary, because minorities can always work to persuade more people to their side. In this way a minority can become a majority by the time of the next election.

This happened in 1800, when Thomas Jefferson defeated John Adams, and power was peacefully transferred from the ruling party to Jefferson's party. Political scientist Harry Jaffa pointed out that nothing like this had ever occurred in world history. Previously, Jaffa writes, vanquished rulers had been executed, imprisoned, or exiled, as in the English Civil War and the Rome of the Caesars.[12] But when Jefferson won, the Federalists quietly vacated office and went back to private life, continuing to organize politically and hoping to return to power in a future election. America, then, invented democracy in its modern form.

What happens, however, if the government, the main instrument of protecting citizens from foreign and domestic theft, itself becomes a thief? This may seem like a very remote likelihood, but the founders did not agree. They recognized at the outset that the same larcenous motives that may cause one man to steal from another could likely induce governments to steal from the people.

"Government," of course, refers to the people running the government. Even in a system of majority rule, the founders knew, government officials could at the behest of a majority of citizens threaten the life, liberty, and property of citizens who were not part of that majority. What is to prevent 51 percent or more of citizens from electing representatives charged with suppressing the liberty or taking away the wealth and possessions of people in the minority?

The founders were acutely aware of this danger. As Jefferson put it in *Notes on the State of Virginia*, "An elective despotism was not the government we fought for."[13] It is not an exaggeration to say that this threat—tyranny of the majority—was one of the founders' main concerns in drafting the Constitution. It was perhaps the chief reason that America has a constitution at all.

The British, by contrast, have no constitution. British law is basically common law and the laws made by the legislature. Those are the supreme laws of the land. But in America the common law and the laws made by the legislature can be overridden by the Constitution, which is the supreme law. The Constitution, in a sense, trumps majority rule. It exists for the purpose of keeping governments—and majorities—in check.

How does the Constitution protect the life, liberty, and property of Americans from the tyranny and larceny of the majority? It does so in two ways. First, it establishes blocking and thwarting mechanisms within government to prevent government from becoming oppressive. Our Constitution establishes separation of powers so that the legislative function, the executive function, and the judiciary function are each distinct.

Then the Constitution installs checks and balances so that each branch, in a sense, becomes a watchdog for the other. The president can veto laws passed by Congress, and the Supreme Court can invalidate laws inconsistent with the Constitution even when both Congress and the president approve them. These blocking and thwarting systems are there to ensure that "factions," as Madison called them, could not by themselves, or even in coalition, effectively steal from the people or thwart the central protective purposes of government.

Second, the Constitution limits the size and scope of the federal government so that it can only do certain things and no more. We have a system of limited government and enumerated powers. Basically the government is authorized to provide for defense and to protect the equal rights of citizens to life, liberty, and property. In addition—and this provision requires careful attention to its wording—government is empowered to make laws for the "general welfare."

The term "general welfare" must be understood in contradistinction to "particular welfare." The government does not exist to advance one group over another but to protect the general or common welfare of all citizens. This, then, is the full scope of what the national or federal government is permitted to do. Beyond this, it is permitted to do nothing. As if to italicize the point, the Constitution clearly declares that all power not specifically entrusted to the federal government is retained by the states and by the people.

The absolute determination of the founders to limit the size and scope of the federal government became clear in the debate surrounding the addition of a Bill of Rights to the Constitution. Hamilton opposed a Bill of Rights, but for a very interesting reason. We don't need one, he said, because why prohibit the government from doing things that it has not been given the power to do? [14] Why say that government shall make no law restricting religion or speech when the Constitution does not grant the government the authority to make such laws?

Advocates of a Bill of Rights so intensely feared a thieving, aggrandizing government that they insisted that many of these rights be specified anyway. That's how we got a Bill of Rights whose provisions typically begin, "Congress shall make no law." The Bill of Rights is manifestly designed to be a limitation on the power of the federal government, which is to say, the majority. The Supreme Court is charged with enforcing these rights in the full understanding that this requires limiting majority rule. Nothing in our Constitution empowers majorities to take away the life, liberty, or property of citizens who happen to be in the minority. The Constitution is our common charter to prevent these forms of stealing.

This interpretation of the limits to majority rule can be confirmed by considering the position of America's supreme student of the founding, Abraham Lincoln. Lincoln is widely understood to be the great champion of government "of the people, for the people, and by the people." He was an unwavering believer in democracy and majority rule. His argument against southern secession was, in large part, that the South was simply attempting to undo the result of a democratic election. How can democracy work if those who lose elections simply break away from the body politic?

At the same time, Lincoln emphasized with utmost clarity that majority rule does not confer upon the majority the right to exceed its constitutional bounds. Elected governments have no more right to usurp powers not delegated to it by the people through the Constitution than nonelected governments do. For instance, majorities cannot take away the fundamental rights of speech, conscience, and assembly because those rights were never surrendered to the jurisdiction of majority rule. Moreover, majorities are not permitted to endanger the life, liberty, and property of minorities while securing their own. The rights of the minority are no less inviolable by the people than by oligarchies and kings. Thus Lincoln assured the people in the southern states that if he were violating any of their constitutional rights, they would have both a constitutional right to secede as well as a natural right of revolution.

But Lincoln insisted that he had not violated any such right. He had not suppressed, and had no intention to suppress, any provisions in the Bill of Rights. Nor, he emphasized, did he have any intention to interfere with slavery in the southern states. Slavery had clearly been permitted there, as part of the founders' original bargain, and Lincoln swore that, putting his personal feelings about slavery aside, he would uphold that bargain. This is critically important because it means that, on an issue absolutely central to his own convictions and to the 1860 election, Lincoln accepted the southerners' contention that to limit or abolish slavery in the South would be to steal their property. Lincoln repeatedly disclaimed any intention on the part of his government to do this.

On the other hand, Lincoln pointed out that the Constitution was silent on the matter of whether Congress could exclude slavery from the new federal territories. In his debates with Stephen Douglas, Lincoln pointed out that this was not a matter of abolishing slavery or taking away anyone's property; rather, it was a matter of preventing slavery from being instituted in the first place. Consequently, Lincoln argued, the open question of whether to permit slavery in the territories was an issue to be decided politically, which is to say, by majority rule. For the South to secede over this was to deny that democratic majorities freely elected can enact their will in their legitimate sphere of governance. In making this—in my view irrefutable—argument, Lincoln demonstrated his keen understanding of the proper scope of democratic rule. Lincoln was completely on board with the founders' anti-theft system.

Lincoln realized, however, that the founders did not limit government power merely to prevent tyranny and theft. They also did so to enable wealth creation as an alternative to theft. Lincoln did not use the term "wealth creation." What he said, rather, was that America is a country where "every man can make himself." [15] For Lincoln, making oneself meant what we would call "making it," improving one's condition in life. In other words, Lincoln was talking about wealth creation.

Yet in earlier eras the idea of wealth creation would have been considered strange, even incomprehensible. Wealth, after all, was believed to consist mainly in land. Obviously the supply of land is limited. Once the available land has been occupied, there is no more. If you get more, that means that someone else has gotten less. This is the very definition of a zero-sum society.

Such societies have existed for millennia. Typically they have been run by caste hierarchies, with aristocrats, priests, and warriors at the top and merchants and craftsmen at or near the bottom. Good examples are the Indian caste system and the feudal hierarchies of Europe. In these hierarchical, zero-sum societies, those at the top of the totem pole generally exploit and steal from those at the bottom, even while reviling them as wicked, lazy, and inferior. Merchants and traders, in particular, have been reviled in just about every culture since the time of the Babylonians.

The American founders, however, got rid of the hierarchical totem pole. In its place they created a new type of society in which government would play a small role and entrepreneurs and workers would play a big role. Such a society would be based on property rights, contracts, and trade. The main business of America would be business. America would become a technological, capitalist society energized by new inventions and their regular applications on the part of entrepreneurs and workers to improve the lot of consumers.

In an 1859 lecture, Lincoln singled out the only right specified in the original Constitution, before the Bill of Rights was added later. This is the right to patents and copyrights. The job of government would be appropriately limited. It would be to merely secure the legal right of inventors to enjoy, for a limited time, the exclusive benefit of their inventions. Lincoln marveled at this; he argued that in protecting the rights of inventors and innovators, America had "added the fuel of interest to the fire of genius, in the discovery and production of new and useful things."[16] Lincoln stood squarely on the side of the wealth creators.

America's system of wealth creation and theft prevention has proven immensely successful. By 1890, Americans had the highest standard of living in the world. And by the mid-twentieth century, America was by far the wealthiest nation on the planet. For the past sixty years, we have been living in the American Era, in which Americans have enjoyed wealth and influence utterly out of proportion to America's size or population. Many countries around the world are copying our wealth-creating, anti-theft formula. And America's system continues to be cherished by productive citizens because it encourages their creativity and labor, and protects the fruits of those efforts from being stolen.

But an anti-theft society is especially unpopular with one group. That group is called thieves. Thieves don't particularly care about wealth creation; they are entirely into wealth confiscation. Thieves would like to see an ongoing transfer from the wealth creators to themselves. In fact, this is their very definition of progress. Consequently the constitutional design that has been the distinctive hallmark of America, and a big reason for America's enviable prosperity, is under fierce attack from a powerful syndicate of thieves, the so-called progressives, who, in their boundless sneakiness, attempt to identify thievery with progress. Let us now investigate their nefarious schemes.

Chapter 5

HISTORY FOR PROFIT:

The Reparations Scam

Yes, my friend it is too true—your eyes is lookin' at this very moment on the pore disappeared Dauphin, Looy the Seventeen, son of Looy the Sixteen and Marry Antonette.[1]

—The Dauphin, in Mark Twain,
Adventures of Huckleberry Finn

I was reclined on my bunk one chilly January night, listening to an inmate named Mfume—who is a reasonably literate guy—tell a bunch of his buddies the story of *The Iliad*. "It starts with Achilles," he said, "a real badass! He's pissed-off because the king, Agamemnon, took the bitch that Achilles was with. Agamemnon wanted to bone her himself. Achilles was like, what the f*ck? I mean, he really loved her ass."

At first I was thinking that this guy should be doing stand-up comedy at the Improv in New York or San Diego. But then I realized that his story was an opportunity to enter into a dialogue with these guys on the subject of reparations. So I jumped out of my bunk and joined the conversation.

"Achilles was angry," I said, "because the girl Briseis belonged to him and not Agamemnon. But Briseis was captured from the Trojans. So do you think that a woman who is taken by force and reduced to being a slave or a concubine actually belongs to her enslaver?"

One of the Hispanic guys said, "F*ck!"

Mfume was not to be easily deterred. "In those times," he said, "homies were allowed to have slaves, and the women who were enslaved were at least not killed. When Agamemnon distributed the booty he gave her to Achilles, so he had no right to take her back. If that happened to me, I'd be pissed-off like a m*therf*cker."

"But what about the cause of the war?" I asked. "The Greeks said they were there because of a past injustice. They wanted restitution for the stealing of Helen. Since the Trojans refused to give Helen back, and pay reparations for their theft, the Greeks threatened to destroy Troy and take Helen back by force."

"That," Mfume said, "is what the Greeks said, but that was not their real reason for invading Troy."

So Mfume wasn't buying the official story. I could barely contain my delight.

"Sure," Mfume continued, "the Greek warrior Menelaus went to Troy to get his wife back. I'm sure he wanted to kill that m*therf*cker Paris, too, for taking her. But his brother King Agamemnon—he didn't give a damn about that. Agamemnon didn't give a f*ck about Helen! He wanted Troy."

"So you mean," I said, at this point ready to write a letter of recommendation for this guy to Dartmouth, "that the whole reparations story was a pretext? The Greeks themselves were the real looters. They had been victims of a theft, and they used that as an excuse to pull off a much bigger theft?"

"Exactly."

And the Hispanic guy listening intently offered his concluding thoughts: "F*ck!"

This chapter is about reparations, the progressive project to restore to people the benefits that were lost to them through historical oppression. In a sense advocates of reparations are just like the Greeks, who claimed their invasion of Troy was a justified attempt to recover what had been taken from them. In this case, progressives claim that reparations are a "taking" that is fully warranted to compensate people for America's historical crimes of theft. The demand for reparations is a "pitch," one of several pitches that I examine in this book.

What is a pitch? It is the con man's sales job that sets up the theft. Pitches are often the most interesting aspect of a con, because they are so creative, so elaborate, so plausible. They draw us into the con, and make us suckers. If we buy into the pitch, the rest of the thief's job is relatively easy.

Some thefts don't require a pitch. If you are going to embezzle money at your workplace, you don't have to convince anyone of anything; you just go ahead and do it. Some thefts require a very brief pitch. If you want to break into an old couple's apartment, beat them up, and steal from them, you may need a pitch to get yourself through the door. Elaborate cons, however, typically require very clever pitches. In movies like *The Sting, Dirty Rotten Scoundrels*, and, more recent, *Focus*, we see how labyrinthine schemes are devised in order to relieve people of their money. A pitch usually involves a very clever person pretending to be a very simple person who wants nothing more than the good, the beautiful, and the just.

In Flannery O'Connor's short story "Good Country People" we meet a Bible salesman who is the very picture of simplicity. He talks simple, acts simple, and seems inept even in pitching his product. The old ladies of the town can hardly believe there are still people around who are so rural and so naïve. Marx's phrase about "the idiocy of rural life" comes to mind here.

Only as the story develops do we discover that the boy is anything but simple. With an artful clumsiness, he cons a handicapped girl with an expensive metal leg to go up with him into a barn. There he paws her and convinces her to unscrew her metal leg. Then, to her horror, he steals her leg! In the closing scene two old ladies see the boy crossing a meadow to make his getaway and one says to the other, "I guess the world would be better off if we were all that simple."[2] And there we have the perfect pitch, one rendered all the more convincing because it is clothed in the garb of such innocence and virtue.

Cunning though he is, this Bible salesman could learn a lot from a progressive. The progressive is after much more than a metal leg. What the progressive wants is the right to come to your house and take your stuff. To do this, he needs a story and it has to seem irrefutable.

In this and the next three chapters, we focus on four ingenious progressive pitches, each one of them aimed at legitimizing a claim to your money. All of these pitches purport to represent "social justice" and come wrapped up in a package marked "fairness."

The first pitch is the "history for profit" pitch, in which progressives claim to be owed almost incalculably large sums to compensate for historical crimes that America allegedly visited on blacks, Hispanics, and Native Americans.

The second is the "inequality" pitch, in which the normal variation of talents and rewards is invoked to justify taxation, regulation, and redistribution, all aimed at restoring some supposedly normal and acceptable state of affairs.

Then there is the "you didn't build that" pitch, in which progressives insist that society, not entrepreneurs and workers, actually built the companies that produce most of America's wealth; the general reasoning is that what society gives, society has the right to take away if it wants.

Finally, there is the Lucky Luciano pitch, which seeks to confiscate people's wealth and resources on the grounds that they are the beneficiaries of undeserved good luck, and apparently the unlucky among us have an equal right to their stuff.

Let's begin with the reparations or "history for profit" pitch. Today this pitch is advanced not merely in the political arena. It also dominates the curriculum of many high schools and most colleges. In my *America* film I associated this critique with Howard Zinn. Zinn didn't come up with it, but he brought together various strains of leftism into a single story line portraying America as the thieving nation par excellence. This story line represents the main narrative of America generated by modern progressivism, and its prevalence testifies to the power of progressives in the American classroom.

The victim class covered by reparations isn't limited to blacks; it also includes Hispanics, Native Americans, women, homosexuals, and the poor. In that respect reparations covers the whole swath of identity politics including race, ethnicity, immigrant status, gender, sexual orientation, and socioeconomic disadvantage. It is about getting even for all the bad things that America has done to people, and attempting to make their descendants whole. Basically it is about dividing America into two classes: the oppressor class and the victim class. This is not to say that the oppressor class today is doing anything to persecute the victim class.

The progressive claim, rather, is that the oppressors are descended from people who stole things—mainly land and labor—and the victims are descended from the people whose land and labor were stolen. The thieves benefited from theft and passed these benefits down to their children and grandchildren; those who were stolen from had less to bequeath to their descendants.

So "oppressor" and "victim" are historical categories. And the basic progressive conclusion is that the oppressor class today owes the victim class a living. Victims should get stuff for free, and this stuff should be extracted from the oppressors. Strictly speaking, from the progressive point of view, this is a just appropriation, because the victims are merely getting back the stolen goods that were once forcibly taken from them.

Think of a team that shows up at your door and claims that all your possessions, including the art on your wall, are actually Nazi stolen goods. Your art is the same art that the Nazis stole from Jewish families. You protest that you had no knowledge of any of this, and nothing to do with any crimes, and your interlocutors hastily agree. Even so, they say, you have inherited this stolen property and you have to give it back. They show you some indecipherable documents that purport to prove their case. You cannot determine the authenticity of the documents or the validity of their claim. Yet by this point they have you on the defensive. You know that any defense you make of your stuff is going to expose you to charges that you are pro-Nazi and anti-Semitic. Your reputation will be ruined. You feel that sense of fear that is a necessary prelude to willingly, even if reluctantly, parting with your stuff.

What does reparations entail in practice? It entails a systematic campaign by progressives to add more and more Americans to the public dole, making them dependent on the government for a living. Government provisions like welfare and food stamps were originally advocated as measures to help widows, orphans, and those who were truly unable to feed and look after themselves. Such provisions were originally portrayed as the hallmark of a compassionate society.

But now, in the Obama era, there is little talk of compassion. Rather, Obama and his progressive allies press an expansion of government benefits as a just inheritance for the victim classes. The basic idea is that victim groups are entitled to live off the rest of us. We owe them a living. Why should the descendants of slaves—whose labor was stolen for two hundred years—have to work for a living? Shouldn't Americans who are the present beneficiaries of past oppression be required to support them? The intellectual arguments of the left, which have penetrated our media and educational institutions, now become the basis for a political project to build an entitled class largely made up of those whose ancestors in America faced historical oppression.

We typically think of reparations in terms of government programs that are specifically race based, such as affirmative action and government contracts for minority groups. Each year the Equal Employment Opportunity Commission (EEOC) extracts tens of millions of dollars in settlements from corporations after threatening those corporations with antidiscrimination lawsuits. These lawsuits are typically not based on any actual proof of discrimination, either past or present; they are based mostly on statistics showing that blacks and other minorities are "under-represented" in that particular company. Even so, corporations are terrified of the EEOC because they are terrified of being accused of racism. They would much rather pay up than endure any taint of the charge of discrimination.

Sometimes reparations is used to justify a feeding frenzy in which minority claimants simply raid the U.S. Treasury en masse while government bureaucrats facilitate a large transfer of wealth from the taxpayer to these so-called historical victims. A scandalous example of this is the Pigford case. Some ninety-one black farmers had sued the U.S. government alleging a legacy of bias against African Americans. Rather than settle the suit and pay the farmers a reasonable compensation, the Obama administration used the lawsuit to make an absurdly expensive settlement. It agreed to pay out $1.33 billion to compensate not only the ninety-one plaintiffs but also thousands of Hispanic and female farmers who had never claimed bias in court.

Encouraged by this largesse, law firms began to conjure up new claimants. Later reviews showed that some of these claimants were nursery-school-age children and even urban dwellers who had no connection to farming. In some towns, the number of people being paid was many times greater than the total number of farms. According to the *New York Times*, one family in Little Rock, Arkansas, had ten members each submit a claim for $50,000, netting $500,000 for the family without any proof of discrimination. Then the Native Americans got in on the racket, and the Obama administration settled with them, agreeing to fork over an additional $760 million. The government also reimbursed hundreds of millions of dollars in legal fees, a cornucopia for trial lawyers who also happen to be large contributors to Obama and the Democratic Party. Altogether the Pigford payout is estimated to have cost taxpayers a staggering $4.4 billion.[3]

But reparations is more than just a racial concept. In a sense, the entire welfare state can be seen as a form of reparation, an atonement for America's past misdeeds. The welfare state, after all, disproportionately benefits minorities even though it is not specifically race-based. I am not speaking here of the New Deal, which was an emergency response to the Great Depression; rather, I am speaking of the programs that began with Lyndon Johnson's Great Society. These were openly justified as measures to correct historical injustices and establish what Johnson famously called the "level playing field."

A good example of a nonracial reparations program that heavily benefits minority groups is the SNAP program, otherwise known as food stamps. Under the Obama administration, the food stamp program has been dramatically transformed. What was once a measure to help feed hungry people, especially during an economic downturn, has now become an entitlement for more than 45 million Americans. In the early 1970s, around 5 percent of the population got food stamps. In the mid-1990s, that number had risen to 10 percent. Now it is 15 percent. When Obama was elected in 2008, the U.S. government spent $30 billion on food stamps; now it spends $77 billion.

The case for this expansion is that the economic slowdown and sluggish recovery has required the federal government to supplement the incomes of poor and working-class Americans so they do not slip further into poverty and deprivation. But the rise in food stamp recipients is not due to changes in the economy. It is not because there are proportionately more hungry people today than before. Even as the economy recovered from the 2008 meltdown, the proportion of food stamp recipients remained steady or continued to rise.

The real reason is that the Obama administration wants more people to depend on the government for their subsistence. Progressive politicians like Nancy Pelosi are positively enthusiastic about expanding the number of people covered by food stamps. "It is absolutely essential that we extend the benefits," she says, because the more people who get food stamps, the better it is for the economy! However strained this argument may be, progressives like Obama and Pelosi clearly want people to feel good about getting stuff for free.

Fraud seems to be widespread in the SNAP program, and the Obama administration does not seem especially eager to stop it. The USDA currently has only forty inspectors to oversee more than 200,000 merchants who accept food stamps nationwide. Prosecutions for food stamp abuse have declined, even as the use and abuse of food stamps has increased. A Seattle TV station reported that SNAP recipients routinely sell their cards on Craigslist and Facebook. A *Milwau-*

kee Journal-Sentinel investigation into food stamp abuse found that "nearly 2,000 recipients claimed they lost their card six or more times and requested replacements." The *Des Moines Register* reported that 30 percent of inmates in the Polk County, Iowa, jail were collecting food stamps that were being sent to their home mailing addresses. Yet when states attempt to crack down on abuse, they are routinely stymied by the Obama administration. Currently the administration is seeking to compel California, New York, and Texas to stop requiring food stamp beneficiaries to provide finger images.

To see how cavalier progressives can be with taxpayers' money, consider the case of Leroy Fick. In 2011, the fifty-nine-year-old Fick won a $2 million lottery jackpot. Still, the Michigan Department of Health and Human Services ruled he could continue receiving food stamps. The Obama administration agreed. The *Detroit News* explained the government's rationale: "If Fick had chosen to accept monthly payments of his jackpot, the winnings would be considered income. But by choosing to accept a lump sum payment, the winnings were considered 'assets' and aren't counted in determining food stamp eligibility."

Food stamps once carried an element of stigma. This was not entirely bad, because the stigma encouraged people to support themselves and not rely on government provision. Under Obama, however, the government has issued so-called EBT cards that resemble bank debit cards. Unlike debit cards, EBT cards can only be used to purchase food and other household items; they cannot be used to withdraw cash. Even so, by using the EBT card, the food stamp recipient can now feel he or she is "paying" no less than the ordinary customer. The removal of stigma has undoubtedly swelled the ranks of food stamp recipients, and in view of the Obama administration, this is a good thing. The progressive assumption: these people deserve it, we are here to provide it, and the rest of you are here to pay for it.[4]

Food stamps are part of a larger progressive project to increase the population of so-called victims who are reliant on government and don't have to support themselves. In a recent study, the Cato Institute found that the total package of welfare benefits under the Obama administration has risen so high that in 35 out of 50 states, it now pays more than a minimum wage job. Liberal states like Massachusetts, Rhode Island, Connecticut, New Jersey, New York, Maryland, and California provide welfare packages around $35,000, which is 70 percent of the U.S. mean income for a family of four. In 39 states, the study showed, welfare pays more than the starting wage for a secretary. In 11 states, it pays more than the first-year wage for a teacher. And in states like Hawaii and Massachusetts, persons on welfare can take home more money than an entry-level computer programmer.[5]

While conservatives find such data dismaying, progressives often respond with delight. While conservatives stress the economic illogic, progressives emphasize the requirements of justice. Conservatives and libertarians argue that when the package of government benefits increases to a certain point, people have no motivation to look for entry-level jobs. It makes economic sense at that point to rely on the state to provide for you, rather than to provide for yourself. This is what the Cato study stresses.

Yet it doesn't seem to have dawned on the authors of that study that many progressives want this. They want people not to enter the workforce. Their reason is that progressives see these people as historically deprived; they shouldn't have to work; the rest of us have a moral obligation to take care of them. This, you may have recognized by now, is the reparations pitch.

Reparations is, in a sense, a great pitch because it relies on a story of things that happened a long time ago. As such, no one is around to verify whether any of this is true, and so if you can get people to buy your story, you are basically home free. The story that progressives tell is one of massive theft. The white man—read "America"—stole the country from the Native Americans, stole the lives and labor of African Americans over several hundred years, and stole half of Mexico from the Mexicans in the Mexican War. In addition, America allegedly oppressed women, homosexuals, and the poor, stifling the identities of these groups and denying them equal opportunity.

The descendants of those victims, so the story goes, are still suffering the effects of deprivation caused by that massive theft, while the beneficiaries continue to enjoy its ill-gotten fruits. Therefore the descendants of the perpetrators—basically all whites, or America itself—are essentially receivers of stolen goods. Accordingly, they must recognize their virtually limitless debt to the blacks, Hispanics, Native Americans, women, gays, and poor people. Pretty much whatever the government wants to do to take money from whites, or from America, can be justified in the name of reparations, because it constitutes a small down payment on the incalculable sums that are actually owed.

I wanted to test out the progressive narrative about reparations among my fellow inmates in the confinement center. I approached the matter cautiously, however. I know that race is a sensitive issue among criminals, and I didn't want unwittingly to get in the middle of any gang associations. It did not escape my attention that, as an Asian Indian, I didn't fit any of the main racial categories. In fact, shortly before I went into confinement, I appeared on *The Kelly File* and told Megyn Kelly that there was no point in me starting an Asian Indian gang because I would be the sole member. At first, I stayed away from the race issue altogether.

But then I saw a black guy, Eldridge, eating with a bunch of Hispanics. I remembered Eldridge from my prison rape class. We had talked a few times. He smiled at me and said, "Looks like desegregation is coming to the confinement center." We got to talking about it. I mentioned that I'd seen members of different groups smoking together outside, or working out together. In prison, Eldridge said, things are very different. "In hard-core prison"—by which he means medium security or high security—"you can't even talk to someone from a different race. Inside, there's a whole protocol. In some places you can play basketball with the Latinos, but you can't eat with them or gamble with them.

"There are leaders from each group that make these decisions. A key-holder is a guy who makes small decisions. A shot-caller establishes policy for a whole unit. Everything has to go through these guys. Even the prison guards take their cues from them. They know it's the best way to avoid trouble. The guards don't really run things; the prisoners do. In Lompoc, I was in medium security and only two of the guard towers had a sniper on the top. Two guards for, I don't know, several hundred inmates."

In Lompoc, Eldridge said, "There were white guys who were not allowed to shake my hand. The South Side Mexicans could not play basketball with me, so I had to wait until they were done to play." For protection, Eldridge decided to join the Black Muslims. Surprised, I said, "You're a Muslim? How come you're always talking about alcohol and women? Is this a branch of the Muslim faith I'm not familiar with?"

He laughed. "I'm not an orthodox Muslim, but in prison I had to be. So I studied the scriptures, prayed five times a day. Normally I don't do any of that. But this was the best way to be safe. There are a couple of hundred Black Muslims in Lompoc, and I saw that no one messed with those n*ggers."

I asked Eldridge about racism in general and, in particular, his view of the white gangs in prison. He said there were three types of white gangs: the Nazis, the Aryan Brotherhood, and the "geos." He described the Nazis as a small cult group, highly disciplined. "Even the other whites know they're a little crazy." The "geos" are geographically defined gangs, like the Long Beach gang and the Santa Monica gang. Basically "they're a bunch of white guys who want to hang out together."

The group for which Eldridge had the most respect—even grudging admiration—was the Aryan Brotherhood. "The AB"—that's what he calls the Aryan Brotherhood—"is the biggest of the white gangs. It uses some Nazi symbols, like the swastika, but these guys are more diverse. They got white supremacists, nationalists, militia guys, the whole thing. Those m*therf*ckers are on the rise, man. It's actually hard to get into the AB; it takes nine months to be admitted. There's a waiting list."

What, I asked, was the secret to their success? "Marketing," Eldridge replied. "They've gone digital. They spend money on recruiting. I have to say, they're really talented."

"Talented," I said. "At what?"

"Music," he said. "I'm serious. It really helps their recruitment."

I asked about Latinos, and here Eldridge became animated. "The Latinos here are savages," he said. "They don't even know how to fight. Brothers fight like men, one-on-one. These people like to fight six-on-one, or ten-on-one."

I asked if he considered that unfair. "I hold to the belief that it takes three Mexicans to fight one black guy," he said. "So three-on-one is fair, but more than that, no."

Latinos are so dense, Eldridge elaborated, that they actually start fights in order to get injured. "They want to show some scars and broken bones. It makes life more exciting for them. It makes them feel strong if they can show some marks on their body. They are like, see, I got a broken rib! Or see, I broke my jaw! I'm telling you, they are some real stupid m*therf*ckers."

Finally I asked about reparations. "I don't know, man," Eldridge said. "These Latinos are into Aztlan—Aztlan this, Aztlan that—but they don't have any idea what they're talking about. You say 'Christopher Columbus' and they are, like, 'Who the f*ck was he?' But now you take the Black Guerrilla Family, those guys are really into history."

Eldridge said he basically accepted the Black Guerrilla Family narrative of white theft and oppression, which for the most part corresponded with the Black Muslim narrative. At the same time, he said, "In prison there's equality, man. We're all just trying to survive. Our real enemy ain't the other groups in here; it's the system, man. The system f*cks us over every time. But I don't want reparations. I want to find the people that's responsible, and I want to beat the sh*t out of them."

The cons may not take reparations seriously, but that doesn't mean we shouldn't. We should take it seriously because it is a story of alleged injustice. Even if the story were coming just from the cons, that doesn't mean they are necessarily telling lies. A criminal in California's San Quentin Prison who is known to be a con artist says that guards are sexually abusing him; he might be lying, but the allegation is serious enough that it deserves to be investigated. Here, too, I propose to investigate the "history for profit" pitch as conscientiously as possible.

Objectively, what would someone have to prove if he were seeking reparations? Imagine the case of a guy who is walking on the sidewalk and a truck runs over his foot, causing him pain and injury, and preventing him from working. The general logic of reparations is: "But for . . ." The man's case goes like this. *But for* the truck running over my foot, I could work normally and earn money and enjoy my day. Now, as a result of the offense, I can't do those things. So I should be compensated for my medical bills, and pain and suffering, and lost wages.

From this example we learn that in order to prove reparations you have to show: a) there has been an offense, b) you have been harmed by that offense, that is, you are worse off than you would have been had the offense not occurred, and c) you suffered actual damages, entitling you to compensation by the party that has harmed you or by its heirs and descendants.

In this chapter I will say a few words about Hispanics and Native Americans, but I'm going to focus on African Americans. I do so because I am addressing the pitch where it seems to be the strongest. In the case of Hispanics and Native Americans, it's not even clear that there was an offense. Consider: Texas legitimately revolted against Mexico and established an independent republic. Mexico can't exactly complain about that, because Mexico had just recently revolted against Spain. Then Texas chose to join the United States. Texas has a disputed border with Mexico, and the Mexican War erupted over that disputed territory. Mexico lost the war, and American troops were in Mexico City. America could have kept all of Mexico; instead, America returned half of Mexico and paid $15 million to settle Mexico's debts. Arguably there is a theft in here somewhere, but it's hardly clear. Moreover, a treaty was signed between the two countries establishing the new borders.

In the case of Native Americans, there have been extensive reparations paid, both in terms of money and scholarships and tax benefits. This is intended to compensate for the undisputed history of broken treaties and unjust displacement and relocation. Still, weren't the Native Americans deprived of a whole country? What about the property rights of America's original inhabitants?

Let's pause to consider what that means. The Native Americans migrated to the Americas in waves, coming originally from Asia. They didn't come together; the migration was over several thousand years. Does that mean that the first group to get to the American continent owned the whole continent? Does the Bedouin who arrives first to the oasis own the oasis? Obviously not. The first native settlers occupied a small territory, and there was plenty of room for others to occupy. What this means is that getting there first certainly establishes a presumptive right to occupation and use, but it doesn't mean you own the whole continent in perpetuity.

When the Europeans arrived, they saw that parts of America were occupied by Native Americans but large parts were virgin territory, that is, not settled by anyone. The Native Americans had no doctrine of property rights; for them the right of occupation was established in a single way, by conquest. When the white man came, he saw land occupied by various tribes. But what the white man didn't know at the time was that pretty much every piece of occupied land had been earlier seized by force by another tribe. Basically the warlike tribes like the Navajo, the Comanche, and the Apache had driven out and displaced peaceful tribes like the Pueblo and the Hopi.

Granted, the white man pushed out these stronger tribes and took their land, but in doing this was he stealing from those tribes, or from the original inhabitants of the land? When possession is legitimized by force, where does the issue of theft arise? I'm not proposing answers to these questions here, merely showing that the issue remains unclear.

Sometimes the oppression narrative, and reparations solution, is advanced with respect to women. Feminists claim that the history of all nations, but especially those of Europe and America, is a story of female oppression by patriarchal authority. Once again, this becomes a matter of unfairness. This narrative is used to justify a wide range of legal reforms and special rights and other provisions.

Certainly, from a legal and political point of view, there is a good deal of truth in the feminist argument. Even so, women wielded considerable power in their own right. It is absurd to compare the plight of women with, say, the plight of Native Americans or African Americans. Moreover, the history of all Western nations including America has been one of expanding freedom and equality for women so that today they enjoy the same rights and privileges as men. No special protections—which is to say no reparations—are now due.

Slavery is an entirely different story. In that case, the theft is undeniable. Of course there were people who sought to deny it. Among southern Democrats, a "positive good" school arose, which attempted to maintain that slavery was good for the slaves. Some slave owners and their Democratic apologists termed it a "school of civilization." Another southern Democratic rationalization was that slavery was justified because the slaves were inferior creatures who did not have the same natural rights as everyone else.

By far the cleverest argument for slavery, however, came from the northern Democrat Stephen Douglas, who argued that slavery was sanctioned by democracy itself. Douglas's argument is worth considering, because even today a version of it is advanced by his successor Democrats to justify their seizures and confiscations. Today's liberal Democrats say that if they can confiscate people's wealth and earnings through the democratic process, then these seizures are fully justified.

Basically this is what Douglas said. He argued for popular sovereignty, which is another term for majority rule. Under this doctrine, each state would decide for itself whether it wanted to have slavery or not.

Douglas professed to be indifferent to slavery itself; he didn't care if it was voted up or down. He insisted, however, that majority rule should decide the question in each part of the country. "The principle of self-government," Douglas said, "is that each community shall settle this question for itself . . . and we have no right to complain either in the North or the South, whichever they do."[6] Sure, the slaves might complain, but Douglas did not think that their opinions counted very much because, in his view, the black man was not equal to the white man.

Lincoln, however, deftly exposed these arguments as specious. To those who said slavery was a positive good, Lincoln retorted, if it is so good, it would be nice to see you try it yourself by becoming a slave. No one took Lincoln up on this offer. If slavery was a school of civilization, Lincoln added, it was apparently a school from which the slaves were not permitted to graduate. "Suppose it is true," Lincoln said, "that the negro is inferior to the white, in the gifts of nature; is it not the exact reverse of justice that the white should, for that reason, take from the negro, any part of the little which has been given him? *Give to the needy* is the Christian rule of charity, but *take from the needy* is the rule of slavery." And when Douglas said that the black man was not the equal of the white man, Lincoln responded, "I agree with Judge Douglas he is not my equal in many respects . . . but in the right to eat the bread, without leave of anybody else, which his own hand earns, he is my equal and the equal of Judge Douglas, and the equal of every living man."[7]

Lincoln said that the same principles that Douglas invoked to enslave blacks could also be used to enslave whites. Were not some whites inferior to other whites? What if majorities in certain states voted to put whites into captivity? Is theft now acceptable because it is approved by a majority of the people who are the very ones carrying out the theft? For Lincoln, the decisions of democratic majorities are only valid if they are within the sphere in which the Constitution authorizes democratic majorities to operate. Otherwise—to put it bluntly—these vaunted democratic majorities are little more than gangs of robbers.

Lincoln compared slavery to "wolves devouring lambs" and pretending it was for the sake of the lambs. Specifically, he regarded the defense of slavery as "the same old serpent that says you work and I eat, you toil and I will enjoy the fruits of it."[8] We see from this analysis that Lincoln understood slavery in terms of theft. Every person has the right to labor productively and to keep the fruit of his or her labor. This applies to whites no less than to blacks. It is the very definition of what Lincoln termed "free labor." Lincoln put this in very simple terms. Each of us, he said, has been given two hands and one mouth. The reason for this is that the two hands should be permitted to deliver their fruits to that mouth. No other person or group of people, however numerous, may justly interfere with this transaction.

The core of Lincoln's case against "popular sovereignty" was that this principle is not up for a vote. Just as your neighbor has no right to take from you what you have legitimately earned, democratic majorities in each state, or for that matter across the nation, don't have that right, either. Sure, government can tax you, and every other person similarly situated, in order to pay for the legitimate purposes of government. But beyond that, to take your wages or savings is nothing more than robbery, because you have worked for it, and someone else is now enjoying it.

Granted that slavery is theft and that Democratic Party arguments to justify that theft are utterly without merit, we now proceed to examine whether America is guilty of allowing—or even perpetrating—that theft. Here we begin with what seems to be a prima facie case. The Constitution permits slavery. The American founders approved the Constitution. Ergo, the American founders were proslavery. Moreover, many of them owned slaves. Consequently, they are responsible both for permitting the theft and for personally engaging in it. This is the core of the progressive indictment of the founders.

That several of the founders owned slaves is undeniable. To this degree, there is personal responsibility for the theft. But it is impossible to fault the founders, as a group, before we consider the actual choices available to them. A group cannot be held responsible for an evil when its members did not have a choice between evil and good, when the only choice available to them was between allowing an evil or bringing about a greater evil. In this case, the choice of the lesser evil is undoubtedly the right one. The evil remains an evil, but the choice to do it is not an evil but a good choice. We don't fault people or punish them for making good choices. It makes no sense to castigate the founders, or make them pay, for doing the best they could do under circumstances that were not of their making.

The founders were, as a group, antislavery, yet they did not have a choice between outlawing slavery or not outlawing slavery. When the founders assembled in Philadelphia, slavery was legal in every single state. Had the founders outlawed slavery immediately, arguably very few states would have joined the union. Certainly the southern states would have stayed out. In that case, slavery might have lasted much longer.

The founders believed that slavery was on a course of extinction. In one sense, they were proven wrong. Eli Whitney's invention of the cotton gin boosted slavery in the American South. Yet the founders were right in the sense that, a few years after the Constitution was adopted, slavery had been abolished in every northern state. By 1800 slavery was no longer a national but only a regional or sectional institution. On this count alone, the founders are vindicated in choosing a course of action that severely restricted the reach of slavery. Systematic theft in one part of the country is preferable to systematic theft across the whole United States.

The black abolitionist Frederick Douglass once wrote that the founders permitted slavery as a "scaffolding to the magnificent structure, to be removed as soon as the building is completed." In that sense the building was completed in 1865, when the Civil War ended and slavery was abolished nationwide. But how was it abolished? It was abolished because Abraham Lincoln and the Republicans took a firm stance against theft and against the Democratic principle of popular sovereignty. Had America gone with the Democrats, slavery would have endured and might still be around in some form today. History proves the Republicans to have been the antislavery, anti-theft party and the Democrats to have been the proslavery, pro-theft party.

While slavery existed all over the world, as part of a universal conquest ethic, the West is unique in being the only civilization to oppose and end slavery. America is the only country to fight a great war to emancipate the slaves. More than six hundred thousand soldiers perished in that war; as I noted earlier, several hundred thousand of them died to achieve for the slaves a freedom the slaves were not in a position to achieve for themselves. This, surely, must count as some sort of reparation. Progressives who say America hasn't atoned for slavery are ignoring the multitude of dead bodies that stand as a bloody testament to the price of freedom for the slaves. Meanwhile, the South that benefited from slavery over those many years was largely destroyed in the Civil War. So by 1865 whatever wealth was accumulated through servitude was largely lost.

This stark reality puts a big hole in the reparations argument that America was built by slave labor. It wasn't. The southern plantation economy was built by slave labor, but that whole system and its wealth was destroyed in the war. Today there are no great southern families or fortunes whose roots are found in antebellum wealth. In contrast, many great northern fortunes were built in the effort to defeat the South and eradicate slavery.

What about the descendants of the slave owners? They are around, but there actually aren't very many of them. Let's recall that slavery had already been abolished in the North. Even in the South, only around 25 percent of white families had slaves. Blacks, too, owned slaves: in the early nineteenth century, there were at least 3,500 black slave owners, who owned upwards of 10,000 black slaves.

Presumably any serious attempt to trace the beneficiaries of slavery would also include the descendants of these black slave owners. Yet no one is proposing such a quest. Even progressives realize it would be ridiculous. Moreover, there is no way to trace how those whites and blacks living today—who are themselves utterly innocent—might have benefited from what their ancestors did more than a century and a half ago.

As for blacks living today, they are clearly better off than they would have been had there been no slavery. The reason is that, absent slavery, they would still be living in Africa. More precise, absent slavery, they would not exist. This is a difficult point to grasp, so let me make it first in the context of British colonialism in my native country of India. Certainly colonialism, like slavery, was established as a form of conquest and rule and, yes, theft. The British came to India to steal. And they did steal. I cannot deny that my ancestors who lived under colonialism for two centuries were worse off than they would have been had the British never come.

But am I, a descendant of colonialism, worse off? Here I would have to say no. The reason is that, whatever the larcenous intentions of the British, they introduced into India ideas and institutions that have greatly benefited my life. I am now a writer and my ability to write and speak English is very probably a direct result of British rule. India is a global leader in technology thanks to scientific principles the Indians first learned from the British, and to an educational system based on British schools and colleges. India is also a democracy, with rule of law, and religious freedom, and a whole infrastructure of roads, railways, and ports that almost certainly would not have been built by the Indians themselves had the British not done it.

On balance, therefore, I have to say that I'm better off because of British colonialism. I might not like to admit this, but it's true. Consequently I cannot with good conscience submit my demand for reparations from the queen. If I did I would be claiming more than my "fair share," and it would be unjust.

Pretty much the same situation applies to the Native Americans living today. Their ancestors perished in large numbers, mainly as a result of diseases contracted from the white man, but contemporary Native Americans have embraced the ideas and institutions that the white man brought to this country. Who knows what the situation of the Native Americans would have been had the Europeans never arrived here? Native Americans understandably regret the loss of an old way of life, but how many now actually want to go back to it? None, because if they wanted to do so, they would have. By their actual choices, the Native Americans affirm that they want to continue living in modern America. They are better off and they know it.

Mexicans who ended up on the American side at the conclusion of the Mexican War did not have to wait for their descendants to enjoy the benefits of living in America. They were better off right away. The reason is simple. In Mexico they lived under tyranny and had virtually no rights; in America they were immediately made citizens and—despite the hardships imposed by a new country, a new language, and ethnic prejudice—enjoyed protections of life, liberty, and property that were simply unavailable in their native country. Their descendants demonstrate their appreciation of life in America merely by remaining here; there is simply no illegal traffic across the border from the United States to Mexico.

As for African Americans, their plight today can be understood in pretty much the same terms. Just as colonialism brought the blessings of Western civilization to India, just as white settlement and the outcome of the Mexican War proved beneficial to the descendants of many Native Americans and Mexicans, in the same way, slavery was the conveyor belt that brought Africans to America. The descendants of slaves, living today, are enjoying the benefits of American freedom and American opportunity. Nowhere in Africa is there a comparable level of freedom and opportunity.

No surprise, the descendants of slaves have no intention of returning to Africa. Led by Frederick Douglass, they realized as early as 1865 that their prospects would be better in America than anywhere else. In staying, these African Americans voted with their feet in the same way that immigrants do when they come to this country. Through free choice, these involuntary immigrants became voluntary immigrants. Recognizing that their ancestors had been victimized by an unconscionable theft, they still opted to remain and thrive in this anti-theft society.

Asked what America should do for the slaves after emancipation, Frederick Douglass replied, "Do nothing with them. Mind your business, and let them mind theirs. . . . The best way to help them is to just let them help themselves." And Zora Neale Hurston, the black feminist and anthropologist, wrote about slavery, "From what I can learn, it was sad. Certainly. But my ancestors who lived and died in it are dead. The white men who profited by their labor and lives are dead also. I have no personal memory of those times, and no responsibility for them. Neither has the grandson of the man who held my folks. . . . I have no intention of wasting my time beating on old graves. I do not belong to the sobbing school of Negroes who hold that nature somehow has given them a low-down dirty deal. . . . Slavery is the price I paid for civilization, and that is worth all that I have paid through my ancestors for it."[9]

These are two intrepid African Americans who deny that America owes blacks—or by extension, any other so-called victimized group—a living. Even though they lived through slavery (in the case of Douglass) and segregation (in the case of Hurston), neither one climbed aboard the reparations brigade. On the contrary, they are standing testaments to the progressive lie about America's past. As a consequence, in our left-leaning educational environment, their views on these topics remain untaught, ignored, erased from progressive propaganda masquerading as history. They are truth-tellers who frustrate the progressive pitch.

As with the Greek pretext for invading Troy, "history for profit" is a scam. It is not a legitimate basis for extracting wealth from productive people and using it to give people stuff for free. America doesn't owe anyone a living, and the leftist project to create a dependent class in this country, living off the public weal, is itself unjust, immoral, and demeaning. While pretending to restore stolen goods, the left is engaging in its own form of theft.

Think of the various scams pulled off by the duke and the dauphin in Mark Twain's *Adventures of Huckleberry Finn*. The huckster tradition is alive and well in America—only then it conned people with the language of religious devotion, and now it does so in the language of fairness and compensatory justice. Either way, it's a pickpocket scheme. Remember the pickpocket in the film *Casablanca* who, while in the process of warning a tourist about "vultures" everywhere, proceeds calmly to lift the man's wallet? If that had been a film about politics, surely that man would have been called a progressive.

Chapter 6

THE THINGS THAT KEEP PROGRESSIVES AWAKE AT NIGHT:

The Greed and Inequality Scam

A man must first make a full confession before beginning this penance; then he must immediately start on a long period of fasting and abstinence, which must continue for forty days, during which he must forgo touching, not only all other women, but even his own wife.[1]

—Don Felice to Brother Puccio, in Boccaccio, *Decameron*

Giovanni Boccaccio was a medieval master of scams, and he out-lined many of these in story form in his great work *The Decam-eron*. I read that book many years ago, and one story stayed with me over the years. It is the one about the dapper con man Don Felice, who has lustful designs on the wife of one Brother Puccio. Through various machinations, Don Felice conveys his feelings to the woman, Mona Isabetta, and finds that they are reciprocated. The problem, however, is that Brother Puccio is always on the scene, and therefore Don Felice cannot fulfill his desires even though Mona Isabetta is receptive to his advances. So he contrives an ingenious diversion.

Knowing that Brother Puccio is "given over to spiritual things," and has taken the trouble to join the Third Order of St. Francis, and moreover that he was a "simple ignorant fellow," Don Felice approaches the target of his scam with disarming camaraderie. "I've often noticed," he says, "that all you desire is to become a saint. Now it seems to me that you're going a very long way round to achieve this, since there is a much shorter way." Don Felice then says this shorter way is only known to the pope and select clergy and of course him. "Because you are my friend and have treated me so well," he informs Brother Puccio, "I would, if I could be sure that you wanted to follow this method and would not reveal it to another soul, teach it to you." Brother Puccio readily agrees.

Then Don Felice gives Brother Puccio an elaborate series of prayers and penances, including fasting and abstinence, all of which have to be carried out at specific intervals, and involve regular presence in church, often for hours at a time, and also several pilgrim journeys, all of these consuming a great deal of time and requiring extensive absences from his home. During all this time Brother Puccio is to stay away from all women, including his wife. Moreover, what these penances and rituals achieve is a full pardon for all previous sins, but Brother Puccio must maintain this new way of life in the future if he wants to be assured of eternal felicity.

As he is laying it on thick, Don Felice professes his reluctance to impose this regimen on Brother Puccio, but by this time Brother Puccio is so convinced that he eagerly embraces it, insisting that this is a very small price to pay to enter paradise. Don Felice even urges him to get his wife's agreement, and Brother Puccio does—the woman quickly figuring out that a scam is afoot, one that she is quite agreeable to being a part of. In this way Don Felice and Mona Isabetta achieve the goal of their desires, attaining, Boccaccio informs us, a sensual paradise somewhat comparable to the paradise sought by the gullible Brother Puccio.[2]

Notice that, for the plot to succeed, Don Felice needed several key elements. First of all he needed moral credibility, because he had to convince Brother Puccio that he was a man of supreme goodness and virtue. Second, he needed to convince Brother Puccio, his gullible target, that he, Brother Puccio, was lacking in that same goodness and virtue. Consequently Brother Puccio would have to make himself, in a sense, Don Felice's student and learn moral virtue from him. Only by following Don Felice's counsel—his pitch—could Brother Puccio reach the higher spiritual plane that presumably Don Felice had already reached.

Another aspect of the pitch is that it involves diversion and entanglement. The pitch draws attention away from what really matters and entangles its target in a completely irrelevant issue. While the target is embroiled in sorting out this irrelevant issue, Don Felice makes his move and enacts his theft. From beginning to end, the theft works beautifully because it is perpetually bathed in an odor of sanctity and virtue.

In the previous chapter we explored a "history for profit" scam. This scam at least seemed to be based on things that actually happened and actually matter. Here we explore a more audacious progressive scam, no less audacious than the one in Boccaccio's book. I call it "the things that keep progressives awake at night" scam. I get the title from an article by a progressive icon and fellow Indian, Amartya Sen.[3] I read Sen's article and also his book *The Idea of Justice* while I did my daily workout on the bike in the confinement center.

Now Sen is an academic superstar who, by Indian standards, lives a highly opulent lifestyle. Given this, I suspect there is virtually *nothing* that could keep him awake at night. But Sen wants us to believe that he is so worried about greed, inequality, and social injustice that he can't sleep! In other words, Sen seeks to establish that he is a man of pure motives, of unimpeachable moral credibility. Sure, it's a pose, but it's a very profitable type of pose. If you disagree, I remind you that Sen has won the Nobel Prize for Economics, among other prestigious awards.

Sen's book *The Idea of Justice* has been hailed as a progressive classic. He sets the tone for the book with a revealing example. Three children—Anne, Bob, and Carla—are quarreling over a flute. Carla wants to keep the flute because, well, she made the flute. Anne claims the flute on the grounds that she is the best flute player of the three. And Bob—there is always a Bob—claims the flute because he is so poor that he has never had a flute of his own.

Now, this is where things take a strange turn. "Having heard all three and their different lines of reasoning," Sen writes, "there is a difficult decision that you have to make." Oh, really? Most sensible people can see there is no difficult decision involved at all. Carla made the flute and it belongs to her. Carla would not have made the flute had she any reason to suspect it would be taken from her and given to someone else. It's Carla's flute. Case closed.

Not for Sen, who informs us that "theorists of different persuasions, such as utilitarians, or economic egalitarians, or no-nonsense libertarians" may each take a different view of the situation. "Bob, the poorest, would tend to get fairly straightforward support from the economic egalitarian." But "Carla, the maker of the flute, would receive immediate sympathy from the libertarian." Probably, Sen says, the utilitarian "would tend to give weight to the fact that Anne's pleasure is likely to be stronger because she is the only one who can play the flute."

Sen remains serenely above the fray. "The different resolutions all have serious arguments in support of them, and we may not be able to identify, without some arbitrariness, any of the alternative arguments as being the one that must invariably prevail."[4] Sen goes on to argue that there is a plurality of ways in which justice can be conceived, all leading to his conclusion that it's fine to take people's stuff as long as it's used for acceptable purposes. Sen even invokes a Sanskrit distinction between *Niti* and *Nyaya*, the former referring to the rules of procedural justice and the latter implying some wider substantive justice that Sen seeks to embrace.

Sen's *Niti* seems to be nothing other than property rights, which he wants to override, and his *Nyaya* is basically theft, which he is wholly in favor of. Like Don Felice, Sen begins by establishing his moral credibility. He is the Eastern yogi of wisdom and virtue, sitting on his sacred pillar. He does this by staying loftily above the fray, while everyone else is in the fray. Others have a theory, while he is the adjudicator of theories. These theories are basically diversions. Most of them have nothing to do with who owns the flute. Rather, they are related to peripheral questions such as "who would like to have a flute" and "who is good at playing the flute." Eventually, Sen declares, "we" are the ones who decide who gets the flute.

This "we" is the giveaway term, and clearly it refers to none other than Sen. Sen decides, but not just for himself; he purports to speak on behalf of society, or government. Sen's entire book can be thought of as an "entanglement." Sen wants us to get entangled in his various diversions, so we don't spot his hidden assumption, which guarantees victory to his position. That hidden assumption is that ownership of the flute has been silently transferred from the person who made the flute to Sen himself, posing as the mysterious "we." Sen—speaking for the government or society—now determines who gets the flute. This is theft, pure and simple, and no less objectionable because it is camouflaged by Sen's academic rigmarole.

I thought of the practical implications of Sen's vision of progressive justice. I was lying on my bunk, reading an article on Obama's latest promise to forgive students their student loan debts. Actually Sen, Obama, and the progressives are the ones who keep me awake at night. Obama likes to portray himself as the savior of the younger generation. In reality, however, college costs are so high in large part because the government subsidizes education with Pell Grants and a whole host of other scholarships and loans. Colleges continually raise tuition because they know that a large portion of the tab is paid for by the taxpayer, not the student. That's how colleges can afford to pay professors six-figure salaries for teaching two days a week and working only nine months out of the year.

So rising college costs, together with government subsidies, represent a collaboration between the government and the schools to take money from the taxpayer. Then, by seeking to relieve student debt, Obama is adding to the national debt. Since the national debt represents a future obligation for younger generations, Obama is offering a benefit to some young people now for which all young people who become taxpayers must pay in the future. Obama's "generosity" is a fraud: he is bestowing on young people money that is actually their own.

Obama has actually stolen that money, because debt, it should be emphasized, is a form of theft. We are of course used to hearing the usual rhetoric about how a huge national debt imposes a crippling burden on future generations. But missing here is the recognition that debt is a form of robbing from young people. Progressives are brazenly ripping off the young, all in the name of "social justice."

Yet young people are in general the poorest segment of the population. Progressive government extracts from them to transfer wealth to other groups, like the elderly, who are by and large a much more affluent group. Notice, too, that young people are for the most part ineligible to vote. They are being saddled with obligations to which they have not consented, and that do not benefit them in any way. This is truly "taxation without representation."

Let's look at the amounts involved.[5] When George W. Bush left office, the federal debt was $9 trillion. That's a huge amount, and Bush added nearly $4 trillion to the total, a disgraceful legacy caused primarily by profligate domestic spending and foreign wars. Bush's second term deficits averaged around $500 billion. But still, the $9 trillion represented America's entire debt accumulated from the founding through 2008.

Now, under Obama, the federal debt is $18.5 trillion. It's larger than America's gross domestic product which is around $17 trillion. The debt will be over $19 trillion when Obama leaves office. While progressives professed to be scandalized by Bush's $500 billion deficits, they have remained silent while Obama racks up trillion-dollar deficits. During the Reagan years the left fretted about "two hundred billion dollar deficits as far as the eye can see." What were annual deficits under Reagan became monthly deficits under Obama. In less than eight years, Obama has doubled the national debt.

If we consider the $19 trillion debt as an obligation being foisted upon the 50 million or so young people in the United States, each person owes $380,000. Obama isn't single-handedly responsible for this rip-off, but he is the prime malefactor. Basically he is charging young people with the cost of a home mortgage—without them getting the home. I am not even considering the cost of unfunded Social Security and Medicare liabilities, which is estimated around $100 trillion. Whenever I think of this intergenerational rip-off, it makes me angry.

I've got a lot of time to read at night. I'm not allowed to bring in my cell phone or my computer, so mainly I read books. I also keep up with social media. Each night I amuse myself by perusing printouts of various leftist attacks on me on social media. I've figured out that leftist groups actually hire people to harass me on Facebook and Twitter. I say this because these people have become my online stalkers. Seconds after I post something, several leftists immediately post comments like "How's prison?" and "You are a felon."

Yes, I am a felon because I broke the law. But justice requires more than a determination that someone broke the law. If a guy is caught speeding and given five years in prison, that's unjust, even though he broke the law. It's unjust because the penalty is disproportionate to the offense, and moreover, no one else who speeds gets that kind of penalty.

So how do my election law offenses compare to those of leading progressives? Well, let's see. Senate Majority Leader Harry Reid took $31,000 in late 2013 from his campaign funds to buy jewelry for his granddaughter Ryan Elisabeth Reid's wedding. In his campaign year-end report, Reid tried to hide his granddaughter's relationship to him by simply listing the transaction as a "holiday gift" to one "Ryan Elisabeth." The impression Reid sought to convey was that he was buying gifts for his supporters.

When it came to light that Reid had funneled campaign money to his granddaughter, Reid agreed to repay the money, but waxed indignant at continuing questions from reporters. "As a grandparent," he fumed, "I say enough is enough." Although Reid's case involves obvious corruption, the Obama administration has neither investigated nor prosecuted a case against this stalwart Obama ally.[6]

Bill Clinton, you may recall, had his own campaign finance contro-
versy. Following the 1996 election, the Democratic National Committee was forced to return $2.8 million in illegal and improper donations,
most of it from foreign sources. Most of that money was raised by a
shady Clinton fundraiser named John Huang. Huang, who used to
work for the Lippo Group, an Indonesian conglomerate, set up a fund-
raising scheme for foreign businessmen seeking special favors from the
U.S. government to meet with Clinton, in exchange for large sums of
money. A South Korean businessman had dinner with President Clinton in return for a $250,000 donation. Yogesh Gandhi, an Indian busi-
nessman who claimed to be related to Mahatma Gandhi, arranged to
meet Clinton in the White House and be photographed receiving an
award in exchange for a $325,000 contribution. Both donations were
returned, but again, no official investigation, no prosecutions.[7]

In 2013, Barack Obama's presidential campaign was fined $375,000
by the Federal Election Commission for violating federal disclosure
laws. An FEC audit of the 2008 records of Obama for America found
the group failed to disclose millions of dollars in contributions and
delayed refunding millions more in excess contributions.[8] Excess
contributions—sound familiar? But the FEC, you see, is a bipartisan
group with an equal number of Democratic and Republican commissioners. As a consequence of both parties having a say, FEC decisions
tend to be more balanced.

My case, you may remember, was deliberately not referred to the
FEC, as such cases typically are. Rather, the U.S. attorney for the
Southern District of New York decided to go ahead and prosecute it.
Unlike Obama, I did not benefit from a scheme involving millions of
dollars in excess contributions; rather, I paid $20,000 in excess of the
campaign finance limit. Yet I ended up in a confinement center, and
Obama, for vastly more serious offenses, paid a token fine.

From these examples, I conclude that progressive justice simply
means justice that benefits progressives. There is nothing proportional
or evenhanded about it. That's why Sen wants the government to own
the flute, which is to say, to own everything no matter who has made

it. If the government owns it, the government can do whatever it wants with it. Progressives determine the outcome, and then solemnly proclaim it "just."

Operating very much in the Sen mode, progressives today press two pitches that I am going to focus on in this chapter. The first is the "greed and selfishness" pitch, and the second is the "inequality" pitch, also known as the pitch of the "rich and the poor." Both these pitches are based on the hidden implication that progressives care deeply about the motives that go into wealth creation and also into the social effects of wealth distribution, while their critics don't. Consequently, progressives are moral people and their targets are morally suspect.

Progressives, in the manner of Don Felice, proceed to instruct entrepreneurs and workers on how they can raise their moral level in society, by turning over the authority for wealth distribution to progressives themselves. In short, the way to become less greedy and selfish is to allow yourself to be ripped off. This pitch, in order to work, requires a good deal of clever diversion and entanglement, drawing people into highly irrelevant issues, and keeping them occupied while the theft is going on. The pitch, as we will see, also requires extremely gullible targets who are suckers in the manner of Brother Puccio.

Let's begin with greed and selfishness. Is capitalism in fact based on these two "low" human motives? The short answer is no. Greed means seeking more than one is entitled to. The whole point of capitalism is to allocate wealth to the person who has created it. Capitalism was actually founded as an alternative to greed. Historically greed has been in the same abundant supply that it is now. And it had a familiar outlet: conquest. People who had the power to take things, took things. They took things to which they were not entitled by force or fraud, much in the manner that Sen wants to appropriate Carla's flute.

Under capitalism, you cannot take things without the consent of the one you are taking them from. If I voluntarily agree to have a mutual fund manager invest my money, and agree to pay him 1 percent a year for his service, he is not "greedy" for accepting these terms, even if his services make him a sizable annual income. Nor am I "greedy" for seeking to profitably employ my money in a manner that will multiply it.

Certainly capitalism is based on self-interest. I, as the investor, am indeed trying to benefit myself, and the mutual fund manager is also trying to benefit himself. Our negotiation is conducted entirely on this basis. Of course we are not solely benefiting ourselves. I am working to support my family, and he, his. "Self-interest," here, has an extended connotation. Moreover, self-interest is not the same thing as "selfishness." Selfishness, like greed, implies excessive self-regard. It is not selfish for Carla to claim her flute, regardless of whether she chooses to share it with anyone else.

Neither is it selfishness to seek to be paid as much as possible for what I do, nor is it selfishness for employers to seek to pay me as little as possible to get their work done. The self-interest that drives capitalism is the same self-interest that drives democracy and all human relations—the basic assumption that people care about themselves and look out for themselves.

Self-interest, Adam Smith writes in *The Wealth of Nations*, comes to us in the womb and never leaves us until the grave. It is a "uniform, constant and uninterrupted effort of every man to better his own condition."[9] Smith contrasts self-interest on the one hand with empathy on the other. Self-interest means thinking about yourself, while empathy means putting yourself in the place of another. Smith has no doubt which is morally preferable. In his other book, *A Theory of Moral Sentiments*, Smith admits, "To feel much for others, and little for ourselves, to restrain our selfish, and to indulge our benevolent, affections, constitutes the perfection of human nature."[10]

At first glance, it may seem that a system like capitalism that is based on self-interest disregards or even repudiates empathy. Smith sagely observes, "It is not from the benevolence of the butcher, the brewer or the baker that we expect our dinner, but from their regard to their own interest. We . . . never talk to them of our own necessities but of their advantages."[11] Smith finds it paradoxical that individuals each working toward their self-interest nevertheless collectively advance the material welfare of society. Smith invokes his famous "invisible hand" to explain how the one leads to the other. The concept of the "invisible hand" implies a kind of magic. Through some necromancy or deus ex machina, self-interest somehow works to make everyone better off.

But in fact there is nothing "invisible" about how the process takes place. Two factors are visibly at work here, and they both serve to tame and temper self-interest. The first is competition. There are several mutual fund managers who want my business. Each of them would like to charge as much as possible. At the same time, only one of them can get it, so they must compete for my business. If some insist upon charging more, others will win my business by charging less. So there is pressure on the fund managers to lower their fees.

This principle applies to me, no less than to the fund manager. I want to pay as little as possible to get a good manager. My research shows that one particular guy is really good. I'd like to get him for free, to pay him close to nothing for managing my money. I know, however, that if I offer such meager compensation his services may end up going to someone else. Then I will have to settle for a less capable custodian of my money. So I compete with other investors for the services of the good manager. Competition helps to temper my self-interest as well as his and bring us to a juncture where both of us are reasonably satisfied. Our consent defines the point of mutual acceptance. Neither of us is being ripped off, because otherwise we would not have agreed to the deal.

There is a second aspect to the invisible hand that Smith did not stress, yet to my mind it is the most important. Even though capitalism may be motivated by self-interest, the capitalist is successful only to the degree that he or she is empathetic. In other words, capitalism works by putting the energies of the capitalist entirely at the service of actual and potential customers. In order to serve customers, the capitalist must always be thinking about them: their wants, their needs, how to make their lives better.

This is operational empathy of a kind that is both rare and morally creditable. The typical intellectual, for example, spends virtually all his time thinking about what interests him and virtually none thinking about the potential customers whom he wants to buy his books. Among the professions, perhaps only the clergy are as dedicated as the capitalist to routinely contemplating and seeking the good of their "customers," who in that particular case are parishioners and church members.

So far I have focused on the motives of the capitalist, but it is worth contemplating for a moment the consequences of the system. Remarkably the capitalist does more to actually improve people's lives than others who seem specifically dedicated to achieving this result. The capitalist, in other words, beats out the professional "servers" and "caregivers." Consider, for instance, Bill Gates versus the Peace Corps. Bill Gates is a self-interested capitalist. The Peace Corps is aimed at helping poor people around the world. Peace Corps volunteers join up for the specific purpose of helping others. Let's assume that Bill Gates developed his computer and software systems primarily for the purpose of benefiting himself.

Yet who has done more to help the poor people of the world, Bill Gates or the Peace Corps? The answer isn't even close: it's Gates. And why? Because Gates is actually more effective than the Peace Corps in envisioning what serves the wants and needs of people. Gates enables the poor to gain access to a world of information that improves their lives in myriad ways, including the prospect of earning a livelihood. The motives of Peace Corps volunteers may be more pure; the results achieved by Gates are clearly superior.

There is no denying that there are plenty of greedy, selfish people who are capitalists. But the greed and selfishness is not in capitalism; it is in human nature. Capitalism takes human nature as it is and seeks to channel it in a way that serves fairness and decency. One may say that capitalism civilizes greed in much the same way that marriage civilizes lust. Lust, like greed, is in human nature; it is foolish and impractical to try to root it out. At the same time, it is widely recognized that these inclinations can have corrupting and destructive effects. So they have to be tamed and steered in such a way that they serve us, and society, best.

The institution of marriage allows for the fulfillment of lust, but within a context that promotes mutual love and attachment and the raising of children. Lust is refined, purified, and in a sense ennobled by marriage.

Similarly capitalism channels greed in such a way that it is placed at the service of the wants and needs of others. Destructive forms of greed, in which we seek to seize and appropriate other people's possessions, are outlawed in a capitalist society. We can acquire what others possess only by convincing them to give it to us, and the only way to do this is to give them something equally or more valuable in exchange. The point isn't just that capitalism makes society better off; it is that capitalism makes us better people by limiting the scope of our vices. So capitalism reduces greed and selfishness while at the same time improving the material welfare of society.

I find it amusing that progressives go on about "greed" and "selfishness" when they are the greediest, most selfish people of all. From the progressive viewpoint, Gates is a greedy, selfish guy because he has more than $50 billion and what can a man possibly want with that much money? (I'm reminded here of Obama's 2010 comment, made in the context of the financial reform debate, "I do think at a certain point you've made enough money.")[12] The progressive solution is to force Gates to part with some, or most, of that money so that they can deploy it as they see fit. This is the progressive equivalent of Amartya Sen's "who gets the flute."

The progressives are right that there is no way Gates can spend $50 billion on himself. He can only eat three meals a day and wear one set of clothes at a time. Even his heirs can be provided for with a fraction of that amount. Gates actually knows this. He has vowed to give away most of his fortune to charity. Nor is he waiting for death to do this. He has already given away billions. He buys mosquito nets for people in poor countries so that they don't get malaria. He invests in medical research. He funds educational projects in America and abroad.

Gates is neither a unique phenomenon nor a modern aberration. Andrew Carnegie gave away $350 million, the vast bulk of his fortune, to a range of charitable causes, from supporting scientific research to endowing several hundred public libraries. Carnegie's philanthropy was a self-conscious expression of his famous Gospel of Wealth: earn as much as you can, then give away as much as you can. And Carnegie practiced what he preached, which is more than we can say of the progressives who criticize tycoons from the past and the present.

Returning to the question at hand, it is not whether a sizable portion of Gates's money is being used to help the needy. It is. The only question is who decides how that money is spent. The capitalist answer is Gates. The progressive answer is progressives. But Gates is the one who earned the money. It's his flute because he made it. Progressives are basically thieves because they are trying to take away his flute by denying his legitimate claim to it. They purport to be champions of the needy, but whether or not this is true, they should be champions of the needy with their own resources. What kind of generosity is it that forcibly seizes and then disburses other people's money? This is not generosity; it's larceny.

To see this more clearly, imagine that I'm walking along the riverbank with a guy who is hungry. I am eating a sandwich. He asks me to share it with him, and so I do. Now, this is a virtuous transaction. I have done a good deed, and he is appropriately appreciative. Perhaps in the future, if he has a sandwich, he will share with some other needy guy. But this virtuous transaction is completely corrupted when it is brought about by the forcible intervention of the government.

Now envision the same scenario as above, but this time Obama shows up on a white horse, dismounts, points a gun to my head, and compels me to share my sandwich. Now I have not done a good deed, since I only shared my sandwich under duress. I gave not out of charity but out of fear. The receiver is not grateful to me; why should he be? He knows that I didn't give voluntarily. So the free sandwich does not provoke a feeling of appreciation; indeed, it is more likely to instill a feeling of entitlement. "I'm still hungry. Why am I getting only half a sandwich?" So even though the result is the same—I and the other guy each end up with half a sandwich—the morality has been completely stripped out of the transaction.

But this does not take into account the most invidious aspect of the transaction: the role played by Obama. Upon reflection, his actions are not only unjust; they are criminal. If he were a private individual, instead of a government agent, I would call the authorities and he would be arrested for assault, extortion, and theft. Unfortunately, in this case I cannot call the authorities because the authorities are the ones stealing from me. So I am doubly deprived: I am being stolen from, and I do not have the recourse of being able to rectify the theft.

Yet Obama is able to get away with it because, for years prior to the theft, he has been convincing people that he is the great apostle of social justice. I am supposed to be "greedy" and "selfish" for possessing a sandwich and he is wonderfully compassionate for taking half my sandwich and giving it to someone else. Notice that, through this process, the recipient of the sandwich is grateful not to me but to him. He becomes the provider even though it is my sandwich that he is sharing.

In fact, Obama is the one who gains the most from the outcome. His gain is not the mere half sandwich he took; rather, it is the allegiance of the fellow he is supposedly helping. That guy is now indebted to Obama, and more likely to vote for him. While the other man gains a meal, Obama gains power. So now we must reconsider the assumption that Obama's actions are motivated by altruism. It's far more likely they are motivated by a will to power. He is the greediest, most selfish one of all because he is the only person among the three of us taking something that does not belong to him. Obama's talk about "greed" and "selfishness" is a fraud; it is simply part of his con man's pitch.

Next we turn to inequality. Here the reigning mantra is that "the rich are getting richer and the poor are getting poorer." If this were true, it would of course be unfortunate. But it still would not follow that the rich are getting richer at the expense of the poor, much less that the rich are therefore exploiting the poor. Progressives, however, intend to leave those impressions without explicitly accusing the rich of impoverishing the poor. Thorstein Veblen gives us the familiar pitch, "The accumulation of wealth at the upper end of the pecuniary scale implies privation at the lower end of the scale."[13]

As with the greed pitch, the inequality pitch is designed to provide a justification for confiscating from those who have more, supposedly to provide to those who have less. Progressives are so attached to this pitch that it has acquired the status of a moral principle or ethic. Stealing of this kind is considered not only permissible, but indeed a good thing to do.

This progressive ethic is not found only in the political realm; we also saw it among slave owners, who insisted that their enslavement of others was a "positive good," and we see it today among criminals. Consider the case of Hero, a South Side Mexican who beat and robbed an old African American woman. I learned about the incident in the confinement center from one of his fellow gang members, Sancho.

"We called the woman Mabs," Sancho told me. Sancho wears a rosary around his neck and has a single earring, a diamond stud. "She had lived in the neighborhood from the time we were kids. We didn't talk to her, because Mexicans don't like to talk to black people, but everyone recognized her, because she was bent over, you know, and walked with a cane and a little dog. Every evening, at the same time, she took the dog for a walk."

Apparently Hero, one of the young punks in the Forty-Fifth Street gang, decided to jump Mabs and take her money. It wasn't as easy as one might expect. The woman put up quite a fight, whopping the guy with her cane and even biting him. Still, what can an elderly woman do against a strapping young man? Mabs took a heavy blow to the back, and another to the head, and she ended up unconscious in the street while the punk made off with her ring and a paltry sum of money.

When word got out in the gang about what happened, Sancho said, "Everyone felt bad. We didn't know this woman, but we thought it was pretty f*cked-up to go after a person who had even less, you know, than we did. We liked this guy Hero. He had pulled off some of the biggest jobs for us. One time he beat the sh*t out of this Asian store owner.

The wife and son showed up, so he beat the sh*t out of them. Then he cleaned out the place. I think he got nearly two grand from that job. We were like, f*ckin' A!

"But this was different, man. I mean, some of us actually wanted to kick Hero's ass. We couldn't do that, you know, because stealing is what gang members do. But I did ask him, what the f*ck, man? And he said, I was high when it happened. Even he felt a little bad about what he did. I told him, leave that bitch alone—don't do that sh*t again."

Actually I was not surprised that Hero beat up the old woman. Violence and robbery are what guys like Hero do. If he could unremorsefully beat up the Asian guy and his family, why should he have qualms about beating up Mabs? The remarkable thing is that Hero was cheered by his peers for harming and robbing the Asian family, while he was on the defensive for doing the same to Mabs.

Certainly the Asians weren't wealthy, but they were perceived to have more than their assailant. Mabs, by contrast, was perceived to have less. While criminals typically steal from anyone from whom they can extract money, inequality provides a pretext for them to take from those who are above them, while no such pretext is available if they steal from those who are below them. In other words, in their mind, it is fundamentally unfair for someone to have more than they do. Therefore it is perfectly fair to rob them. The same principle, it seems, applies to modern progressivism.

Before we ask how much inequality there is in society, and whether it has gotten better or worse, let's explore at the level of first principle how inequalities come to exist in the first place. Imagine a society with 100 members, and each of them has $50. There is perfect equality. Now one of those members—let's call her J. K. Rowling—publishes a Harry Potter book. She prices each book at $5. For some reason, and the reason is not important, everyone wants this book. Indeed all the other 99 members of the society are willing to part with $5 apiece to purchase the book. So badly do they want the book that they ignore the possibility of pooling their resources and sharing a few books among the group. Each one wants his or her own book. So 99 people all fork

over $5, and J. K. Rowling gets nearly $500 in exchange for her product. Rowling now has nearly $550 while the others now have $45 each.
Suddenly we have inequality, and there is a yawning chasm between
Rowling and everyone else. Nor is this a one-time event; when Rowling's next Harry Potter installment appears, the inequality is sure to
increase.

Even so, has any injustice been perpetrated? No. The inequality is
directly in proportion to what Rowling has provided the others. Not
only are they fine with the inequality; they are actually the ones responsible for causing it. They voluntarily gave their resources to her
because in their minds her book was worth at least $5. She has their
money because they wanted her to have it.

What we learn from this example is that there is nothing inherently
objectionable about inequality. Nor is increasing inequality by itself a
problem. What matters is how this inequality came about. Progressives
who insist that J. K. Rowling is a crook and is depriving people of their
"fair share" are themselves crooks who are trying to take the justly
earned fruits of her labor. In Lincoln's terms, she works and they eat. It
doesn't matter whether these crooks then share the money with others,
in exchange for votes and power, or keep the money for themselves. In
both cases their conduct is equally reprehensible and their inequality
pitch must be recognized as being part of the political thief's standard
bag of tricks.

The problem of inequality must be distinguished from the problem
of poverty. The two are quite distinct. A society in which everyone is
poor has no inequality and lots of poverty. A society in which there are
lots of rich people and few poor people has considerable inequality but
very little poverty. Americans who respond to the progressive moral
appeal about inequality are usually thinking about the need to allevi-
ate poverty.

Yet there are comparatively few poor people in America. This statement may seem shocking. What about all the progressive data that show
that nearly 15 percent of people are poor? That number is determined

without taking into account government benefits. Once government benefits are factored in, there are very few poor people in America.

Moreover, when progressives tell us how little money the poor have, they are once again not counting the government benefits they currently receive. So when you hear that "it's nearly impossible to make ends meet for a family of four on $12,000 a year," be assured that no one is actually making ends meet for a family of four on that amount. In reality, the family making $12,000 a year is getting subsidized housing, food stamps, free health care, and a host of other benefits. If we added these up, we'd find that this family is actually making ends meet on closer to $30,000 a year. We taxpayers are the ones who are paying for the difference.

Progressives realize, however, that it doesn't sound quite so convincing to say "it's nearly impossible to make ends meet for a family of four on $30,000 a year." After all, the mean income in this country is $50,000 a year, so getting by on 60 percent of the national average does not seem to be a case of extreme deprivation.

Let's now examine the progressive pitch about inequality. Progressives typically begin by dividing America into three groups: the rich, the middle class, and the poor. Then progressives point out that the middle class appears to be shrinking. Consequently, progressives say, inequality must be increasing. The rich are getting richer and the poor are getting more numerous. Indeed, the rich must be benefiting at the expense of the poor. The progressive solution is to give progressives free rein over rich people's money. Progressives then pledge to implement a series of government measures to reduce inequality.

As I consider the progressive tripartite division of people into poor, middle class, and rich, I ask myself where I fit into these camps. Then I realize that, when I reflect on the course of my working life, I fit into *all of them*. I came to America with $500 in my pocket. That sum had to last me for my first year as an exchange student. As it turned out, it was also the total of my discretionary spending throughout my four years of college. When I was admitted to Dartmouth I had no idea how I could afford to go; Dartmouth made that possible by giving me a package of scholarship grants, student loans repayable after graduation, and fifteen hours of work-study employment per week. Dartmouth in those days cost $30,000 a year, half of what it costs now.

During this period of my life, I was so poor that I could not afford to eat at McDonald's. I don't mean I couldn't eat regularly at McDonald's; I couldn't eat there at all. I found it ridiculously expensive. By contrast, poor people in America eat at McDonald's all the time. They don't even know what it means to be poor in an absolute sense. It's funny to recall now, but there was a period in which my circumstances were so modest that I envied the poor because they had so much more than I did.

Things didn't improve dramatically with my first job, which paid just over the poverty line. But as I became a magazine editor in Washington, D.C., and then secured a coveted job in the White House, my salary rose and I entered the comfortable middle class. Eventually when my books hit the bestseller list, and I was invited to give speeches, and later when I made successful documentary films, my earnings rose even further and I accumulated enough to qualify as rich, or at least very well-off.

Mine is undoubtedly a success story, yet this upward trajectory of earning is hardly uncommon. It defines the path taken by typical families in America. People start out with meager earnings, then they do better, and they reach the peak of their earning power in their fifties or sixties. Yet progressives would count them as poor in one stage, middle class in the second, and perhaps rich in the third. This hardly describes one class of person exploiting another, or benefiting at the expense of another; rather, it describes the same person moving through the familiar stages of life.

This pattern shows we must be careful in evaluating the progressive inequality pitch; it doesn't prove the pitch untrue. One aspect of it is clearly true. The middle class as a group is indeed shrinking. At one time it described virtually the whole of American society; now it describes less than half of it. Why is that? It's because over the past few decades, many people have moved from the middle class to the ranks of the affluent. In other words, they haven't moved down; they have moved up.

Previously it was a rarity to find a millionaire—a person with a net worth of $1 million. Today there are nearly 5 million families with a net worth exceeding $1 million. I wouldn't call these people "rich," because being rich today, unlike in the past, requires more than $1 million in total assets. Even so, these people are certainly well-off in that they have capital to invest and they have a good deal of discretionary income. In a sense, they make up a new class in between the middle class and the rich. We can call it the upper middle class or the affluent class.

In departing the middle class, these successful Americans have widened the gap between themselves and those they have left behind. So inequality is greater. But far from being a bad thing, this is a very good thing, because so many people now have access to the privileges that were once the prerogative of the very few.

Over the past century and a half, the great achievement of the West was to create a middle class, allowing the common man to escape poverty and live in relative comfort. Now the United States has performed an equally impressive feat. It has created the first mass affluent class in world history. A mass affluent class is just starting to emerge in several European countries as well. And this mass affluent class is now large enough in America that it outnumbers the poor.

What about the people who have not moved up, the ones left behind? Their condition certainly hasn't worsened; it has improved. Nor has the condition of the poor worsened; it too has improved. Poor people have amenities today that would in previous eras clearly establish them as middle class or better. Being poor today means having a place to live, home appliances like refrigerators, washing machines, and microwave ovens, decent clothing, a car, cable television, and a cell phone. Poor Americans today are better housed, better clothed, and better fed than average Americans were half a century ago; in many respects they live better than the average European does today, and of course by world standards they are in the very upper echelon.

When so many in the middle class have prospered and moved up, why have so many others stayed put? Why have their incomes stagnated? Here the main problem isn't rich people; it's poor people. Middle-class Americans have seen the price of their labor driven down, or at least held constant, by the competitive pressure coming from three different directions: globalization, immigration, and technology. A guy making steel today isn't typically being exploited by his wealthy boss; rather, his problem is that some other guy in another country can make steel more cheaply. So either his plant has to close down, or it has to pay its workers less in order to stay competitive.

Similarly, new immigrants are willing to work for less and therefore they exert a downward pressure on the price that labor commands. Many Americans are not willing to do those jobs anymore at the price that the market is able to bear. Finally, technology replaces workers by doing, more quickly and cheaply, what humans were previously required to do.

Of course, progressives could call for a slowing down of the pace of technology or for restrictions on immigration or globalization. This, however, would pose serious political risks. Silicon Valley, which has been quite friendly to the Democrats, would likely turn against them. Hispanics, an important voter bloc, would also recoil if the Democrats proposed to reduce legal and illegal immigration. Finally, there is no easy way to stop the global exchange of goods and services that puts downward pressure on certain types of jobs but also produces goods and services more cheaply and thus benefits American consumers.

Consequently, progressives pretend not to notice these factors and even when they do, they don't do much about them. In some respects, they advocate policies, such as immigration amnesty, that make the problems worse. But at the same time progressives point to CEOs and entrepreneurs and blame them for the plight of those whose incomes are stagnant. More broadly, they demonize the rich and the successful. This is pure scapegoating. It is a devious scheme to target innocent people for public venom so that progressives can steal from them and come across as the good guys for doing it.

I mentioned that technology was one of the factors responsible for suppressing the wages of certain types of workers, and thus a contributor to the income gap. Yet at the same time, technology ensures to people across the swath of American society access to products that even rich people didn't have in the past. Contemplating the vast range of technological wonders that even poor people have today, the novelist Tom Wolfe once observed that they would, if he could see them, "make the Sun King blink."

Moreover, while technology may contribute to certain types of short-term inequality, long-term it is a powerful instrument of social equality. Consider: A century ago a rich man traveled by horse and carriage, while the poor man traveled on foot. That's a huge difference. Today a rich man might drive a Jaguar, and his poorer counterpart a Honda Civic or a Hyundai. That's not such a huge difference. A century ago the rich could escape the bitter cold of winter, or the scalding heat of summer, by escaping to holiday retreats; the poor, by contrast, had to endure the elements. Today most homes, offices, and cars are temperature-controlled and the benefits are enjoyed by rich and poor alike.

These examples could be multiplied, but here's the most telling one of all: a hundred years ago, the life expectancy of the average American was around fifty years. The gap between rich and poor was about ten years. It was not uncommon for a wealthy person to live into his late sixties or seventies but quite rare for a poor man or woman to do so. Today the average life expectancy is just over seventy-five years, and the gap between rich and poor has narrowed to 2–3 years. So the poor have not only made huge absolute gains; they have also made huge gains relative to their more affluent counterparts.

Now, progressives may attempt to argue that these improvements are due to government policies, such as medical allowances for the poor, but it was technological capitalism that produced the medical improvements in the first place. Moreover, when it comes to inventions like the car, the computer, the cell phone, and a whole arsenal of lifesaving drugs and treatments, rich people paid the exorbitant initial prices that financed the research and development over time that made those products better and cheaper and brought them within the reach of virtually the whole society.

Summing up, we can see that the progressive pitches about greed, selfishness, and inequality are basically diversions. They seek to deflect us away from the core issue, which is that the creators of the wealth are the ones who deserve the wealth they have created. To put it in primitive terms, the farmer who grew the crops gets to keep the crops and the hunters who killed the deer get to eat the deer.

Progressives, however, have always had their eye on those crops and that deer. Through an elaborate flimflam—"that greedy selfish farmer who wants to keep the food he planted and harvested," "look how much meat those hunters have compared to those who didn't go on the hunt"—the progressives seek to establish themselves as the moral arbiters in adjudicating an issue that needs no adjudication, namely, who has the right to the crops and the deer. The moment we enter into their pitch, we have unwittingly transferred ownership of the crops and the deer to the government, which is to say, to the progressives. This is the biggest theft of all, one that is especially diabolical because it marches behind a banner of justice.

Chapter 7

YOU DIDN'T BUILD THAT:

The Society-Did-It Scam

If you've got a business, you didn't build that. Somebody else made that happen.[1]

—Barack Obama, on the 2012 campaign trail

In this chapter we explore one of the central claims of modern progressivism, that wealth is created not by entrepreneurs and workers but rather by society, and therefore the proceeds can be allocated by the state according to its perceived benefits to society. Of course, if the premise is not true, then the conclusion doesn't follow, and the progressive redistributive project is built on a fallacy. Therefore progressives like Obama are very keen to inform entrepreneurs, "You didn't build that." Obama's explicit claim is that "society did it" and the implicit suggestion is that "society could have done it without you."

Interestingly there is a confinement center corollary to the idea that "society did it." It is the idea, sometimes heard among the criminal class, that "society did it to me." Or, to put it a bit differently, "society made me do it." These two ideas—attributing wealth creation or criminal behavior to society in general—seem to be based on the undeniable truth that the outcomes of our actions depend on many factors outside ourselves. "Society" becomes a stand-in for the innumerable, sometimes untraceable influences that contribute to our choices and the results of those choices.

The two ideas have something else in common: they both subtract from the idea of personal responsibility. In one case the businessman or entrepreneur doesn't get the credit; in the other the criminal or wrongdoer doesn't take the blame. A closer look can help us see the dangers inherent in granting to society outcomes that would never have occurred without specific individuals freely undertaking specific courses of action.

We can appreciate those dangers without denying that, in many cases, society does in fact give people a very hard shake. This happens all over the world. In Suketu Mehta's account of the Mumbai underworld, he describes one vicious murderer, Satish, who might be described as a therapist's dream. "When Satish was seven years old, in 1981," Mehta tells us, "he saw his mother burning alive in front of him." Mehta asked how it affected him. "The next day," Satish nonchalantly replied, "I was eating chocolates." To make matters even worse, the police said Satish's father had killed his mother. The father contended it was a suicide. The father was suspended from his job, jailed, tried, and sentenced to life in prison. Years later, he was acquitted on appeal, but by this time Satish had left the home and was part of the youth crime population of the city.[2]

Satish's experience may be especially horrific, but even in America we can see how circumstances can conspire to push people to the edge of their endurance. One of my confinement center peers is an older guy who reviews the case files of inmates and helps them draft letters to their lawyers, probation officers, and sometimes even judges. "These guys," he tells me, leaning back in his plastic chair in the restroom as another guy put drops in his eyes, "whether white, black or Latino, have horrible backgrounds. It's beyond tragic."

I said that I suspected that most of them, perhaps 90 percent, had serious family problems. "Ninety percent?" he said, blinking ferociously to let the drops sink into his eyes. "No, one hundred percent." He estimated that 25 percent of the inmates he had known had been molested by a parent or someone close to them. "Something happens to them that f*cks them up, and then they spend the rest of their lives f*cking up other people."

I wonder, what will my experience here in confinement do to me? I had this thought about halfway through my captivity. It was January 2015, and I was really feeling the weight of my sentence. I'd been confined through Thanksgiving, Christmas, and New Year. I'd done three months, but I still had five to go. Routines that seemed amusing when I started became just dreary.

Every few hours, for example, there was count. We were a bunch of guys confined in two dormitories, yet for some reason it took nearly an hour to count us. Clearly there were no math majors on the staff. We had to stand around our beds the whole time while they did their thing. Some guys were asleep. Inevitably the staffer would prod them "Jimenez?" "What? Yes, it's me." But they *knew* that was Jimenez. I think, they were just screwing with him. That's the sadism of bureaucracy. This is why some people like to work in these jobs. Ordinarily a puny man or woman could not push a tough guy like Jimenez around. Here, they can.

Not only am I frustrated with the place, I'm increasingly frustrated at this point with Judge Berman. At a hearing following my sentencing, he said he was not satisfied with my weekly counseling with a licensed psychologist. He insisted I be examined by a full-fledged medical psychiatrist. He demanded I take one of the standard psychological assessments, such as the Minnesota Multiphasic Personality Inventory (MMPI).

So I took the MMPI, and with my probation officer's consent, had the results sent to Roger Gould, a renowned psychiatrist in New York. Gould's field of expertise was relevant to my situation. As he wrote Judger Berman, "The bulk of my professional writing the last 25 years has been about the lifecycle, the various adaptations and challenges that take place during defined age transitions."

I had seen Gould the previous year, over the period of four months, in connection with a tumultuous love relationship I was then involved in. Consequently he had had the opportunity to get to know me first-hand. In addition, Gould conducted interviews with me over the phone about how I got involved with the law in this case.

Based on his examinations, Gould wrote the judge to say, in part, "Mr. D'Souza is very well developed in his professional life and functions at a high level without much conflict.

"Mr. D'Souza at this point in time is quite well-adjusted to the difficult circumstances of his probation and the stigma associated with his penalty. He sleeps well in noisy crowded conditions and does not report any significant anxiety or depression.

"I see no evidence of psychopathology and certainly no need for any kind of psychotropic medication. He is not an angry person with an impulse disorder. I do not believe he is hiding anything. He is what he presents himself to be.

"He is a man who made a mistake for good motives that led to bad judgment. He is very ambitious and dedicated to his work which consumes most of his mental energies. He had very little time to give to his old friend and gave too much money instead. He is paying for that mistake and has accepted the penalty without rancor or resentment."

Although he could not question Gould's credentials, Berman seemed suspicious that this report had been produced by a psychiatrist in private practice. Berman apparently felt this made his conclusions a bit suspect. Berman ordered that I should be examined by a *government* psychiatrist.

So Kathy, my probation officer, identified a government psychiatrist and I went to see him. As I walked in the door, he said, "Are you Dinesh D'Souza?" I confessed that I was. He expressed surprise. "Why on earth are you here?" I told him.

"That's it?" he said. "You gave twenty grand over the limit. That's all there is to it?"

"Yes."

"I ask because it's very unusual to have a psychiatric examination in this sort of a case."

"I know." Then I told him about the Obama connection.

"Oh, I see," he said. "You pissed off the higher-ups."

"I sure did."

"Well, I'm sure there's nothing wrong with you. But still, I have to examine you. So fill out this test, and we'll see what it says."

I answered about two hundred questions on his survey. A few days later, I heard from Kathy that the test showed I was completely normal.

I suspected the judge would not be happy to hear this. It seemed at this point that the guy was looking for a pretext to proclaim me mentally deficient and administer medications to "cure" me of my chronic lawbreaking tendencies—or perhaps, we should honestly admit, my conservatism.

Judge Berman continues to torture me in other small ways. Obviously I had not been able to perform my community service of teaching English classes during the holidays, because the Catholic school that administers those classes was closed for Christmas and New Year. Kathy had reported this to Judge Berman, and to Kathy's surprise, he said he wanted me to do makeup classes. I asked Kathy, "I wonder if he does makeups when the court closes for the holidays." She replied, "What do you think?"

Fortunately I figured out a way to turn Berman's recalcitrance to my benefit. I went to my case officer at the confinement center. I had been assigned a new case officer by this time, a very pleasant woman named Leilani Haslop. I reminded her that I already had a late check-in at 10 p.m. for Mondays, because that was my teaching day. But now I had to do makeups, so I also needed a late check-in for Wednesday. She changed my form to extend my return time to 10 p.m. on Wednesday in addition to Monday.

This meant, however, that I could check in at 10 p.m. on Wednesday for the remaining duration of my confinement. I got to return late every Wednesday for twenty more weeks. This may seem surprising, because you might expect the guys at the front desk to allow me late check-in only when I am actually doing makeup classes. This, however, is not how things work in the bureaucracy.

The inmate sheet is like the Bible; what it says is how it goes. If it says 10 p.m. return, then there is no point trying to explain anything different. If I told them I should return early on a given Wednesday, because there is no makeup class that day, they would give me blank stares. Recognizing by now how the system worked, I took advantage of it. I enjoyed the extra hours of freedom.

I began to wonder if I was myself learning to scam the system. In this case, not really. There was actually no way I could change my sheet, even if I wanted to. Once they modified my Wednesday return time, I had to return at 10 p.m., just like it said on the paperwork.

I return now to progressive justice and the familiar concept of "society did it." Let's see more specifically how society did it to two guys in the confinement center, a South Side Hispanic named Ricardo and a Mexican gang member named Popeye. Ricardo and Popeye are friends, which is unusual since South Siders and homegrown Mexicans don't typically get along. They even look alike—with their narrow eyes, elongated faces, and slight goatees. In any case, both Ricardo and Popeye seem to have an attachment to their Catholicism; I see them cross themselves before they eat.

Ricardo was sent here after completing a seven-year sentence for possession and selling of drugs. He has also done time for other things. Ricardo told me that his father was, from his earliest memory, an alcoholic and a schizophrenic who was in and out of mental institutions. His mom, he said, raised him and his brother, but she often took off for days at a time. "We ran in the streets for as long as I can remember," Ricardo says. And then, when he was around seven, "my mom just woke up one day and checked out. When we got home from school she was gone."

"I'm so sorry," I said. "That must have been terrible for you."

"Oh no," he said. "My brother and I were relieved. By this point she wasn't even looking after us. We had been living off the street. She mainly brought men home and they would curse us or beat us. One of them used to play with me, you know, molest me when my mother wasn't around. But I never told her. I never told nobody. My mom would drink a lot, and she also got high, and she would yell at us a lot. Sometimes we couldn't even understand what she was saying. So when my mother left, we were very happy. We were free."

Ricardo said, "I was adopted by a family for a year, and that would have worked out good for me, but they moved to Oregon, and so I was back on the street. I was doing drugs by thirteen. I did what I could to sell them, and if I couldn't, then I'd smoke them. The drugs helped me—they were a way to forget my past."

Ricardo also learned to fight. "Fights were my way to prove myself." In school people would come to him to solve a situation. "But I never wanted to solve the situation. I wanted it to happen. I wanted people to think I was crazy. Then they would feel intimidated." Eventually he joined a gang in Southern California. "We did robberies and sold drugs and sh*t," Ricardo said, "but mainly we got into fights, sometimes fights that left people injured or dead."

These fights, Ricardo said, often revolve around female gang members called *cholas*. "If you drive through the barrio, you'll see them. Some of them wear fedoras. They wear tank tops, no bras, and they are tough girls, with attitude. These girls also like to beat up the new girls, I mean really mess them up, you know. One girl had her face disfigured and everyone was like, f*ck, but you know, sh*t happens.

"It's sad for the girls, because we use them as sex toys. Most of the *cholas* we use for trains," Ricardo said, explaining that a "train" is when a girl has sex with two, three, or ten people, all in a row. "That's the easiest way for girls to get into a gang. But some *cholas* prefer to get in by doing murders.

"A lot of the fights," Ricardo said, "are started by the *cholas*." On one occasion, Ricardo's girlfriend was standing around with a bunch of her friends, and some guys drove up in an Impala. Someone said something insulting about one of the *cholas*, and so the girls gave the guys the finger, and told them to f*ck off. There was a lot of shouting.

"We heard the noise and came out. I wasn't armed but my friend had a shotgun and a .44 Magnum Colt. The guys drove off, but when they got some distance away they popped their trunk and turned their headlights off. My friend handed me the loaded shotgun. The guys got back into the car. When the car started toward us, I didn't wait—I fired my shotgun and there was glass all the way down the street. I don't know what I hit. What I know is that the car swerved and crashed and we turned and ran. So like I say, the *cholas* usually get these things started, and it's our job to finish them."

Ricardo wasn't caught selling drugs; he was actually arrested, he said, for "beating up this pimp." The pimp, he explained, "was harassing my girl. So I kicked his ass. Now he knows he deserved it. I told him to say nothing. But he went and told the cops everything. He told them I was a dealer and da-da-da-da-da. Then they talked to my girl and she gave them the rest of the story. I was arrested while I was in the bathtub."

Ricardo does not blame his circumstances for his current incarceration. "My brother blames my mom," he says. "He is now a drug addict. He drives a truck but he can't keep a job. He's messed up in the head. But me, I don't blame no one. I'm in NA—Narcotics Anonymous—and I've got a part-time job. I'm saving my money for when I get out. So I'm up to it, n*gger. But can you believe the sh*t I've been through?"

I could. By this time I had been more than three months in confinement. I had spent the holidays—including Thanksgiving and Christmas—in this strange place. I knew the routines. I knew the kind of people who get stuck in here. How far I had come since my first days when I could barely get my combination locker to work and when I slept with one eye open, jerking my body to attention every time a door opened or someone tumbled out of their bunk to go to the bathroom.

Now I've got one of the best bunks in the place—lower bunk, right by the wall. As the real estate brokers say, "Location, location, location." Some South Sider vacated his spot, and I was in there before anyone else made their move. Now I don't care who's making a racket; I sleep soundly, hearing nothing.

Another character in my confinement center was Popeye, the Mexican. He was raised in Tijuana, where his grandfather was apparently a local gangster. "They called him El Tigre—the tiger." El Tigre owned several businesses, including a gas station. One day he was standing at the pump, talking to a friend, when another car pulled up and a man got out. He walked up to El Tigre and shot him in the face. Then he got back into the car and drove off.

"After my grandfather was killed," Popeye says, "my family's fortunes went down. My father, my uncles, they all worked for El Tigre. So they all lost their jobs." His father, not surprising, continued his career of crime. "I remember the time—I was around ten years old—when he pulled up to our house in a Jaguar. Now, we didn't own a Jaguar. But he said to me, get in. I asked him if he had stolen the car. He said, no, he had gone to work for another gangster named Fulgencia and he was driving that man's car."

Popeye said, "My dad borrowed everything from other people. He borrowed money all the time. He even borrowed guns." Eventually he accumulated a heavy debt of money and guns, and so his creditors kidnapped Popeye's older brother. The father couldn't pay, and so they dropped the brother into a barrel of acid. "He just disappeared, you know," Popeye told me. "I mean, his body literally went to nothing. Nothing was ever recovered. I couldn't respect my dad after that happened."

Popeye went in search of a new family that he could respect. He found one in a Tijuana gang that had ties to the Mexican mafia. Popeye described the gang's system of first diminishing, and then building up, self-esteem. "First the gang guys jump you and beat you up," Popeye said. "They want to break you down, to leave you with no defenses at all. Then they put their arms around you and give you their shirts and say that you are their homeboy. You become one of them by learning to depend on them. Your whole life now becomes the gang. They are your new family."

As part of his gang identity, Popeye got a special tattoo on his face. "It was a triangle of three dots. The first dot stands for Life. The second stands for Prison. The third stands for Death. Basically the triangle means that I am signing up for a life that includes prison and death. In this way I showed my loyalty to the gang. I was ready to be locked up, even to die, for my brothers."

Popeye wanted me to understand that it takes discipline to be in a gang. "The gang demands your complete loyalty and your complete respect. If you f*ck up, it won't be some stranger who comes to threaten you. Your closest friend—the guy who brought you into the gang, the guy who gave you his shirt—that's the guy who will walk up to you and hit you in the face. He may even take out his gun and shoot you. I know, man, it's harsh. But those are the rules and you learn them fast. The whole system is based on respect, which is another word for fear."

I asked Popeye what he feared most. "I fear being alone. I fear having nothing. I fear losing face." The gang, he said, replaced those fears with a single one: "fear of the gang leader." Thus it is incumbent for a gang member to be swaggering and tough in front of everyone else, cowering in front of the gang leader. What the gang leader says is law. "When you join a gang," Popeye explained, "you have to follow orders. If they tell you to take a guy out, you take him out. If they tell you to stab a corrections officer, you do it. If you don't do it, you put your life in danger."

Popeye became one of the leading drug operatives for the gang, with a reputation for ruthlessness and violence. Soon he came to the attention of one of the Tijuana drug cartels. At this point, Popeye looked around the confinement center dining room to make sure no one was listening to him. He also lowered his voice. "They offered me a job as a contract killer," he said. "Three thousand dollars a week."

Popeye was tempted, but he was also smart. "I did some research, and I figured out that they pay you for the first couple of weeks. Then they don't pay you for a while. Sometimes they send you into a shootout where you are almost certain to be killed. That way you are most useful to them—hopefully you kill two or three guys, and then you are killed and they don't have to pay you."

So Popeye politely declined the contract killer offer, and instead took an assignment to run drugs across the border. "That was fifteen hundred dollars a week," he said, "and I knew there was a risk of being caught. I also knew that the cartels themselves might turn me in—they like to hand over some small fry so that the authorities are happy and their big guys are left alone. This was a risk I was willing to take."

The risk paid off the first couple of times, and then Popeye got arrested. "You ask me whether I blame my family, or society, or myself," he told me. "I don't really think about it that way. I'm just telling you my story. It's a sad story, but we don't yet know the ending." He smiled. "Mine may turn out to be a sad story with a happy ending."

I'm not hopeful. But I said, "Time will tell." He nodded in agreement.

One thing we can say for both Ricardo and Popeye, they don't try to blame their sins on society. These two guys, for the most part, recognize that they have been dealt a tough hand, and yet they accept responsibility for how things have turned out for them. I know, and I suspect they do, too, that society had a role in shaping them. Yet they also know that their actions are the result of their choices. Society dealt them a hand, and they figured out how to play that hand. Ricardo and Popeye seem to recognize they are being punished not for who they are but for what they did. One may say of their rap sheets: they built that! Progressives, I think, can learn a lot from these two criminals.

Progressives have been trying for decades to figure out how to discredit American business and American capitalism, so that they can confiscate the profits and feel good about themselves. The latest progressive pitch comes not from professors or intellectuals but from Barack Obama, Elizabeth Warren, and Hillary Clinton. Their claim is, in Obama's famous words, "You didn't build that." Warren's way of putting the same thing is, "There is nobody in this country who got rich on his own." And Hillary chimed in, telling a Massachusetts audience in late 2014, "Don't let anybody tell you that it's corporations and businesses that create jobs."[3]

What are Hillary, Obama, and Warren saying? Their main argument seems to be that society, not business, creates wealth. In particular, it is government, not business, that gets things made. Finally, even within businesses, it is the employees and workers—not the entrepreneurs—who are responsible for whatever business contributes to the overall affluence of society.

Obama and Warren give several examples. Obama points out that successful entrepreneurs probably had a public school teacher somewhere who inspired them to their current pursuits. Warren notes that businesses use the public roads to transport their goods to market, and call on the police and the fire department when things go wrong. "You moved your goods to market on roads the rest of us paid for. You were safe in your factory because of police forces and fire forces the rest of us paid for." Both Obama and Warren insist that companies are highly dependent on the social infrastructure—indeed on the federal government—to stay in business. Consequently, society has a claim on the profits of these businesses. Government can justly say that it owns a portion of the gains, and these can legitimately be seized through taxation, regulation, mandates, or other instruments of the state.

Now, business is made up not just of entrepreneurs but also of employees and workers.

Taking this into account, progressives have put forward a corollary to "you didn't build that." That corollary is the leftist claim that within companies, entrepreneurs and CEOs cheat the workers and greedily claim the lion's share of the profits. Hillary attributes the notion that businesses create jobs to "that old theory, trickle-down economics. That has been tried and failed. It has failed rather spectacularly." Hillary here seems to object to the notion that businesses are the wealth creators and that some of that wealth should filter down to employees; she seems to think that the employees create the wealth, and the entrepreneurs illicitly take it for themselves.

Let's consider a couple of examples of how the government—figuring that it, not business, "built that"—proceeds to appropriate money from the private sector and do things that are supposed to promote fairness and social justice.

In 2008–2009, the government put into effect a stimulus package designed to jump-start the economy. By 2010, the Obama administration reported, the government had spent $1.4 trillion and created 800,000 jobs. This figure is probably exaggerated, but let's go with it. Dividing 1.4 trillion by 800,000, we get 1.7 million. So the Obama administration spent $1.7 million on average to create a job.

In order to reduce the embarrassment caused by this ridiculous cost, the administration insisted the stimulus "saved" 2.4 million jobs. It arrived at this number by adding to the 800,000 jobs created an additional 1.6 million jobs "saved." Supposedly these are jobs that *would have been lost* had there been no stimulus.[4] You can only imagine the statistical legerdemain that must have gone into this calculation. Yet even taking the dubious 2.4 million figure, the Obama administration's cost per job is $583,000. Keep in mind that most of these jobs pay around $50,000, so the worker gets $50,000, and the rest goes down rat holes that are virtually impossible to identify.

Now economists estimate that in the private sector, it costs somewhere in the range of $120,000 to $140,000 to create a job. This is the average cost for creating jobs that pay between $30,000 and $50,000 a year. So taking the higher figure of $140,000, the U.S. economy could have used $1.4 trillion to create 10 million new jobs!

Why, then, would the government prefer to spend the money to create fewer jobs? Because the government's goal is not employment per se but also—indeed primarily—a transfer of resources from the private sector to the public sector. "You didn't build that," in other words, becomes a pretext for appropriation. And thieves don't care that the reallocation of resources from others to themselves has undesirable macroeconomic effects. What matters to them is that they get the money.

How valid, then, is the progressive critique that "you didn't build that"? The pitch itself has two parts. The first is that society did it, not business; the second is that workers did most of it, not CEOs and entrepreneurs. Both these arrows strike at the same target: entrepreneurs. Consequently an exposé of the progressive pitch requires a refutation of this dual attack and also a defense of the entrepreneur, an explanation of what it is that entrepreneurs actually do.

This explanation is, oddly enough, lacking. Adam Smith didn't provide it in his *Wealth of Nations*, and most entrepreneurs, for reasons we will explore, don't provide it today. One of the few writers to celebrate entrepreneurs was Ayn Rand; she unapologetically defends capitalism, the system, and also capitalists, the people! In my view, the most insightful defender of entrepreneurs was the economist Joseph Schumpeter, and we will be learning a lot from him in this chapter. Ultimately, we will see the progressive pitch for what it is, an ingenious scam aimed at depriving wealth creators of the wealth they have created. Rand calls them the "looters," and this is basically a clinically accurate term for a group that is very much with us today.

Let's begin with this notion that society, not entrepreneurs, is primarily responsible for the success of an enterprise. What is the evidence for that? Actually there is very little. Consider the great inventions and innovations of the nineteenth century that made possible the Industrial Revolution and the rising standard of living that propelled America into the front ranks of the world by the mid-twentieth century. Who built the telegraph, and the great shipping lines, and the railroads, and the airplanes? Who produced the tractors and the machinery that made America the manufacturing capital of the world? Who built and then made available home appliances like the vacuum cleaner, the automatic dishwasher, and the microwave oven? More recent, who built the personal computer, the iPhone, and the software and search engines that power the electronic revolution? Entrepreneurs, that's who.

Government played a role, but that role was extremely modest. In the nineteenth century, the government did little more than grant licenses to companies to operate on the high seas or to go ahead and build railroads. As is often the case when there are government favors to be had, such licenses and contracts were attended with the usual lobbying, cajoling, and corruption. In the twentieth century, the government refused to help the Wright brothers because it had its own cockamamie idea about how airplanes should be built; the Wright brothers, on their own, actually went ahead and built one that could fly, and the government was so angry that for a long time it simply ignored this stunning new invention.

True, the federal government built the highway system after World War II—one of the few unambiguously good things the federal government has done—and the Defense Department was the first institution to develop a crude type of Internet. Still, the plethora of Web innovations and applications that have transformed people's lives—that only happened when the Internet went private.

What about today? I offer as my exhibit several important structures that bear the name of a single individual: the late West Virginia Democratic senator Robert Byrd. There is the Robert Byrd Academic and Technology Center at Marshall University, the Robert Byrd Cancer Research Laboratory at West Virginia University, the Robert Byrd Health and Wellness Center at Bethany College, the Robert Byrd Conference Center at Davis & Elkins College, the Robert Byrd Library, the Robert Byrd Industrial Park, the Robert Byrd Visitor Center at Harpers Ferry National Historical Park, the Robert Byrd Bridge, the Robert Byrd Expressway, the Robert Byrd Freeway, the Robert Byrd Highway, the Robert Byrd Interchange, and the Robert Byrd Transportation Center. This is a sample of the fifty or so constructions, public and private, which bear the name of this great man Robert Byrd. Another dozen or so are named after his wife, Erma Byrd.[5]

How did the Byrds get to have their names on all that real estate? The reason is that Byrd was instrumental in appropriating the money to get these projects built. Since he was responsible for allocating the money, naturally he got to stick his name, and occasionally his wife's name, on the facilities. In a sense, Byrd is like someone who endows a wing or building for a college and then gets that wing or dormitory named after him.

At Dartmouth, for example, there are buildings called Wheeler, Thornton, and Reed. Presumably that's because Wheeler, Thornton, and Reed coughed up the money. But there is an important difference. Wheeler, Thornton, and Reed donated their own money. Byrd simply used his power in the Senate to direct taxpayer money toward favored projects in his state. Whatever we think of Byrd's role—benign or invidious—the one thing we can agree on is that Byrd didn't build any of that.

I'd like to focus in specifically here on Obama's and Warren's arguments, and in order to test these, I select two companies to examine more closely: FedEx and Facebook. I'm going to go with Obama's assumption that the founders of both companies, Fred Smith and Mark Zuckerberg, respectively, benefited from the services of a charismatic public school teacher. Clearly both companies move their goods through extensive use of the public roads. Naturally they also take advantage of a whole range of public services, including the police and fire departments. And I can hear Obama and Warren triumphantly saying, who provided that whole ensemble of services? The government, that's who.

Yes, but when Fred Smith and Mark Zuckerberg were sitting in those public school classes, surely there were other kids sitting with them. So apparently they got something out of that teacher that those other kids didn't. Moreover, FedEx and Facebook have access to the public roads and public services, but so does everyone else.

What does Warren mean when she says, "You moved your goods to market on roads *the rest of us* paid for"? Didn't entrepreneurs also pay for those roads through taxes? As Warren well knows, they did; in fact, they pay the bulk of the taxes. Even so, Warren falsely implies that "the rest of us" are paying the entrepreneur's bills. Her sleight-of-hand is aimed at suggesting the entrepreneur has an unpaid debt to the rest of us. Entrepreneurs have an obligation to reimburse society, and the more successful the entrepreneur, the greater the obligation.

Yet who deserves the credit for FedEx and Facebook being more profitable than the other companies out there? The simple answer is: the managers and employees of those companies. And who is responsible for Fred Smith and Mark Zuckerberg learning more in school than the other students who got the same instruction? The simple answer is: Fred Smith and Mark Zuckerberg. Society and government merely provided for them the same infrastructure that they provide for everyone. They took advantage of this infrastructure, in a way that others didn't, to do things that others wouldn't or couldn't. So they built their companies; society didn't. They are responsible for their success; the government isn't. And consequently they deserve the rewards of that success, and progressives don't have the right to appropriate it.

If we step back from the progressive argument and put it in any other context, its absurdity immediately becomes apparent. Imagine if I were to say to my daughter, who got a high score on the SAT, "You don't deserve your scores at all. You didn't build that. After all, young lady, you had teachers who helped you with vocabulary and math. Moreover, you took the public roads to the test. Had your car been held up along the way or caught fire, you would count on the services of the police and the fire department. So society deserves a large part of the credit for those scores. They don't reflect your accomplishment but society's accomplishment." If I said this I am sure my daughter would think I was talking like an insane person. In fact, of course, I would be talking like a progressive.

So far I have dealt with the easy part of the progressive argument. This is a defense of the companies against the claim that they didn't fully earn their profits. Now we turn to the stronger progressive argument that workers, not entrepreneurs, are the ones within the company that make the company successful. Yet entrepreneurs make off with most of the profits.

This argument owes its origin, and fullest expression, to Marx. Today Marx's name is out of fashion—it is creepy to think that, just a half century ago, nearly half the population of the world was governed by communist regimes that took his name—but the Marxist argument lives on without attribution in the work of progressive thinkers and pundits. "We ought to have much more democratic enterprise," economist Richard Wolff recently said in an interview with Bill Moyers. "We ought to have stores, factories and offices in which all the people who have to live with the results of what happens to that enterprise participate in deciding how it works."[6]

This is the usual socialist mantra that workers should exercise control over the means of production. Wolff is invoking it to advocate not socialism per se but rather much greater worker control over how business operates. He also advocates strong government regulation to strengthen the bargaining power of workers over entrepreneurs. In order to examine the merits of this, we will do better to leapfrog over Wolff—a derivative scribbler—and take on Marx himself.[7] Marx argued that all products are produced through a combination of capital and labor. The capital is provided by the "capitalist." The labor is provided by the "worker."

Capital, Marx said, is basically money. And money has a rental value, which is called interest. If you borrow money from a bank, you have to pay a certain percentage—say 5 percent—annually for the use of that money. So Marx concluded that capital is worth 5 percent. In this sense it is simply a cost of doing business. Businesses need land and equipment and they also need capital: all these costs must be taken into account in starting any company. Let's call them the capital costs.

What happens, however, when the company starts making and selling products? Marx said that the capitalists, who run the company, hire workers for the lowest price that they can afford to pay them. Basically this is the cost of keeping the worker alive and working. Collectively, this is the labor cost borne by the capitalist.

Yet Marx noticed that when businesses sell products, they do not merely seek to recover their capital and labor costs. Rather, they sell products for the highest price that they can get away with. Consequently there is a surplus that businesses typically accumulate: this is the revenue over and above the capital and labor cost. Businesses call this "profit." Marx called it "surplus value."

For Marx, the crucial question is: Who gets this surplus value? Who is entitled to the profit that businesses accumulate? Marx insisted that this profit belongs wholly to the workers. They earned it, so they deserve to share it. In reality, however, the entrepreneur or the capitalist gets it. If he has investors, they too share it. Marx regarded this as the most scandalous form of exploitation. He insisted that workers spend only part of their day working to benefit themselves; the rest of the time they spend working to benefit the capitalists. Basically the capitalists are stealing from the workers. Yet Marx recognized that this was the essence of capitalism. Only a workers' revolution, Marx believed, would end this unjust arrangement.

Notice that Marx isn't condemning the capitalist for taking "excessive" profits; he is condemning the capitalist for taking *any* profits. Marx, I want to emphasize, was not a progressive con man. He passionately believed that capitalists were greedy, corrupt exploiters. The reason he felt that way was that he was a complete ignoramus about business. He simply had no idea how businesses actually operate. Marx never ran a business. He never even balanced his checkbook. He was a lifelong leech. He had all his expenses paid for by his partner, Friedrich Engels, who inherited his father's textile companies. Progressives like to portray Engels as a businessman but in fact he too didn't actually operate the family business. He had people to do that for him. Freed from the need to work, Engels was a man of leisure and a part-time intellectual. Ironically Marx and Engels were both dependent on the very capitalism they scorned.

This is one reason progressives love this peculiar duo, and especially Marx. They too have little understanding of what entrepreneurs do. Nor do they really care. They have no aspiration to become entrepreneurs themselves. Rather, they prefer occupations like community activist or professor of romance languages at Bowdoin College. And they aspire to be, like Marx, lifelong leeches. They would like to rip off the gains of capitalism and agitate against the system that subsidizes their rip-off and agitation.

But what is it that Marx and the progressives are ignorant about? Here we turn for insight to the great early twentieth-century economist Joseph Schumpeter. Schumpeter was hardly an apologist for capitalism—he is famous for his essay on "the cultural contradictions of capitalism." In that essay he argues that capitalism unleashes a gale of destruction that undermines traditional institutions like the family and local communities. Schumpeter has been proven largely right about this. Schumpeter was also, in a way that is not widely recognized, a student of what entrepreneurs actually do. He published his insights in a remarkable but little-known book, *The Entrepreneur*. As is evident from this book, Schumpeter spent time with entrepreneurs in a way that Marx never did. While Marx theorized about capital, Schumpeter described the actual lives of capitalists.[8]

Capitalists, Schumpeter says, are not primarily suppliers of capital. In fact, very few people who start businesses use their own funds. Typically they borrow the funds or they seek investors who provide them with the necessary capital. And this is not easy, Schumpeter says, because the value of a new product is not apparent prior to its making. The entrepreneur must convince people who have not witnessed him succeed that he is going to succeed. He must, in a sense, talk his way into getting money. But it is typically not his money. So Marx's notion that capitalists are merely suppliers of capital is dead wrong.

The first thing that entrepreneurs provide, Schumpeter says, is the idea for the business. Without the entrepreneur, there would be no business. Of course, not all those who run businesses have actually started them. CEOs typically rise up within a company, or are recruited from another company; they didn't found the company. But originally there must have been an entrepreneur who was also a founder.

The most successful businesses are not merely a more efficient way to supply existing goods to existing markets. Rather, they arise out of a type of exploration or discovery. They are based on new ideas that generate new products, and the most successful products are not merely responses to consumer demand, but things that were supplied before there was a demand for them. The rewards of starting and operating such a business can be staggeringly high.

Think about the Sony Walkman or the iPhone. No one wrote to Sony or Apple demanding these products. Rather, entrepreneurs conceived them and made them and only then did we realize we couldn't live without them. "People don't know what they want until you show it to them," Steve Jobs said. "I never rely on market research. Our task is to read things that are not yet on the page." This foresight, operating in advance of public opinion, was just as true of the automobile in the early twentieth century as it is of Apple products today. Jobs's hero, Henry Ford, once commented, "If I'd asked customers what they wanted, they would have told me, 'A faster horse.'"[9]

Entrepreneurs of this type are true visionaries. In the case of Silicon Valley, these are guys who take sand and oxygen, two of the most abundant materials on earth, and convert them into silicon chips, making possible the whole communications revolution. Sometimes, like Jobs, they are also artists who make things that have an almost sensuous beauty. To suggest that Jobs or Apple is "ripping people off" is something only an idiot, or a progressive, would think of. Actual iPhone users are delighted with the product and would pay much more, if they had to, for it.

Schumpeter concedes that with some notable exceptions—Thomas Edison comes to mind—most entrepreneurs are not inventors; rather, they are innovators. Henry Ford didn't invent the automobile, but he figured out how to build one that would serve the needs of the masses. As this example illustrates, the typical entrepreneur is not a scientist who makes a new theoretical discovery or even makes a new invention. Rather, he is a master of application who takes an existing discovery or invention and figures out how it can be used in a new way.

He is also what Schumpeter calls a "man of action," one who actually carries out his ideas. And while every generation seems to produce a Henry Ford or a Bill Gates, typically entrepreneurs don't seek to broadly change the way things are done or the way people live; instead they focus narrowly on one aspect where they think they can make a difference.

This is the essence of entrepreneurial imagination and insight—knowing where to focus. Schumpeter calls it "a certain narrowness." Its object can be quite unspectacular, something as trivial as "Where is the driver who heads out to work in the morning going to put his coffee?" Then, with a kind of unnatural obsession, the entrepreneur zooms in on that and spends his days thinking about it; indeed, says Schumpeter, he thinks of little else, making him seem to his family and friends to be a bit of a bore.

What the entrepreneur seeks to do, according to Schumpeter, is to exploit this perceived opening, this business opportunity. This is extremely difficult because everyone, including the entrepreneur, is accustomed to the old way of doing things. Most people are creatures of inertia and habit. Most of our lives are governed by customary, relatively mindless operations. The entrepreneur is not exempt from these routines.

In order to succeed, therefore, the entrepreneur must overcome the resistance of society—the inevitable chants of "it can't be done" and "this will never work." The entrepreneur cannot possibly convince the critics; he must show them. But being human, he feels the force of their objections. He must also learn to overcome the resistance within himself. Schumpeter says that entrepreneurs are typically willful and somewhat self-centered, and they need to be to keep going.

Entrepreneurs must also seek a new type of knowledge, knowledge that must be sought out in order to enable him to blaze a new trail. After all, Schumpeter says, the entrepreneur is one who seeks to make a new road, not walk along the old road. Consequently the old maps won't work for him anymore. The knowledge the entrepreneur seeks may have a theoretical component but it is ultimately practical; it is ultimately about getting something done. The entrepreneur sets out to acquire this relevant knowledge, recognizing that he must make himself a kind of world expert on the topic, whether it is a new source of raw materials, a new method of production, a new type of product or service, a new market, or a new form of organization.

To others this may seem like a tiny matter, a small niche, but for the entrepreneur it is a veritable empire. Schumpeter writes that entrepreneurs seek above all "to found a private kingdom" and they seek, in the manner of a medieval lord, to become the overlord of that kingdom. What drives the entrepreneur is not primarily money, although the entrepreneur may consider the amount of money he makes to be an index or measure of his success.

But entrepreneurs are rarely super-lavish consumers, even if their means permit; everyone close to the entrepreneur can see he derives more satisfaction from being a producer than from being a consumer. Schumpeter remarks, in a way that every entrepreneur will instantly recognize, that these are people who are mainly motivated by the experience of freedom, the joy of creation, a feeling of pioneering something new, and, finally, an indomitable will to succeed. This is conquest of a sort, but conquest that cannot be had without satisfying the will and winning the consent of the consumer, who is the ultimate decider of the entrepreneur's fate.

We can see here why entrepreneurs are such poor defenders of the free market system. They are narrowly focused on what they do. What they do operates within the free market system, but it is scarcely concerned with the system itself. They no more think about the free market system than a basketball player thinks about who prepared the court for him to play. If basketball players encountered people who said that the rules of basketball were unfair—that they discriminated against Koreans, or that they deprived obese people of their "fair share"—they would stare uncomprehendingly; they would not know how to respond.

So it is with many entrepreneurs; they are used to taking for granted the system of capitalism that makes their success possible. Historically, this is a system of finance, insurance, and transportation that entrepreneurs themselves built. Even so, today's entrepreneurs take the existence of that system for granted, in the same manner that fishes presume the existence of water.

Capitalism is also a system of ideas, and many entrepreneurs are not familiar with what those ideas are. Indeed they become defensive and inarticulate when progressives attack those ideas. Ironically the defense of capitalism is left to people other than the capitalists themselves. Progressives have discovered this vulnerability on the part of entrepreneurs and businesspeople, and they ruthlessly exploit it. They make it seem like because those people cannot defend what they do, what they do is indefensible.

Second, the entrepreneur organizes the business. He (or she) assembles the capital, the insurance, the physical plant or facility, the equipment, and the labor. Workers—even specialized workers—don't do this. And specialization here doesn't help because organizing a business requires such a varied range of skills. The entrepreneur has to make decisions that involve land values, equipment values, taxes and insurance, labor negotiations. Entrepreneurs must figure out not only how to make things but also how to finance them, market them, and sell them.

Most of the people he contracts with will have little understanding of what he is up to; they merely agree to sell specific goods or services. The entrepreneur must integrate all those into a functioning, successful enterprise, an enterprise whose full scope is frequently only comprehensible to him and no one else. Moreover, doing all that is not enough; it must be done as well, or better, than every competitor, or else the entrepreneur faces the prospect of going out of business. This function Schumpeter calls entrepreneurial leadership. It takes highly capable people to do this, and that is another reason why successful entrepreneurs earn relatively large rewards.

Progressives and union bosses frequently insist that they could run the business as well, if not better, than the entrepreneur does. Yet this is merely a talking point; there seems to be no example in the history of the world of any actual demonstration of this principle. If unions could do without entrepreneurs, why don't they? This would be a guaranteed way to keep all the profit for themselves. Evidently the reason they don't is that they can't. The job of actually organizing a business is too difficult, too complex, for them to manage. It's much easier to *say* you can run Delta Air Lines than to actually ensure that, every single day, all those planes land safely and on time. Taking responsibility for the lives of hundreds of thousands of people who board the airlines every day—that's not an easy thing.

Third, the entrepreneur takes risks. These risks are of two kinds: known risks and unknown risks. This distinction I don't get from Schumpeter but from the early twentieth-century economist Frank Knight. Toss a coin, Knight said, and you have a 50 percent chance of getting "heads." This is a risk, but it is a known risk. Uncertainty, in this case, can be gauged and weighed. Consequently, the entrepreneur can to some extent anticipate it and plan for it. Capital risk, Schumpeter points out, is borne not by the entrepreneur but by the investors and financiers of the business. For the most part, capital risk is a known risk, an uncertainty whose parameters are recognized in advance.

But some forms of uncertainty cannot be gauged, because the future is unknown and unknowable. Take my own case. After two successful documentary films, I am currently moving into also making feature films. The former are nonfiction; the latter are fiction. It's a completely different deal. What is the chance that I will succeed in making an animated film or a horror film? I cannot—no one can—even venture to guess. There are too many unknowns. Here, Schumpeter points out, the entrepreneur can be guided only by intuition—intuition that accepts risk and yet is balanced by sound judgment that seeks rationally to minimize it. Schumpeter says that part of the high reward for successful entrepreneurs is payment for taking this type of unknown risk.

Notice that workers do not take this risk. A worker does not take a risk of putting in effort and waiting to get paid; a worker wants to be paid at the end of two weeks or at most a month. Entrepreneurs, by contrast, must wait before the business makes a profit, a process that sometimes takes many months, even years. The entrepreneur, in other words, enters the market before the worker and long before the consumer, who is the end user who will ultimately pay the entrepreneur for his effort. If the consumer doesn't show up, the entrepreneur is finished; he must go out of business.

This risk does affect workers, of course; if a company goes out of business, the workers lose their jobs. Even here, though, workers may have contractual rights that are enforceable. Workers, however, don't hitch their ordinary fate to the vicissitudes of the company. An entrepreneur cannot say to his workers, "We had a bad quarter and lost money, so I expect you all to return a part of your wages." Workers, like elderly folk who deposit money in a bank, highly value security and must recognize that security typically comes at the price of a lower financial return. That's why unions were started—to provide enhanced worker security.

Workers, Schumpeter says, know that they cannot do what entrepreneurs do, but they have little appreciation for the full extent of what entrepreneurs actually do.[10] Think of the valet who parks a car at a resort. He thinks to himself, "The customer pays $25 a night to park his car. I parked 100 cars today. So I earned $2,500 for the resort. But how much did they pay me? A measly $100. So where does the other $2,400 go? Probably to the rich bastard who owns the resort. He's ripping me off."

It seldom occurs to the valet that people are paying $25 a night to park because they are at a resort. The rich bastard had to think of the idea for the resort, he had to raise the money, he had to get the permits and the insurance, he had to hire the employees—including the valet—and he had to market the resort to get people to come. Without all of that, no one would pay $25 to park there. They would pay what I would pay if someone offered to park my car, a whopping 25 cents. Worker resentment is understandable—Schumpeter does not expect the myopic valet to appreciate what it takes to run a resort—but that does not make it justified. The valet is being paid pretty much what his labor is worth in this context, namely $100 a day.

Schumpeter also recognizes that many people who witness the entrepreneur's success from the outside—and here we can envision progressive academics and pundits—view that success with incomprehension and incredulity. "The entrepreneur's performance is inaccessible to immediate observation from a distance. You cannot see the entrepreneur at work in the same way as the worker or farmer. Moreover, the practical knowledge that intellectuals have of this activity basically comes from newspapers written by other intellectuals. . . . The opinion is widespread that entrepreneurial profit is nothing but the consequences of social causes that have nothing to do with the entrepreneur's activity, and would have been available to the community without the entrepreneur." [11] By this time in Schumpeter's analysis we are laughing with him at how out-of-it these observers are.

Entrepreneurs deserve their success, and they succeed by producing new and better things and thereby satisfying their customers. In fact, as we will see in the next chapter, it is the customer, not the businessman, who has the real power and who benefits the most from entrepreneurial capitalism. The customer is, in fact, the entrepreneur's boss, and, not surprising, entrepreneurs take all their cues ultimately from the customer.

It would be good for workers to try harder to understand entrepreneurs, because, after all, the entrepreneur is the worker's sole customer. Entrepreneurs sell products and workers also sell a product, namely, their labor. The entrepreneur must work to satisfy all his customers; the worker must satisfy only a single customer, his employer. People in government, too, should cultivate a better understanding of business and the constructive role played by both entrepreneurs and workers. Government is utterly dependent on entrepreneurs and workers, because the cost of government is after all the overhead of society, and who pays that overhead except entrepreneurs and workers?

The one group that no one can expect to satisfy is the progressives, because these are the con men whose pitch is aimed not at understanding business but at shaking it down, not at justice or efficiency but rather at extortion and robbery. This group, if it is credited at all, should be credited with organizing a highly successful theft operation; that's something, I must say, that they have built entirely by themselves.

Chapter 8

SILVER SPOONS AND GENETIC LOTTERIES:

The Lucky Luciano Scam

No one deserves his place in the distribution of natural assets any more than he deserves his initial starting place in society.[1]

—John Rawls, *A Theory of Justice*

In this chapter we turn to the final progressive pitch, what I call the Lucky Luciano scam. The Sicilian-born mobster Charles Luciano was called "Lucky Luciano" for surviving innumerable close calls, including several beatings, a throat-slashing, and a couple of assassination attempts, mostly caused by his refusal to join a rival mob boss. Luciano was arrested twenty-five times for assault, illegal gambling, blackmail, and robbery but never spent any time in prison. In short, he had what Machiavelli terms *fortuna* on his side.

What Machiavelli meant by *fortuna* is the twists and turns of fate. While Machiavelli conceded that luck has a role in all things and is inherently unpredictable, he insisted that it should not be cursed but rather embraced. *Fortuna*, he argued, can be at least partly steered through ingenuity and force of will. Criminals, I discovered during my confinement, understand this. Like Machiavelli, they are realists. They rejoice at good luck and attempt to work around bad luck as best they can. Progressives, however, rail at luck as a form of injustice and seek to use government to correct the vicissitudes of fortune.

Let's remember, however, that this is a pitch. Progressives aren't actually confused about luck; they are using luck to sell their ideological formula. In this respect, progressives are doing exactly what Machiavelli advocates and what criminals do. They have converted the omnipresence of luck in society to justify an omnipresent government role as the arbiter and regulator of luck. Luck has become a profit-center for modern progressivism.

We can see this quite clearly if we follow the fortunes of Hillary Clinton. She is a woman who has clearly had *fortuna* on her side, and in addition, she and her husband have ingeniously and ruthlessly manipulated their circumstances for personal gain.

Hillary rode her husband's success to become first lady of Arkansas, then first lady of the United States. Then she won an easy race in liberal New York to become its junior senator. As a senator she accomplished, well, nothing. Then she ran for the Democratic presidential nomination, losing to Barack Obama, who appointed her secretary of state. Despite extensive travels, Hillary's achievements as secretary of state are essentially nil. As with Benghazi, most of her notable actions are screwups. In an apparent confirmation of the Peter Principle, however, Hillary is now back as the leading candidate for the Democratic nomination for president in 2016.

Hillary is fortunate, not merely in her career path, but also in being the surprise recipient of hundreds of millions of dollars that have been rained on her and her husband both directly and through the Clinton Foundation. The Clinton Foundation has raised more than $2 billion in contributions. A substantial portion of that came from foreign governments. Some sixteen nations together have given $130 million. In addition, through speeches and consulting fees, more than $100 million has ended up in the pockets of the Clintons themselves. The foundation, although ostensibly a charitable enterprise, gives only one dollar out of ten to charity. It has also been disclosed that the Clintons have developed a penchant for traveling in high style, and use a substantial amount of donation money on private planes and penthouse suites. The rest of the loot seems to have been accumulated into a war chest that is at the behest of the Clintons and the Hillary presidential campaign.

How did the Clintons get so lucky? The story is told in Peter Schweizer's book *Clinton Cash* and associated news reports, from which I extract a few choice details.[2] Canadian billionaire Frank Giustra gave $31 million to the Clinton Foundation. His business partner, Ian Telfer, directed another $2.3 million to the foundation through his Fernwood Foundation. Following these donations, things began to happen. Bill Clinton and Giustra met with the dictator of Kazakhstan. Mukhtar Dzhakishev, who oversees Kazakh mining, claimed that Hillary Clinton pressured Kazakh officials to sell uranium assets to Giustra's firm and said that Hillary refused to meet with him until he agreed to approve Giustra's deal. He did so.

After a series of mergers, Giustra's firm was acquired by a Russian conglomerate that built the Bushehr nuclear reactor in Iran. This conglomerate applied to the Committee on Foreign Investment in the United States, a small group of high-ranking officials including then–secretary of state Clinton, to buy a controlling interest in U.S. uranium mines. Despite obvious national security concerns, the committee approved the Russian takeover. Giustra and his partners got more than a lucrative Kazakh deal; they also got a controlling interest in the entire U.S. uranium mining industry. Remarkably, Bill and Hillary's good fortune also extended to their benefactor Frank Giustra.

Mining tycoon Stephen Dattels in 2009 donated two million shares of stock in his company to the Clinton Foundation. Two months later, with the support of the U.S. government, including one Hillary Clinton, the U.S. ambassador to Bangladesh pressured that nation to reauthorize a mining permit that benefited Dattels's company. The Clinton Foundation never disclosed Dattels's donation.

In 2008, the Swedish telecom company Ericsson found itself under investigation by the U.S. State Department for selling telecom equipment to the regimes of Iran, Sudan, and Syria, all considered state sponsors of terrorism. In 2011, Ericsson was named in a State Department report proposing to include telecom restrictions as part of its new sanctions against terrorist regimes. That year, Ericsson sponsored a speech by Bill Clinton and paid him a whopping $750,000, around three times Clinton's fee at the time. Ericsson had never previously sponsored a Clinton speech. Ericsson's timing could not have been more fortuitous, since later that year the State Department unveiled its new sanctions list for Iran. Telecom sanctions were not on it.

Douglas Becker is CEO of Laureate Education, a for-profit education firm that provides online instruction to students in several foreign countries, including Brazil, China, and Saudi Arabia. Laureate named Bill Clinton as "honorary chancellor" and paid him to speak several times a year, netting him around $1 million in speech income from Laureate alone. On disclosure forms, Bill says only that he has been paid "more than $1,000" by Laureate.

Becker also runs a nonprofit group called International Youth Foundation (IYF). Once Bill Clinton got on the Becker payroll, and Hillary became secretary of state, U.S. government funds through USAID to IYF increased dramatically. From 2010 to 2012, IYF received annual grants exceeding $20 million, for a total of nearly $65 million. In addition, the International Finance Corporation, a division of the World Bank—headed by Clinton pal Jim Yong Kim—made a $150 million equity investment in Laureate. Once again the Clintons' luck corresponded with good fortune for Douglas Becker.

In 2012, Bill Clinton received a whopping $250,000 for a single speech he gave in Boston to the Global Business Travel Association. But a review of documents filed by Bill Clinton's office showed that one of the sponsors of that talk was the aircraft giant Boeing. As secretary of state, Hillary was a strong advocate for Boeing. She pressed a state-owned airline in Russia to buy Boeing jets.

Jeffrey Epstein gave $3.5 million to the Clinton Foundation in 2006, shortly after the FBI began investigating him for participating in the exploitation of underage girls as sex slaves. Flight logs show that in 2002–2003, Bill Clinton made more than a dozen trips on Epstein's jet—nicknamed the "Lolita Express" because it apparently came equipped with teenage prostitutes. Somehow the Epstein investigation was concluded in 2008 with a secret settlement. Epstein pleaded guilty to one count of soliciting underage girls, for which he served a year in prison. All other charges were dropped, and all the records in the case were sealed. Only Swiss bank records leaked by a whistle-blower brought the incident to public light.

Somewhat more blatant was President Clinton's pardon of Marc Rich, a wealthy financier and oil trader who faced life in prison for illegally trading with the government of Iran and for evading $48 million in taxes. These crimes got him on the FBI's Most Wanted List. Rich's ex-wife, Denise, had been pressing Clinton for a pardon, but Clinton reportedly said he was having difficulties, even though he was "doing all possible to turn around" the White House counsel on the subject. Rich got his pardon, finally, after Denise Rich gave $100,000 to Hillary Clinton's 2000 New York Senate campaign, $400,000 to the Clinton Library, and another $1 million to the Democratic Party.

The Clintons came to Washington poor and are now extremely rich. One may say that they came professing to do good and left making out very well. The Clintons now have a net worth exceeding $100 million and they control assets exceeding a billion dollars. What did the Clintons have to do to earn this largesse? According to the Clintons, *nothing*. There were no bribes involved or deals made. People just happened to give them money, and then favorable things just happened for those people. Neither Hillary nor Bill caused those things to happen, or if they did, it was not because of the money flowing into their pockets. In other words, the Clintons have had better luck than Lucky Luciano, with a much bigger take than Luciano ever got.

Luck, of course, plays an important role in human success, and one

of the cleverest pitches of the progressives is to insist that since luck is
arbitrary, we don't deserve the fruits of our own luck. Since luck cannot
be *earned*, some progressives say, the benefits of luck should by justice
be widely *shared*. The redistribution of luck is, in the progressive mind,
a requirement of equal opportunity. By this logic, Luciano had no right
to escape so often with his life and freedom while other gangsters, by
contrast, were not similarly fortunate. The progressive solution is to
take all the fruits of our individual luck, pool it in one huge reservoir,
and turn it over to them. Then they pledge to ration this bonanza in
an equitable manner, minus of course the usual administrative charge.

Here we explore the logic of this remarkable line of thought, taking
up the reasoning of two of the most interesting progressive figures,
the left-leaning tycoon Warren Buffett and the philosopher John
Rawls. Buffett has become a poster boy for the Obama administration.
In effect, Obama trots out Buffett as an example of an "enlightened
tycoon." His usefulness is that he is a traitor to his class. After all, Buffett is a capitalist who wants higher taxes on capital. (He has famously
said that his secretary pays a higher rate of income tax than the capital
gains rate he pays on his investment income.) Buffett uses this example
not to urge that his secretary pay less, but that he pay more.

Buffett is also an advocate for the estate tax. Even though he has
pledged to leave virtually all his wealth to charity, he seems to think
that other rich people may not be so generous. In sum, Buffett is a progressive dream because he is a rich guy who wants the government to
do more to soak the rich: higher capital gains taxes, higher income
taxes, higher estate taxes.

On the surface, Buffett seems to be suggesting that government acts
on behalf of the people, while rich people act mostly on behalf of themselves. Government—the collective—can allocate resources in a more
disinterested way than individuals, and thus we can trust government
to use wealth to promote the public good. Market allocations may
be efficient but they are also unfair; only the state can confer justice.
Therefore the state has the right to take—ideally by persuasion, but if

necessary by force—as much of your accumulated wealth and income as it wants. Your money becomes its money.

On what basis does Buffett justify his progressivism? His central point is that the rewards of capitalism—including his own rewards—are basically unearned. They are the fruits ultimately of luck. As we will see, Buffett draws his ideas largely from the philosopher John Rawls. Rawls, who is widely considered the most influential political philosopher of the last half century, proposes a basic redesign of our society—his own remaking of America—in order to make sure that the rewards of luck are widely shared. Since the early 1970s, Rawls has been the darling of the progressives, because his arguments provide an intellectual basis to justify wealth confiscation and wealth redistribution.

Here we examine those arguments. Our purpose in considering Buffett's and Rawls's Lucky Luciano pitch is not so much to figure out whether it's a good deal—I think we know the answer to that one—but to figure out how we can deconstruct and debunk this ingenious progressive scam.

The medieval thinker Boethius writes of luck in his *Consolation of Philosophy*, "You are wrong if you think Fortune has changed towards you. Change is her normal behavior, her true nature. In the very act of changing she has preserved her own particular kind of constancy."[3] Boethius should know. He was raised in a patrician family and had, from a young age, a spectacular career under the Ostrogoth king Theodoric. He became consul, then head of the administrative service, and finally chief of all palace officials.

Then his luck turned. Theodoric intercepted some incriminating letters written by a senator named Albinus, and when Boethius defended Albinus, he was implicated. Evidence—quite likely forged—was produced against him. He was arrested, condemned, and sent to exile. When Theodoric confirmed the sentence, Boethius was tortured and then bludgeoned to death. I had read Boethius in college, but I reread the *Consolation* in the confinement center. (Prison literature makes a quite different impression when one is in captivity.) Boethius's life and work both bring to light not only how luck is fickle but also how it is undeserved. Whatever Boethius's virtues and vices, he was surely lucky to see the success that he did; he was just as surely unlucky to see his career plummet so dramatically.

My own luck in the confinement center turned about halfway during my stay. One of the staff, a big guy named Felipe, was working the night shift when he happened to see a rerun of *The Kelly File*. He did a double take. Is that D'Souza! Holy sh*t, it is! The next day the guy came up to me and said, "I watched your videos online for about six hours last night." The guy had seen my political debates, my debates with leading atheists, he had watched TV interviews, read excerpts from my books, even knew all about my case.

His verdict? "You rock, man." Within days he had informed everyone behind the counter that I rocked. He started calling Obama "Baracksucker" and his wife "Hochelle." The staff—100 percent Hispanic—began to treat me like a celebrity. The actual benefits of this were minimal, but at least I knew that if there was any trouble I could count on a hearing. Luck, as I say, was with me the day that guy turned on the Fox News Channel.

My luck also turned in another way that would probably not make Judge Berman happy. Right in the throes of my confinement, I fell in love. No, this was not a case of me falling for one of the other guys in the confinement center. In that case, you may ask, where does a guy who sleeps nights in a halfway house have a chance to meet a good woman?

I met Debbie Fancher in Texas just prior to my sentence. We began to work together on a project to get my *America* film shown in schools and colleges in Texas. Midway through my confinement, I fell in love with her. A forty-nine-year-old divorced mother of two, she is a Venezuelan immigrant who came to America speaking no English at the age of ten. She is a patriot who is also active in Republican politics. On Twitter she goes by "Conservative Latina."

Once we started dating, Debbie would come to San Diego to visit. We would spend days together, working and hanging out. Unfortunately, I had to say goodbye at 7 p.m. and check back into confinement at 8 p.m. She started calling me "Cinderella Man." Even though our time was sorely restricted, my relationship with Debbie was a solace to me during those long months in confinement when I could not yet see the light at the end of the tunnel. We found we had so much in common and the love we both have for this country blossomed into a love for each other.

Luck also plays its unpredictable hand for the folks in the confinement center. Consider Chris, who joined us from a white-collar prison camp in Florida. A clean-cut white guy who liked to wear extremely long short pants that went below his knees and T-shirts with very upbeat messages, Chris had served a year for tax fraud. Chris didn't cheat on his taxes, but he was apparently very good at advising businesses on how to cheat on theirs. This came to the notice of the IRS, and criminal charges were filed against Chris.

Except Chris was nowhere to be found in the United States. His business was carried out entirely over the Internet. He was eventually tracked and captured in Panama, and returned to the States in a paper suit and leg irons—a very humiliating way to travel! They stuck him in a holding center in Florida, and there, Chris told me, he almost got killed.

He was sitting in front of the TV, chomping on a sandwich, when another inmate grabbed him from behind and started choking him. Chris tried to fight him off but the other man was much bigger and stronger. Chris felt the consciousness draining out of him. Just then, a corrections officer happened to look into the TV area, and he struck the man across his head, breaking his grip.

"We were both thrown into solitary confinement," Chris said.

I was puzzled. "You, too?"

"Yeah, for two days. Whenever there is a fight, they always throw everyone involved into solitary, until they figure out what happened. Sometimes it can be a week before they do. In this case, the guy was off his meds. I'm just lucky the CO came in when he did. Otherwise the guy could have killed me."

Luck also favored the Mexican gang member Cojones in his encounters with members of rival gangs. Cojones was a squat guy with a square face and very thick glasses. He was just twenty-two, but I could see in his face that he had been through a lot. "I've been hit with a rock on my cheek," he told me. "If that rock had been two inches lower, it would have completely broken my jaw. Another time I got hit with a hammer on the back of my head. See the scar? That could have killed me. Then there was the time when these guys hit me several times across the back with a bat. I could have broken my spine, if someone up there wasn't looking out for me.

"But the luckiest was when I got trapped by this gang member in an alley, and he pulled out a nine-millimeter and aimed it at me. I was with another guy, an Original Gangster . . ."

"Original gangster?" I interrupted.

"That's a gang member who is too old to be in the gang anymore," Cojones explained. "When you get too old you become a kind of older statesman and people call you OG, or Original Gangster. Well, this OG saw the gun and he just took off and ran."

"He ran away?"

"Yeah, man. Can you believe it? He's supposed to be an OG, a tough guy, but even he saw what was coming. He just took off on me and ran across the parking lot. Then I saw the guy point at me and fire three shots.

"Bang, bang, bang. I heard the shots, and I felt them hit me in the chest, the stomach, and on my thigh. I fell back.

"The guy dropped the gun and left. I looked for blood, but there wasn't any. He missed all three times. I don't know how, because he was only a few feet away, just from here to that door, man, and yet he didn't hit me.

"It's unbelievable, I know. When I tell guys that they say, 'You must have been mistaken, maybe it was a toy gun or something.' Homie, I grew up around guns, and I have shot guns, and I know a bang when I hear one and fire when I see it coming from a gun. Was it luck? Was it destiny? I don't know. I just know that I should not be here talking to you, and yet I am."

Less fortunate was the guy who got into a physical fight with his girlfriend. I don't know his name—I'll call him Jude. I heard about Jude from another guy in the confinement center who was in prison with him. Evidently, Jude's girlfriend hit him with an umbrella and he punched her in the face, and she called the police so he was arrested and charged with domestic abuse. Both had struck blows, but hers didn't show and his did, and besides, he was a guy. So he got a year sentence.

While Jude was in prison, he heard that his girlfriend was driving his car and had taken up with another guy, and he burned with rage. Then he got to talking to the guy in the next cell, and Jude told him how much he hated the bitch and how she had screwed him over and how much he would like to beat the hell out of her.

What happened next could be a scene in a movie. The cellmate said he had two friends who could make that happen. In fact, they would be happy to kill the bitch. Jude didn't have to do anything—it would just be a favor to him. He said, great. The two guys came to see him and told him how they would do it, and, still consumed with bitterness and hatred, he said, sure, go ahead. Then they came back a week later and showed him pictures of the girlfriend lying in a pool of blood, and he said, serves her right.

Little did Jude know that his cellmate was using the conversation to obtain leverage with the authorities. He told them that a fellow prisoner intended to murder his girlfriend. The FBI set up the "hit" and the girlfriend agreed to cooperate in order to make it look real. Because of his knowledge and complicity with the scheme, Jude was charged with conspiracy to commit murder. He is currently serving a life sentence.

Now, granted, here was a guy who went along with a purported scheme to murder his girlfriend. Still, he didn't actually come up with the idea, nor did he carry it out. It's not clear that he would have attempted anything of the sort had he been out of prison. His rage, disproportionate as it was, has cost him his freedom for life. Surely Lady Luck was frowning on Jude the day he got to talking with the wily guy in the next cell.

I also met in the confinement center a guy in his forties named Udo who had just served a ten-year sentence for drugs. Udo was an extremely tall fellow seemingly of Eastern European origin—I couldn't tell for sure—but was entirely broken when I met him. I tried to console him that he would soon be out, but he said, "It doesn't make any difference to me at this point. My wife has already left, and my kids are grown up now."

So what did Udo do to get ten years? He was apparently in possession of a few thousand dollars' worth of meth when his car was pulled over by the police in the San Francisco area.

His bad luck was that the arrest was in the part of San Francisco called the Presidio. The Presidio, you see, is an area constructed on federal land. The federal government doesn't actually use that property, and it isn't marked as federal land. It has long been leased out to private businesses, restaurants, and shops. It's a regular tourist spot now.

But since the land is still owned by the U.S. government, this guy had committed a federal offense. Consequently he got ten years. "If I had been arrested a mile away," Udo said, "it would not have been a federal offense and I would have gotten one year, with six months in a rehab center. For the same crime."

What could I say? "Bad luck, man."

"That's putting it mildly, wouldn't you say? That single piece of bad luck has completely destroyed my life."

Criminals are somewhat fatalistic; they accept luck as part of the way life is. They rejoice when they have good luck and complain when they have bad luck. But they don't rail against luck itself, or believe that society should be redesigned to curtail the influence of luck. In this respect criminals are different than leading progressives.

Even so, there is a resemblance in how the two groups justify their conduct. Think of it this way: if your success is all due to luck, then I have every right to take your stuff, because I'm not depriving you of something to which you are justly entitled. This is the justification for criminal activity; it is also the justification for progressive wealth confiscation and wealth redistribution.

America has attempted for many decades to replace luck with just deserts. America has been striving to become a more meritocratic society. One may see our civil rights laws, as well as efforts to open up higher education and job opportunities to more classes of people, as efforts to reduce the scope of luck. Even so, luck endures in so many powerful ways, notably in the chances available to the children of those who are highly successful. Think of Bill Gates's children, or Chelsea Clinton, or one of the Bush progeny. Isn't it unfair that they enjoy the benefits of being born into rich, influential families?

Not necessarily. It was Marx who emphasized more than a century ago that capital is merely "stored labor." What Marx meant is that any reserve of cash or influence, even though it may be gifted or passed down to someone through inheritance, has to be originally earned. Someone, at some time, had to work for it and to save it. Gates, obviously, made all that money. So it's his money. He has every right to give it to whomever he wants. This is the point of having money: it confers on people the discretion of being able to spend it as they will. Gates has publicly announced he is bequeathing only a small fraction of his wealth to his children, but even if he decided to give most or all of it, no one has any legitimate grounds for complaint. We—not having earned it—have no claim on his money.

But if rich people are allowed to leave everything to their kids, what becomes of the ideal of equal opportunity? I suppose the answer is, it remains an ideal. In a free society, there is simply no way to ensure that everyone's children have the same chance. Society simply does not have the resources to give everyone the opportunities that Gates can afford to give his children. The only way to ensure a truly level playing field is not only for the government to pull everyone else's children up, but also to pull Gates's children down. Only progressives are willing to entertain such notions. Basically they amount to a theft scheme, with Bill Gates and other successful people as the target.

The progressive justification for appropriating people's wealth is typically that rewards in a capitalist society do not conform to any objective measure of "merit" or "just deserts." In other words, people do not get what they truly deserve. America is unfair. Obama even compares America unfavorably to Russia and China. He points out that in some countries like China and Russia, teachers get paid as much as doctors. His implication is that it is simply arbitrary that doctors make much more than teachers in this country. The market, in Obama's view, is whimsical and arbitrary. Luck, not merit or just desert, determines how capitalism's rewards are allocated.

This may seem like anathema to defenders of the free market, but Friedrich Hayek did not think so. He would have agreed with Obama that capitalism is not based on merit or just desert. Hayek wrote in *The Constitution of Liberty*, "In a free system it is neither desirable or practicable that material rewards should be made generally to correspond to what men recognize as merit."[4] Hayek conceded that at first glance this seems like a shocking statement, but nevertheless he showed in what sense it is true.

Objectively considered, teachers are just as valuable as doctors to any society. The education of the young—their preparation to assume the leadership and functioning of society—is no less important than conserving the health of people in a community. Thus, merit would seem to dictate that teachers should be paid roughly the same as doctors. This seems to be what Obama was getting at.

Yet Hayek insists that in a free market system, rewards are distributed not in proportion to intrinsic merit or just deserts but only in proportion to value, and value is entirely in the eye of the beholder—which is to say, the customer. The question of why people want things, or whether they are right to want them, is of no interest to entrepreneurs or to capitalism generally.

Consider an extreme example: Let's say I can throw sharp objects into the air and catch them between my teeth. Ordinarily this talent would make me a barroom curiosity. In a capitalist society, however, I could put my skills up for public consumption. If for some reason millions of people are fascinated by my skill—and, even more important, if they are willing to pay to watch me—then my peculiar talent suddenly becomes marketable. Now it has the potential to make me very rich. So here, as in all cases, the verdict lies with the customer. The rewards under capitalism depend on what people vote for, using ballots that are otherwise known as dollar bills.

Warren Buffett—the so-called Sage of Omaha—knows this as well as anyone. Indeed he banks on it when he makes investments in various companies. He is also the beneficiary of this system of capitalist wealth allocation. His investors find value in what Buffett can do in picking profitable companies, and thus, over time, by investing his own money and theirs, Buffett has become a multibillionaire. Even so, Buffett emphasizes that much of his success is not due to his honed profit-spotting skills, but rather to luck. Progressives have jumped on this, saying, "See—clearly the Sage of Omaha knows what he is talking about." No doubt. Let us look more closely, however, at why Buffett would say this.

In several interviews, Buffett makes it clear that he does have a remarkable set of skills. He has a very good antenna for figuring out which companies are likely to grow and become profitable. This, he stresses, is not purely a function of intelligence. Equally important is good practical judgment and a level head, invulnerable to wild swings of emotion. Buffett doesn't know how he got this way; as long as he can remember, he was this way. And this set of skills just happens to be one "that pays off huge in this society."

Buffett points out that if he had been born in prehistoric times, his skills would have been entirely useless and he'd probably have ended up as some animal's lunch. If he had grown up in Paris in the Middle Ages, he probably would not have provided much competition for Anselm or Aquinas. Even today, would Buffett have enjoyed his legendary success if he had been born and raised in, say, Uruguay or the Seychelles? Doubtful, and Buffett knows it. He recognizes he had the fantastic good fortune of being born and living in the United States and of "being wired in a particular way that I thrive in a big capitalist economy with a lot of action."[5]

Buffett's point can be illustrated—and debunked—by considering the very similar example of Richard Santulli. Santulli is a math whiz who discovered his abilities quite by accident. "All my friends would spend hours on history and philosophy. To me, I hate to say it, math was the easy way out." After a stint at Goldman Sachs, where he put his math acumen to use doing computer analyses of companies, Santulli became interested in airplanes. He figured out a way that corporate executives and other well-off people, who didn't want the cost and hassle of owning a jet, could buy fractional ownership. Through Santulli's company, Executive Jet, they could now get a private aircraft when they needed one for a certain number of hours per year. Santulli's company was eventually acquired by none other than Warren Buffett's Berkshire Hathaway, netting Santulli in excess of $100 million.[6]

Was Santulli lucky? Yes. Imagine a Richard Santulli figure in the year 1910. He has incredible math skills. He can perform amazing gymnastics with numbers. But what can he do with that skill? In 1910, virtually nothing. He can perhaps impress his friends by calculating probabilities on a gambling spree. But not much else. Quite likely our math whiz would have become a math teacher in his hometown. Today, however, those same skills are in high demand. Suddenly a talent that was once nearly useless becomes, in the electronic era, extremely valuable. Today if you can figure out a way, like Santulli did, to put your math skills to work, you too can become a centimillionaire.

All of this may seem like a full confirmation of Buffett's point, but actually it shows that Buffett's statements are entirely beside the point. What matters is the wants of the consumer. Consumers in 1910 didn't want anything out of math geniuses of that time, and so they were unwilling to pay them handsomely for supplying an essentially useless product. Consumers today, by contrast, can markedly improve their lives by using the skills that math geniuses can provide them. Consequently Richard Santulli today offers measurable value to people that his counterpart in 1910 simply didn't. Similarly Warren Buffett today contributes far more to the lives of people than a prehistoric Warren Buffett could and would have.

None of this is to deny the role of luck. It is merely to make two points about it. First, Santulli may have been lucky but he is also someone who took advantage of the available opportunity. Many people are good at math; Santulli figured out fractional ownership. A few other guys may have done the math; he actually built the company. Santulli confirms Machiavelli's point that *fortuna* may be unpredictable but she can be subdued through force of ingenuity and will.[7]

Second, the luck that benefited Santulli and Buffett doesn't just benefit them; it benefits lots of other people. While in one sense Santulli and Buffett are lucky to have customers around who appreciate them and pay well for their services, in another sense those customers are also lucky to have Santulli and Buffett around to do things for them that others cannot do, or do as well. Capitalism brings together buyers and sellers who are both fortunate to find and profit from each other.

I sense that a market-savvy guy like Buffett appreciates these points, even if some of his more thick-headed progressive allies don't. Consequently, Buffett seeks to lift his luck argument to higher ground. "Let's say that it was 24 hours before you were born, and a genie appeared and said, 'What I'm going to do is let you set the rules of the society into which you will be born. You can set the economic rules and the social rules, and whatever rules you set will apply during your lifetime and your children's lifetimes.' And you say, 'Well, that's nice but what's the catch?' And the genie says, 'Here's the catch. You don't know if you're going to be born rich or poor, white or black, male or female, able-bodied or infirm, intelligent or retarded.'

"Now," Buffett asks, "what rules do you want to have?"[8]

It may appear as if the Sage of Omaha has been doing some truly hard thinking about our social problems, but actually he has taken his paradigm directly from the philosopher John Rawls. In his treatise *A Theory of Justice*, first published in 1971, Rawls asks us to construct the rules for a just society by standing, as it were, behind a "veil of ignorance." Rawls's conditions are pretty much the same as Buffett's, but his argument is much more deeply conceived. Rawls's radical premise—the reason we are even talking about genies and veils of ignorance—is that he considers all the qualities that are normally described as merit actually to be the product of pure luck.

What does he mean? Consider two examples: Roger Federer and Albert Einstein. Tennis champion Federer has marvelous athletic talents, to be sure. But how did he get them? He inherited his basic physique, thus prevailing in the genetic lottery. No doubt he works hard and practices a lot, but who taught him to do that? Probably these skills were socialized into him at an early age. So in this analysis Federer deserves no credit either for his physique or his work ethic; both are part of his inheritance. The same applies to Einstein, who had the good fortune to be born intellectually gifted and curious.

Rawls holds that all success is the product of "accidents of natural endowment and the contingencies of social circumstance" and that these are "arbitrary from a moral point of view." From this premise, Rawls concludes that people have no right to the fame or money generated by their efforts. In this view, markets may be efficient but they are profoundly unfair, because they reward people purely for their good luck.

Rawls does not, however, call for absolute egalitarianism, a division of rewards into precisely equal shares. He recognizes that such a measure would inhibit growth and make everyone worse off. So what is Rawls's solution? He argues that since some people have greater ability, the fruits of that ability should be used for the common advantage. Choosing from behind the veil of ignorance, Rawls contends that the basic structure of society should be designed in such a way that inequalities of wealth are permitted only when they serve the interests of the disadvantaged members of society.[9]

The radicalism of Rawls's argument can be seen by taking up a distinction I made earlier in this chapter between Bill Gates's wealth and the wealth he may bequeath to his children. Now, I defended Gates's right to provide for his children as he sees fit. But even so, there is no question that Gates earned his wealth, while his children will receive a part of it as a windfall. Rawls denies that this is a meaningful distinction. From his point of view, the children are lucky, because they get money like manna from heaven, and Gates is also lucky, because he was born smart and developed productive habits that were socialized into him. From Rawls's perspective, the savvy, industrious Gates has no more right to his money than his offspring do.

What is one to make of Rawls's argument? The first thing to say is that it is based on a complete denial of human responsibility. If what he says is true, shouldn't we empty all the prisons and let all the convicts go free? Every criminal choice is the product of nature or nurture, or some combination of the two. But whatever the combination, Rawls insists that our endowments are "arbitrary from a moral point of view." After all, we are not responsible for choosing our parents, nor do we have any role in determining our early childhood socialization. Therefore we are not responsible for who we are and what we do. (Reading Rawls in the confinement center, I chuckled at the thought of having him as my defense counsel, urging my exoneration by quoting passages from *A Theory of Justice*.) Consequently, we cannot hold criminals—or anyone else—to be acting wrongly. But if criminals aren't accountable for actions, how can we justify punishing them and locking them up? Consequently we must free them.

This simply is not going to happen. No society can function that treats the actions and choices of its members as accidents of luck, exempt from accountability. So Rawls's scheme is unworkable. Still, isn't there a powerful strain of truth in it? Isn't luck behind most, if not all, of what we do? More important, if we were being honest with ourselves, would we say we are entitled to the fruits of our fortune? To this last question, Rawls emphatically answers no. I intend to emphatically answer yes.

Rawls assumes that people have no right to the benefit of their luck, but let's see if this is true. A group of ten people is walking through the forest and one of the ten happens to glance down and finds a $100 bill. She picks it up and puts it in her purse. Now, here's the question: Does she have a right to the money? Or is she morally obliged to share it with the others? And why limit it to the other nine, who just happened to be on the scene? Must she share her winnings with the entire society on the grounds that this money isn't hers and therefore everyone has an equal right to it?

This is absurd. The money wasn't earned, to be sure, but she found it, and absent any prospect of locating the original owner, the money is rightfully hers. Yes, it's fortune, but fortune happened to be winking in her direction that day. She may not have a moral right to the funds, but even less does anyone else have a moral claim upon them. Therefore, for all practical purposes, the money does and should belong to her, and the question of whether she should share it depends entirely on her goodwill.

Put this way, luck seems churlish, even undemocratic, but a bit of reflection will show that the opposite is true. In reality luck is the most democratic of all forces, precisely because it is so arbitrary, undiscriminating, whimsical. One of the ten found the $100 bill but any of the ten could have found it. In this sense, luck is a perfect expression of equal opportunity.

This is true whether the luck is good or bad. Two of us are in a boat in the middle of the ocean, and the boat develops a leak. Only one can stay on board, or else the boat will sink and both will drown. So how do we decide who stays and who gets off? We toss a coin. Let's say you win and I have to disembark. Luck has smiled on you, and frowned on me. But has either of us been cheated? No. Why? Because in this scenario both of us had an equal chance to succeed. Thus even though luck has produced a winner and a loser, the outcome is just. Rawls's point that you don't deserve your luck because you didn't do anything to deserve it is both irrelevant and idiotic: the very meaning of luck is that it is unexpected, undeserved, entirely dependent on chance.

This chance element of luck is precisely what makes it so democratic, so egalitarian, and so just. Contrast the guy who wins the 100-meter dash in the Olympics with the guy who wins the lottery. Both contests are fair, in the sense that they are open to all and conducted according to an evenly applied set of rules. Even so, the first is a merit outcome and the second is a luck outcome. The Olympic winner obviously requires a whole set of physical and perhaps even mental abilities to secure the victory. Presumably he must be strong, lean, long-legged, and fast.

By contrast, the lottery winner does not have to be anything; he or she only has to be in possession of the winning ticket. When it comes to the lottery, everyone can enter and anyone can win. Moreover, everyone with a ticket has the same prospect of success. Unlike contests of merit, which require a whole host of rare talents and abilities, luck gives hope to all, and a chance to everyone: what could be more fair than that?

Rawls's only comeback is his fabled "veil of ignorance." He insists that from behind the veil of ignorance, everyone would vote for his particular outcome. I, for one, would not vote for it. Rather, I would vote for precisely the anti-theft model that the founders established in America. I would vote for a society that may provide less security than Rawls would like, but at the same time would provide more opportunity. I prefer living in a country where we make our own luck and seek our own fortune.

I can see why progressives love Buffett and Rawls. Buffett has become the entrepreneur whom progressives endlessly flatter, because he flatters their prejudices and enables their scams. Rawls has become regular assigned reading for progressive educators in the colleges. Why? Because he provides them with a pretext for confiscating the wealth of everyone who has it, however they managed to get it. Rawls's arguments are seriously defective, but at least he was serious about them; progressives, by contrast, have adopted them because they are such a valuable addition to their Stealer's Handbook. What Rawls intended as philosophy, progressives have converted into a Lucky Luciano pitch.

However seriously we rebut these pitches—and I have taken the trouble in these past chapters to rebut them in detail—we should not forget that, in the end, they are part of a scam. In this respect they are reminiscent of the scams pulled off by the duke and the dauphin in Mark Twain's *Huckleberry Finn*. In one scene, Huck sees the duke putting up a poster announcing that "the celebrated Dr. Armand de Montalban of Paris" is scheduled to give a "lecture on the Science of Phrenology" at a given time and place. Admission is ten cents, although Dr. Montalban would "furnish charts of character at twenty-five cents apiece." Another poster announces the sale of tickets for a performance by the "world-renowned Shakespearian tragedian, Garrick the Younger, of Drury Lane, London." It is the duke, of course, who is pulling off these impostures.

Huck is initially taken in by these two rogues, in the same manner that many Americans have been conned by progressives. The progressive scams, however, have endured for a while. Huck, however, is a quick learner. He soon figures out what his high-titled compatriots are up to. "It didn't take me long to make up my mind that these liars warn't no kings or dukes either, but just low-down humbugs and frauds."[10] Assessing the pitches that progressives have been putting forward for at least the past seven years, from the reparations pitch to the inequality pitch to the "you didn't build that" pitch to the Lucky Luciano pitch, it is difficult to come to a different conclusion.

Chapter 9

THE GODFATHER:

Saul Alinsky's Art of the Shakedown

I feel confident that I could persuade a millionaire on Friday
to subsidize a revolution for Saturday out of which he would
make a huge profit on Sunday even though he was certain to be
executed on Monday.[1]

—Saul Alinsky

In the last four chapters we have surveyed various con man pitches
that show the ways progressives sell their cons. Now we turn to the
cons themselves.

Scams don't occur spontaneously; they require planning, leadership, and strategy. In the case of the mafia, a single man performs that
role: the godfather. In this chapter we examine a special type of godfather. This godfather is a visionary and a strategist, but he is unable to
pull off the big rip-off. Rather, he is himself a small-time hood. He operates from the margin, from the outside, shaking down corporations
and local government agencies and making a handsome, though not
extravagant, profit for himself.

By themselves his shakedown schemes would be unremarkable. But they turn out to be the instruction manuals for many others. So this godfather's supreme achievement is in the area of mentorship. He becomes the inspiration and trainer of two talented students who grow up to be big-time hoods. The godfather's name is Saul Alinsky. His most famous students are Barack Obama and Hillary Clinton.

Hardly anyone recognizes this, but Alinsky and the Alinsky method is the hidden force behind the 2008 economic meltdown. The meltdown was the worst economic crisis since the Great Depression; it was the main cause of median wealth in the United States in the subsequent three years declining nearly 40 percent. While the meltdown is routinely attributed to Wall Street "greed," its real cause was government and activist pressure on banks and banking agencies—like Fannie Mae and Freddie Mac—to change their lending and loan guarantee practices. Yes, the 2008 crash was actually the result of an Alinskyite scam—actually a series of Alinskyite scams, carried out over many years.

Basically the Alinskyites were trying to steal money from the banks and, in the process, force the banks to make loans to people that they had no intention of making loans to. The banks acquiesced, and eventually the whole scheme came crashing down. It was toppled not by greed but by the sober reality that when you loan money to millions of people who cannot afford to pay, those people are very likely to default on those loans. That's how Alinskyites almost destroyed the U.S. economy a few years ago. If Alinsky had never lived, none of this would have happened.

Progressives blamed the 2008 meltdown on Wall Street greed and bank shenanigans. Economist Joseph Stiglitz regurgitates the standard line. "Banking had long been based on trust. In the years leading up to the crisis, though, our traditional bankers changed drastically. Commercial lenders hard-sold mortgages to families who couldn't afford them, using false assurances. Trust went out the window."[2]

This, however, explains very little. Greed, admittedly, is a staple of Wall Street. But in all their investments, greedy people are tempered by fear. Precisely because they want money, greedy people don't like to lose their capital. Consequently, over many decades, as Stiglitz well knows, Wall Street and the banks had developed quite conservative procedures for making their real estate loans. Typically they required borrowers to put between 10 and 20 percent down. That way even if the home and property dropped in value, the banks and investment houses wouldn't lose money. Fannie Mae or Freddie Mac, quasi-public institutions that purchased mortgages and provided loan guarantees to banks, were known for their strict underwriting standards, including minimum down payments and detailed credit histories. This is how home loans used to be made in America.

So what changed? What changed is an aggressive campaign, conducted by progressive politicians and community activists, to force banks and financial institutions to lower their lending standards. This goes back to the early 1970s.[3] Before that, progressives had focused their political energies in getting government money to build large housing projects for the poor. These projects, however, soon became dens of dilapidation, decay, and criminal activity. They symbolized the failure of the liberal welfare state.

Progressives needed a new idea, and Alinsky came up with one: force banks and financial institutions to loan money to unqualified applicants so that they can buy homes. Alinsky's own idea was to terrorize the banks by having thousands of activists walk into banks and open up accounts of one dollar each, in effect paralyzing the bank's normal operations. This became the model for a number of leftist groups that took up the cause of bank intimidation, notably an Alinskyite organization called ACORN.

The ideological justification for this tactic was "social justice." Starting in the 1970s, ACORN and other leftist groups protested that banks were "discriminating" against poor and minority home loan applicants. Even though such applicants had less wealth, less income, and less reliable credit histories, these groups insisted that banks should lower their lending standards to accommodate them. According to these activists, home ownership was a "right" and getting a mortgage to buy a home was a matter of "fairness."

In 1977, a liberal Democratic Congress obligingly passed, and President Jimmy Carter signed into law, the Community Reinvestment Act (CRA). This law, aggressively promoted by liberal icons like Senator Ted Kennedy and Senator William Proxmire, imposed on banks an "affirmative obligation" to make loans in their own neighborhoods, even if those neighborhoods were poor credit risks.

One might suspect that an administrative apparatus, put into place by the government, would be adequate to ensure compliance with the law. For progressive activists, however, social justice requires outside activism in order to be enforced. Over the next couple of decades, ACORN and other activist organizations protested and picketed banks, demanding a modification in lending practices and more loans to people with no assets and dubious credit. ACORN pushed for banks to make mortgage loans not only to poor Americans but also to illegal immigrants. Some banks and financial institutions yielded to this pressure, but others didn't.

In the 1990s, there were a few highly publicized studies, such as one by the Federal Reserve Bank of Boston, and another by the *Atlanta Journal-Constitution*, showing that banks were more likely to make home loans to whites than to blacks, even when income levels were the same. For the most part these studies were flawed, because banks don't simply make loans on the basis of income. They also consider such factors as net worth, savings, credit history, outstanding debt, and market value of the home. When these criteria were factored in, the racial gap narrowed greatly or disappeared altogether. Even so, the Clinton administration hired Alicia Munnell, the lead author of the Boston Fed study, as assistant secretary of the Treasury, and made the faulty redlining studies a pretext to push for a renewal and wider application of the Community Reinvestment Act.

The Clinton team went further. For the first time, the government began to pressure Fannie and Freddie to modify underwriting standards and facilitate more home loans throughout the country. The Clinton administration also pushed through a bailout of several failed financial institutions, conveying a message to banks that they should comply with the government's relaxed lending proposals because if they lost money the government was there to protect them. Clinton's hatchet team included Attorney General Janet Reno; Deval Patrick, who headed the Civil Rights Division of the Justice Department; and directors of the Department of Housing and Urban Development (HUD) Henry Cisneros and Andrew Cuomo. All of them pressured banks to loan money to previously unqualified applicants, and got the government more deeply involved in backing risky, so-called subprime loans.

Starting in the Clinton era and continuing through George W. Bush's two terms, progressive activists mounted direct pressure—either in the form of public protest or lawsuits—against banks. This was aimed at intimidating banks to adopt new lending standards and also to engage the activist groups themselves in the lending process. In 1994, a young Barack Obama, recently graduated from Harvard Law School, joined two other attorneys in suing Citibank for "discriminatory lending" because it had denied home loans to several bank applicants. The case was called *Selma S. Buycks-Roberson v. Citibank*.

Citibank denied wrongdoing, but as often happens in such situations, it settled the lawsuit to avoid litigation costs and the negative publicity. Selma Buycks-Roberson and two of her fellow plaintiffs altogether received $60,000, and Obama and his fellow lawyers received nearly a million dollars in legal fees. This was a small salvo in a massive fusillade of lawsuits filed against banks and financial institutions in the 1990s.

ACORN, the most notorious of these groups, had its own ally in the Clinton administration: Hillary Clinton. (Around the same time, ACORN was also training an aspiring community activist named Barack Obama.) Hillary helped to raise money for ACORN and also for a closely allied group, the Industrial Areas Foundation. The IAF had been founded by Saul Alinsky and continued to operate as an aggressive leftist pressure group long after Alinsky's death in 1972.

Hillary lent her name to these groups' projects and met several times with their organizers in the White House. ACORN's efforts were also supported by progressive politicians like Nancy Pelosi, Barney Frank, Jon Corzine, Chuck Schumer, and Harry Reid. These politicians berated the banks to make loans easier to get. "I do not want the same kind of focus on safety and soundness," Frank said at a September 25, 2003, hearing. "I want to roll the dice a little more."

As Peter Schweizer shows in his eye-opening book *Architects of Ruin*, Frank, Pelosi, and Reid blocked efforts to reform Fannie and Freddie during George W. Bush's two terms. Indeed Schweizer writes that by this time Fannie and Freddie "were effectively hijacked by liberal activists." Fannie, which owned or guaranteed nearly half of all home mortgages, was headed by Franklin Raines, who portrayed banking practices less as a form of productive commerce than as a form of social equity and wealth redistribution. In 2001, Raines said that under his leadership Fannie Mae was a "mediating structure that bends the financial system to create homeowners." Fannie Mae no longer viewed itself as a tough gauge of good loans; it now became a vehicle to help generate, and then insure, bad loans.

Many banks succumbed to pressures from the government and from Fannie and Freddie, but some held out. These businesses were systematically targeted by ACORN and other leftist activist groups. ACORN discovered that the best time to threaten pickets and protests was when banks were conducting merger negotiations. Such negotiations were widespread in the 1990s and early to mid-2000s. During such periods banks sought desperately to avoid negative publicity.

ACORN found that it could extract not only lending policy concessions but also direct financial contributions. The group took in millions of dollars from Citibank, J. P. Morgan, Bank of America, and Washington Mutual. In 2004–2005 alone, ACORN received $175,000 from Washington Mutual, $400,000 from Citicorp, $1 million from J. P. Morgan, and $1.3 million from Bank of America. ACORN even got money out of Freddie and Fannie, showing how deep its tentacles stretched into the American home mortgage industry.

By 2008, the entire banking and home mortgage lending industry had been corrupted by the left. It was hardly a commercial industry anymore; rather, it was a kind of progressive racket. And the racket came to an end when, first by the thousands, and eventually by the millions, the people who lacked the ability to pay back their loans stopped making their loan payments. This caused the panic of 2008, followed by the crash of 2008.

The government used the crash to justify a series of measures expanding government control of the banking and investment industries, and indeed of the U.S. economy. This began in the last months of the Bush administration, and continued through the Obama administration. Bush officials apparently convinced themselves that, without bailing out big banks and financial institutions, the entire economy would grind to a halt.

With the benefit of hindsight, this seems far-fetched. Certainly the financial institutions had major problems, in that they now owned hundreds of billions of dollars in toxic assets, that is, mortgages that were no longer being repaid. But so what? Why should the liabilities of the private sector become a problem for the American taxpayer? The taxpayer doesn't benefit when banks make profits; why should the taxpayer be on the hook when banks make losses? Moreover, why would Obama and the progressives—who were no fans of banks, investment houses, and Wall Street—go along with such measures?

The reason can be seen in what Barney Frank said when the meltdown occurred: "The private sector got us into this mess. The government has to get us out of it." Frank realized that this economic crisis, despite being caused by the progressives themselves, provided progressives with a unique political opportunity. Frank was not the only one to see this. Obama adviser Rahm Emanuel famously said, around the same time, "Never let a crisis go to waste." The Obama administration led the effort to convert a government-generated crisis into a massive expansion of the power and reach of the federal government.

Thus progressives became the unlikely advocates for government bailouts of Wall Street, largely because they saw that these bailouts would become the mechanism for establishing government control of the financial sector. Progressives had long sought this; here was their chance to make it happen. The Dodd-Frank legislation, scandalously named after two of the actual perpetrators of the problem, gave the government, through the FDIC, the power to identify a bank as "troubled" under vague and arbitrary criteria and then take it over and manage its assets, merge it with another bank, transfer its assets or liabilities without consent, remove existing managers and employees and also move shareholders down the list of priorities in terms of getting back their money.[4]

The federal government also took Fannie Mae and Freddie Mac into "conservatorship." Reaching into the federal Treasury, the Obama administration injected massive amounts of money into the banks. Citigroup and Bank of America, for example, each received $45 billion. The total Troubled Asset Relief Program (TARP) bailout package cost a staggering $700 billion. Some banks didn't want or need bailouts; the government insisted they take them.

Later, as banks began to improve their balance sheets, several attempted to pay back their government loans. The Obama administration refused to accept the money, on the grounds that banks would first have to pass a "stress test." Of course the "stress test" was simply a way for the government to maintain control of those banks.

So if banks gained by getting free money, and the government gained by extending control over the financial sector, who lost? The taxpayer! The taxpayer was the sucker in this whole transaction. His money stood guarantee for the depositors and investors and bank officials who had taken risks and made bad loans and were now facing crippling losses. Instead of them suffering, the taxpayer suffered. And who raided the Treasury and stuck the taxpayer with this bill that was not the taxpayer's bill to pay? The very federal government that is responsible for managing the Treasury and protecting the revenues provided by the taxpayer.

A second group lost out—ordinary citizens whose homes plummeted in value. This group numbered in the millions. After the meltdown, they discovered to their dismay that their mortgages now exceeded the market value of their homes. To this date many of these people live in homes "underwater."

A third group also suffered—poor borrowers who defaulted on their loans. A typical loser was Catrina Roberts, a single mother of four, who was told that she could afford a house. Roberts was earning $880 a month after taxes. Yet she got a fixed-rate mortgage in Cleveland with virtually no money down. Six years later, she went into foreclosure. "I know when you buy a house, eventually you have to put work into it," she said. "But I didn't know it would lead me here, because if I did, I would never have bought it. So I'm at a point right now that I don't want to buy a house, ever again."[5] People get hurt in rip-off schemes, and ironically the people most hurt in this one were the very people progressives claimed to be helping.

To understand Alinsky, it helps to recall the mafia film *Goodfellas*, which begins with a young boy, Henry Hill, who lives in a poor miserable tenement building. Every night he stays up late and through his window watches the "wise guys" in the street and in the alley and in the restaurants below. There they are, enjoying the good things in life: they've got the money, they've got the booze, and they've got the girls. Even more spectacular, they do just what they want. When they break the rules, by making a big noise or throwing beer bottles or kicking people around, nobody—not even the cops—stops them. They are truly above the law. How wonderful, Hill thinks, to be able to live like this.

Hill knows right away what he wants to be when he grows up. And when he becomes a "wise guy" himself, he begins to see what that life means in practice. In the most famous scene in the movie, he takes his girlfriend, Karen, into a posh nightclub. He walks right past the line and goes in through the service entrance, past the security guards, and although the place is full, a table is lifted into the air and set up right in front of the stage. Karen can hardly believe it, and Hill gives her that serene, confident look that says this is the way he lives, the kind of royal treatment she can expect when she is with him. This is a tiny glimpse of the theft payoff, the special treatment even beyond what money can buy, that highly successful crooks and politicians aspire to.

Henry Hill could have been named Saul Alinsky.

This comparison may seem shocking to those who have only been exposed to the progressive propaganda narrative about Alinsky. According to that narrative, Alinsky was tough and brash, but basically motivated by a love of people and a passion for justice. He fought tirelessly against greedy corporations and insensitive government agencies to improve conditions in the urban ghettos, then became a labor organizer, then proved himself on the battleground of civil rights, and finally specialized as a community organizer, bringing hope and justice to the disadvantaged in cities like Chicago, Detroit, Rochester, and St. Louis. This is the "official story."

The real story is much more interesting, and interestingly, it comes from Alinsky himself. I'm not referring to Alinsky's two books, *Reveille for Radicals* and *Rules for Radicals*. Those are books of strategy, and since part of Alinsky's recommended strategy is camouflage and deceit, we can be sure that there is a fair amount of both in these books. Conservatives routinely denounce Alinsky's books for their blatant Machiavellianism; liberals celebrate them for their hard-boiled realism. The books are certainly worth reading: they bristle with worthwhile insights that can be used by the left or the right. But they say little about Alinsky himself.

Happily for us, there is a text that examines Alinsky's life as a whole. In March 1972, just two months before he died, Alinsky gave a detailed, tell-all interview to *Playboy* magazine. At this point Alinsky was at the top of his game. He was rich, he was famous, and he could take justified pride in the success of his operations. This seems to have been Alinsky's chosen occasion to speak candidly and spill the beans. He tells things about himself that appear in no other source. While the *Playboy* interview is very revealing, it is also damning, and not surprisingly it has been largely ignored in hagiographic accounts of Alinsky, such as Sanford Horwitt's *Let Them Call Me Rebel*, a book partly financed through grants from Alinskyite organizations.

Let us follow the Alinsky story, as narrated by Alinsky himself in the interview. Born in 1909, Alinsky grew up on the South Side of Chicago. His parents were Orthodox Jews who had emigrated from Russia. "Poverty was no stranger to me," he recalled. "We lived in one of the worst slums in Chicago; in fact, we lived in the slum district of the slum, on the wrong side of the wrong side of the tracks, about as far down as you could go."

Alinsky's father was a tailor, then ran a deli, and then a cleaning shop. "But whatever business he had, we always lived in the back of a store. I remember, as a kid, the biggest luxury I ever dreamed of was just to have a few minutes to myself in the bathroom without my mother hammering on the door and telling me to get out because a customer wanted to use it."

The era from 1910 to 1929 was a prosperous one for America, but it was also harsh for those at the bottom who were struggling to make it. Alinsky's father never did, and there is an obvious bitterness in Alinsky's tone as he recalls those years. From his father Alinsky seems to have learned a lesson that capitalism draws the life out of you, while never delivering on its promise of success and leisure. As Alinsky saw it, there is no correlation between hard work and reward. The system is based on a lie. The elder Alinsky's failures also seem to have earned him the contempt of his son.

Alinsky's father divorced his mother and left the family while Alinsky was a teenager. Alinsky says that he despised his father and that his father felt the same way about him. The two barely spoke to one another. At one point during the Depression, Alinsky says, "I had exactly four bucks between me and starvation, so in desperation I sent a registered letter to my father, asking him for a little help, because I didn't even have enough for food. I got the receipt back showing he'd got the letter, but I never heard from him. He died in 1950 or 1951 and I heard he left an estate of $140,000. He willed most of it to an orchard in Israel and his kids by his previous marriage. To me, he left $50."

What Alinsky didn't get from his dad, he decided to take from others. From his earliest years, Alinsky recalls, he disliked rules and had limited respect for other people's property. "In little ways, I've been fighting the system ever since I was seven or eight years old. I mean, I was the kind of kid who'd never dream of walking on the grass until I'd see a sign, KEEP OFF THE GRASS, and then I'd stomp all over it." At sixteen, Alinsky moved out of the house and, in his words, "was shackin' up with some old broad of twenty-two." On the slum streets he learned the art of petty thievery and put his skills to work when he enrolled at the University of Chicago.

With evident relish, Alinsky describes one of his scams for eating big meals in the university cafeteria system while only paying for a cup of coffee. He would go up to the cashier and order a cup of coffee; at that time, it cost just a nickel. The cashier would write him a ticket listing the price, and he would take the coffee and keep the ticket. Then he would go to another university cafeteria—part of the same chain—and order a full meal. The waitress would then give him his check for the meal. In those days, customers didn't pay the waitress; rather, they went up to the cashier and paid. Then Alinsky would pocket the bill for his meal and submit his nickel ticket to the cashier. By switching checks, Alinsky was eating full meals and paying just for his cup of coffee.

This is of course the kind of scam that one can see any clever, im-poverished slum kid pulling off. What makes Alinsky original is that he developed a whole system based on this scam. It included maps of the various university campuses with all the cafeterias marked on it. Alinsky then put up signs on the university bulletin board and invited people to meetings. "I stood on the lectern and explained my system in detail." Pretty soon, he says, he had whole teams of students signed up for his ingenious scam. "We got the system down to a science," Alinsky says, "and for six months all of us were eating free."

Unfortunately for Alinsky, the university changed its payment system and the scam didn't work anymore. Asked whether he had moral qualms about ripping off the university, Alinsky erupted, "Are you kidding? There's a priority of rights, and the right to eat takes precedence over the right to make a profit." Even here, we see in the young thief that sense of entitlement and organizational zeal that would expand into a whole rip-off program. He feels perfectly entitled to game the system, and takes pride in teaching others how to do it. He doesn't even bother to publicly justify the theft by calling the university evil or discriminatory. He figures out a way to steal, and he goes ahead and does it, and then shows others how to do it.

One may call Alinsky a theft educator, like Fagin in *Oliver Twist*, an instructor in the art of taking stuff without paying for it. His educational program would ultimately guide a whole political movement— the whole progressive movement—and inspire two of the most important figures on the American, and world, stage.

Alinsky realized, however, that he didn't want to spend his life on petty rip-off schemes. He wanted to learn how the big-time criminals do their thing. So he changed his academic focus to criminology, not so much, it seems, to reform crime but to understand how to be a more effective thief. He proposed to his professors a unique project: an in-depth study of Chicago's criminal gangs. At first his teachers were skeptical that Alinsky could penetrate those gangs, but ever the schemer, Alinsky was fully up to the task.

One such gang was a group called the 42 Mob, made up of Italian youths who, Alinsky says, "were held responsible by the D.A. for about 80 percent of the auto thefts in Chicago" and were "just graduating into the outer fringes of the big-time rackets." Alinsky tried to get to know the leadership, but they were a tight-knit group "with hair trigger tempers." Alinsky finally got his chance when the gang's leader, Thomas Massina, or Little Dumas, was shot and killed in a drugstore holdup. Alinsky went over to Dumas's house, where he heard his mother "weeping and wailing, repeating the same thing over and over in Italian. I asked one of the kids what she was saying and he said she was bemoaning the fact that she didn't have any pictures of Dumas, nothing to remember him by.

"So I left right away, picked up a photographer friend of mine, and rushed down to the morgue. The attendant took us to the icebox, where Dumas was laid out on a slab. We took a photograph, opening his eyes first, then rushed back to the studio to develop it. We carefully re-touched it to eliminate all the bullet holes, and then had it hand-tinted.

"The next morning, I went back to the wake and presented the photograph to Mrs. Massina. 'Dumas gave this to me just last week,' I said, 'and I'd like you to have it.' She cried and thanked me, and pretty soon word of the incident spread through the gang. From that moment they began to trust me and I was able to work with them, all because of the photograph." Recalling the incident, Alinsky refuses to consider it cynical or manipulative. "It was an improvised tactic and it worked. Everybody got what they wanted. Mrs. Massina got something to hold onto in her grief and I got in good with the kids. It was a simple example of good organizing."[6]

Alinsky had an easier time getting in with the Sholto Street gang, whose leadership he befriended: Felix the Cat, Step-and-a-Half (a thug so called because he had a limp), Chickenman, Rags, and Stiff. Alinsky's biographer Sanford Horwitt writes that Alinsky had a particular tough-talking style that appealed to young hoodlums.

"When he first took the boys out to lunch at the neighborhood delicatessen," Horwitt writes, "he instructed them that when you order in a restaurant, you don't say, 'I would like' such and such, or 'May I'; rather, you say, 'I'll have' that sandwich. The boys appreciated the subtle distinction, the aggressiveness." Alinsky often took gang members out to lunch—"Gold's for corned beef, Spino's or Tufano's for spaghetti"—and "sometimes he would give the boys money to set up a spread at one of their houses for the whole gang."[7]

Of course Alinsky's "generosity" was a means for winning the trust of gang members so that Alinsky could study their criminal schemes, but regardless they appreciated it. Pretty soon they looked at Alinsky as one of their own, a kind of honorary uncle, and even kidded him for dressing like a dandy and making the gang look bad.

Eventually Alinsky even got gang members to cooperate in extensive "life histories" that he prepared. He'd hand out sheets and ask gang members to write down their recollections about when they first stole eggs or had their first encounter with the police. These detailed personal histories would prove useful not only for getting him academic credit but also for learning firsthand how people stole stuff and got away with it.

It's one thing to penetrate a small-time Chicago gang, but quite another to get inside the most notorious criminal operation in the city and indeed the country at the time, the Capone mob. With single-minded determination, Alinsky set out to get in with Capone's mobsters. As he recounts the experience, "My reception was pretty chilly at first—I went over to the old Lexington Hotel, which was the gang's headquarters, and I hung around in the lobby and the restaurant. I'd spot one of the mobsters whose picture I'd seen in the papers and go up to him and say, 'I'm Saul Alinsky, I'm studying criminology, do you mind if I hang around with you?' And he'd look me over and say, 'Get lost punk.' This happened again and again, and I began to feel I'd never get anywhere.

"Then one night I was sitting in the restaurant and at the end table was Big Ed Stash, a professional assassin who was the Capone mob's top executioner. He was drinking with a bunch of his pals and he was saying, 'Hey you guys, did I ever tell you about the time I picked up that redhead in Detroit?' and he was cut off by a chorus of moans. 'My God,' one guy said, 'do we have to hear that one again?' I saw Big Ed's face fall—mobsters are very sensitive, you know, very thin-skinned. And I reached over and plucked his sleeve. 'Mr. Stash,' I said, 'I'd love to hear that story.' His face lit up. 'You would, kid?' He slapped me on the shoulder. 'Here, pull up a chair. Now, this broad, see. . . .' And that's how it started.

"We became buddies. He introduced me to Frank Nitti, known as the Enforcer, Capone's number two man, and actually in *de facto* control of the mob because of Al's income-tax rap. Nitti took me under his wing. I called him the Professor and I became his student. Nitti's boys took me everywhere, showed me all the mob's operations, from gin mills and whorehouses and bookie joints to the legitimate businesses they were beginning to take over. Within a few months, I got to know the workings of the Capone mob inside out."

Alinsky seemingly had no problem with the mob murdering people as part of its business; in fact, he argued with mobsters about the most cost-effective way to get the job done. "Once, when I was looking over their records," Alinsky says, "I noticed an item listing a $7500 payment for an out-of-town killer." This by itself is pretty incredible, but it is exactly what Alinsky says. Indeed if Alinsky himself is to be believed, he was so close to the mob that they would let him look over their assassination plans, even before they were carried out. This must have required a deep level of trust, because Alinsky could have sent the inner circle of the Capone mob to prison.

Puzzled by what he saw in the mob's records, Alinsky contacted Frank Nitti. As Alinsky recalls the incident, "I said, 'Look, Mr. Nitti, I don't understand this. You've got at least 20 killers on your payroll. Why waste that much money to bring somebody in from St. Louis?'

"Frank said patiently, 'Look kid, sometimes our guys might know the guy they're hitting, they may have been to his house for dinner, taken his kids to the ball game, been the best man at his wedding, gotten drunk together. But you call in a guy from out of town, all you've got to do is tell him, "Look, there's this guy in a dark coat on State and Randolph; our boy in the car will point him out; just go up and give him three in the belly and fade into the crowd." So there's a job and he's a professional, he does it. But if one of our boys goes up, the guy turns to face him and it's a friend, right away he knows that when he pulls that trigger there's gonna be a widow, kids without a father, funerals, weeping—Christ, it'd be murder.' "

Alinsky recalls that when he stuck to his guns about using a local guy and saving money, even a hardened criminal like Nitti was shocked and regarded Alinsky as "a bit callous."[8] We might expect the student to be shocked by the callousness of the high-level mobster, but in Alinsky's account it is the high-level mobster who is shocked by the callousness of the student. At least this is how Alinsky apparently wants us to view him.

In reading his account, I'm reminded of guys in the confinement center who speak laughingly about the people they've beaten up, the women they've abused, and in some cases the murders they've witnessed or committed. These seem to be people who have lost their humanity, who have become sociopaths in that their conscience has been so dulled it is virtually nonexistent. I suspect Alinsky would feel right at home in their company.

Alinsky plainly admired how the Capone gang could shake down various merchants and commercial establishments and essentially extort from them or rob them at will. "They had Chicago tied up tight as a drum," Alinsky recalled. "They owned the city, from the cop on the beat right up to the mayor. Forget all that Eliot Ness sh*t; the only real opposition to the mob came from other gangsters, like Bugs Moran or Roger Touhy. Capone was the establishment. When one of his boys got knocked off, there wasn't any city court in session, because most of the judges were at the funeral and some of them were pallbearers."

Alinsky wasn't a mob operative himself, so he didn't get to enjoy the full rewards of being a member. "I was a nonparticipating observer in their professional activities," he says, "although I joined their social life of food, drink and women. Boy, I sure participated in that side of things. It was heaven."[9]

Heaven! Here is Alinsky indulging in that Henry Hill moment, when the young protagonist of *Goodfellas* goes beyond wistfully watching mob revelries from his window; he actually gets to participate in them.

Alinsky also remembers Capone showing up at Chicago ball games and being cheered by hundreds of people. Here was the ultimate bad guy—Lucifer, one might say—but Lucifer certainly had his admirers. Capone was known to be a thug—he didn't even pretend to be a good guy—yet in Depression-era Chicago, he was also a hero for flouting laws that most Americans agreed were foolish and unrealistic. In one sense Capone was an extortionist, a shakedown man, but he was also providing services—gambling, alcohol, and prostitution—that were illegal but for which there was a definite demand. Alinsky even likens

Capone to a "public utility." No wonder Capone had a constituency and a devoted following. Seeing all this, and getting himself a taste of the fruits of mob high life, Alinsky not surprisingly resolved to become a professional shakedown artist himself.

To see how mafia shakedowns work, we might recall Don Fanucci from Mario Puzo's *The Godfather*. This local mafia chief is described in the novel as "a heavy-set, fierce-looking Italian who wore expensive light-colored suits and a cream-colored fedora." Fanucci was known as the Black Hand. This was the part of the mafia that extorted money from storekeepers and from successful individuals and families. Puzo stresses that since many of the Italian immigrants of the early twentieth century were violent themselves, extortion could not work through simple threats of violence. Rather, Fanucci and other successful extortionists had to be choosy about their victims, and also smart in the way that they got money from them.

Fanucci, for example, usually picked on elderly couples without male children to defend them. He scavenged off other criminals, such as those who sold lottery tickets or ran gambling operations in their homes. Mostly he got his money from small storekeepers, extracting a price they figured was easier to pay than it would be to risk what Fanucci might do to them. Every now and then Fanucci showed what it meant to cross him. In one case, a group of men resisted Fanucci and one of them slashed his throat with a knife. Fanucci shot the assailant and killed him, whereupon the others paid up and made their peace with Fanucci.

We meet Fanucci in the novel because he intends to collect from Vito Corleone and his two friends Tessio and Clemenza after the three of them have pulled off some petty robberies. Fanucci approaches Corleone almost gently. "Ah young fellow," he says. "People tell me you're rich. But don't you think you've treated me a little shabbily? After all, this is my neighborhood and you should let me wet my beak." Corleone did not answer. Then Fanucci smiled and unbuttoned his jacket to show the gun he had tucked away in the waistband of his trousers. Then he moderated his demands. "Give me five hundred dollars and

I'll forget the insult." [10] Fanucci was merely doing what he had found to work. Most people paid his ransom; they figured it was better than tangling with Fanucci.

There was only one problem with Alinsky's career goal to emulate criminals like Capone and Fanucci in their shakedown schemes: mob shakedown men sometimes get knocked off. Even in *The Godfather*, Fanucci tries to shake down Vito Corleone and his two accomplices and gets murdered. Alinsky wanted to figure out how to emulate the mob's shakedown operations without getting killed. He said to himself, "Here I am, a smart son of a bitch, I graduated cum laude and all that sh*t." He knew he could figure a way. "And then," he says, "it came to me, that little light bulb lit over my head."

Basically Alinsky realized that the answer was politics. In politics, you can steal from people without getting knocked off. In politics, there is such a thing as legal theft. What better way than this to wet your beak? So Alinsky moved on to politics, yet he patterned his political operations on what he had learned from the Capone gang. In a very revealing quotation, Alinsky told *Playboy*, "I learned a hell of a lot about the uses and abuses of power from the mob, lessons that stood me in good stead later on, when I was organizing." [11]

For Alinsky, politics is the art of intimidation from the outside. This is basically what a community organizer does. Alinsky himself explains. A community organizer must first identify the target, which may be a local business, a national retail chain, a public school system, even the mayor's office. The target must have resources, or money, or jobs to hand out. Extracting those benefits without working for them now becomes the organizer's mission.

Power, Alinsky writes, never gives in without a fight. The only way to get stuff from the people who have it is to make it easier for them to give it to you than to fight you. "Very often the mere threat," Alinsky says, "is enough to bring the enemy to its knees." Getting the target to the point of submission—forcing it to pay up—is the supreme challenge of a political organizer.

Before attempting the extortion, the organizer must recruit allies.

In Alinsky's words, "To f*ck your enemies, you've first got to seduce your allies." These allies may be unions, disgruntled workers, sixties leftists, activist clergy, homeless bums, inner-city gang members, professional malcontents, anyone you can get. In Chicago, working the Back of the Yards area near the city's stockyards, Alinsky was able to find powerful allies in the Catholic Church. While the church in that city was politically liberal, Alinsky knew that many priests wanted to stay away from the kind of hardball extortionist politics that he had in mind. He decided that he could not bring them into his fold with an appeal to Christian charity.

Alinsky explains: "Suppose I walked into the office of the average leader of any denomination and said, 'Look, I'm asking you to live up to your Christian principles, to make Jesus' words about brotherhood and social justice realities.' What do you think would happen? He'd shake my hand warmly and say, 'God bless you, my son,' and after I was gone he'd tell his secretary, 'If that crackpot comes around again, tell him I'm out.'

"So in order to involve the Catholic priests, I didn't give them any stuff about Christian ethics, I just appealed to their self-interest." Basically Alinsky told them that if they backed him he would make sure that more money flowed in their direction, and this meant government grants for the church and personal donations for the collection plate. "Now I'm talking their language," Alinsky crowed, "and we can sit down and hammer out a deal. That's what happened in Back of the Yards and within a few months the overwhelming majority of the parish priests were backing us, and we were holding our organizational meetings in their churches."

While the church helped Alinsky in Chicago, he realized that on the national scale the biggest challenge was to recruit and radicalize members of the white middle class. This, he frequently said, was the largest and most powerful group in the country. Consequently it could apply strong political pressure to extract benefits both from government and from corporations. At the time Richard Nixon was courting the white middle class, and many people considered that group to be politically conservative. But Alinsky felt confident that he could make headway with it.

Of the white middle class, he said, "Right now they're frozen, festering in apathy, living what Thoreau called lives of quiet desperation. They've worked all their lives to get their own little house in the suburbs, their color TV, their two cars and now the good life seems to have turned to ashes in their mouths. Their personal lives are generally unfulfilling, their jobs unsatisfying, they've succumbed to tranquilizers and pep pills, they drown their anxieties in alcohol, they feel trapped in long-term endurance marriages, or escape into guilt-ridden divorces. They're losing their kids and they're losing their dreams. They're alienated, depersonalized, without any feeling of participation in the political process, and they feel rejected and hopeless. Their society appears to be crumbling, and they see themselves as no more than small failures within the larger failure. All their old values seem to have deserted them, leaving them rudderless in a sea of social chaos. Believe me, this is good organizational material."

The way you win recruits from this group, Alinsky writes, is not by solving these people's problems but by aggravating them. In Alinsky's words, "The despair is there; now it's up to us to go in and rub raw the sores of discontent." This is done by directing people's frustration not against government but against business. "We'll show the middle class their real enemies: the corporate power elite that runs and ruins this country."[12] What has this corporate power elite done that is so reprehensible? For Alinsky, this is the wrong question. The real question is a very simple one: who has the money?

For Alinsky, morality is a scam. Morality is the cloak of power. Activists appeal to the language of morality but recognize that it is a mere disguise. As Alinsky puts it, "Ethical standards must be elastic to stretch with the times. . . . In action, one does not always enjoy the luxury of a decision that is consistent with one's individual conscience. . . . You do what you can with what you have, and then clothe it with moral garments."[13]

In his book *Reveille for Radicals*, Alinsky takes up the fashionable liberal cause of "reconciliation." He proclaims the very idea totally un-realistic, "an illusion of the world as we would like it to be." In the real world, Alinsky says, "Reconciliation means that one side has the power and the other side gets reconciled to it."[14] Alinsky was determined to have the power on his side, so that his opponents would become recon-ciled to being shaken down by him.

Alinsky's contempt for traditional morality can also be seen in the figure to whom he dedicated his book *Rules for Radicals*. That figure is the devil. Alinsky calls Lucifer "the first radical known to man who re-belled against the establishment and did it so effectively that he at least won his own kingdom." He goes on to say, "If there's an afterlife, and I have anything to say about it, I will unreservedly go to hell. Hell would be heaven for me."[15] Progressives detest the comparison between Alin-sky and Lucifer, because they know it makes him look bad, but we can see here that Alinsky, in taking his hat off to the devil, wasn't simply joking. On the contrary, it is safe to say that a man who wrote two books on radicals—*Reveille for Radicals* and *Rules for Radicals*—would have a lot to learn from the "first radical."

Rules for Radicals contains several Luciferian principles strewn throughout, such as "Life is a corrupting process from the time a child learns to play his mother off against his father; he who fears corrup-tion fears life." On another occasion, Alinsky admiringly cites Lenin. "Lenin was a pragmatist," he writes. "When he returned to what was then Petrograd from exile, he said that the Bolsheviks stood for get-ting power through the ballot but would reconsider after they got the guns."[16]

What Alinsky meant by this is that activists should invoke prin-ciples like free speech and equality under the law in order to protect themselves, but once they come to power they can ignore those princi-ples and not extend them to their opponents. Modern progressives in the Alinsky mode seem to have taken this lesson to heart.

While Alinsky attempted to direct middle-class frustration against private corporations, he was not above targeting the government for his shakedown schemes. He gleefully described the way he forced Chicago mayor Richard J. Daley to give in to some of his extortionist demands to increase minority hiring through Alinsky's own activist network. Daley was a very powerful man who regarded Chicago as his personal domain. In this, Alinsky found Daley's Achilles' heel. Daley was especially proud of the efficiency of Chicago's O'Hare Airport. Now in those days, before 9/11, anyone could go through security and enter the main airport. Alinsky's scheme involved deploying several hundred activists to completely immobilize all the airport's restroom facilities. He knew that passengers usually wait to get off the plane before heading for the bathroom.

Alinsky's idea was to have activists take up every stall, armed with, as he put it, "box lunches and reading material to help pass the time." Male activists would be positioned at every urinal, with other activists waiting to replace them as they finished their business and moved to another men's restroom. "What were desperate passengers going to do?" Alinsky said. "Is some poor sap at the end of the line going to say, 'Hey pal, you're taking too long to piss?' "

Alinsky was confident that his "sh*t-in," as he called it, would completely paralyze the airport. "O'Hare would become a shambles." Alinsky didn't even have to carry out the scheme: he leaked it to the press, and Daley caved. The city agreed to increase its hiring and to use Alinsky's network to provide the new recruits. On another occasion, Alinsky got Daley to give in to another shakedown—this one involving government contracts and jobs funneled throughout Alinskyite organizations—through a rat deployment strategy, and once again, he didn't actually need to carry it out. "We threatened to unload a thousand live rats on the steps of city hall. Daley got the message, and we got what we wanted."

Alinsky didn't mind that these tactics seemed absurdist or puerile, as long as they worked. Horwitt describes an occasion in the spring of 1972 when Alinsky organized a student protest at Tulane University's annual lecture week. A group of anti–Vietnam War protesters wanted to disrupt a scheduled speech by George H. W. Bush, then U.S. representative to the United Nations, and an advocate for President Nixon's Vietnam policies. While the students planned to picket the speech and shout antiwar slogans, Alinsky told them that their approach was wrong because it might get them punished or expelled. Besides, it lacked creativity and imagination. Alinsky advised the students to go hear the speech dressed up as members of the Ku Klux Klan—complete with robes and hoods—and whenever Bush said anything in defense of the Vietnam War, they should cheer and holler and wave signs and banners saying: "The KKK Supports Bush." This is what the students did, and it proved very successful, getting lots of media attention with no adverse repercussions for the protesters.[17]

On another occasion, Alinsky targeted government welfare agencies that in his view were trying to administer programs themselves rather than funnel the money through Alinskyite organizations. Alinsky framed this as an issue of the government deciding for itself what poor people need, rather than trusting the poor to run their own lives. In reality of course, Alinsky wanted himself—rather than government bureaucrats—to allocate the money. In order to pressure the government to change its approach, however, Alinsky urged black activists to dress in African tribal costumes and greet government officials flying into Chicago from Washington, D.C. This action, he said, would dramatize the "colonial mentality" of the antipoverty establishment. I learned about this particular Alinsky caper from Hillary Clinton's Wellesley College thesis.[18]

Alinsky met with tactical success, not only in tackling government agencies and government representatives, but also in shaking down the private sector. In Rochester, New York—at that time a company town, home of Eastman Kodak—Alinsky organized a campaign called FIGHT and attempted some stunts at the corporate headquarters, but they didn't work. Ostensibly Alinsky was asking that Kodak hire more blacks, but company president Louis Eilers detected a larger agenda. "It is more and more clear," he said, "that all the talk about unemployment is only an issue or device being used to screen what FIGHT is really doing—and that is making a drive for power in the community."[19]

Eilers was onto Alinsky. But Alinsky was not done with Eastman

Kodak. He realized that the city and Kodak took great pride in the Rochester Philharmonic Orchestra, which the company helped to fund and on whose board top officials of the company sat. Alinsky organized a group of a hundred blacks to attend concert performances. Before the performances, he planned a "pre-show banquet consisting of nothing but huge portions of baked beans." The plan was basically to have an organized "fart-in." Alinsky found that his activists were excited to participate. "What oppressed person doesn't want, literally or figuratively, to sh*t on his oppressors?"

But this wasn't just for the psychological benefit of the participants; it was also to force the establishment to back down. Alinsky explains, "First of all, the fart-in would be completely outside the city fathers' experience. Never in their wildest dreams could they envision a flatulent blitzkrieg on their sacred symphony orchestra. It would throw them into complete disarray. Second, the action would make a mockery of the law, because although you could be arrested for throwing a stink bomb, there's no law on the books against natural bodily functions. Can you imagine a guy being tried in court on charges of first-degree farting? The cops would be paralyzed." With tactics like these, Alinsky brought Eastman Kodak to the negotiating table, and he got most of his demands met. These demands included the hiring of Alinsky cronies and also the steering of city contracts through Alinsky's activist network.

On another occasion, Alinsky was working in his home base of Chicago to force Chicago's department stores to give jobs to black activists who were Alinsky's cronies. On this issue of course Alinsky was competing—or working in tandem, however we choose to view it—with Chicago's number-one racial shakedown man, Jesse Jackson. Jackson mastered a simple strategy of converting race into a protection racket. He would offer to "protect" Chicago businesses from accusations of racism—accusations that the businesses knew were actually fomented by Jackson himself. The businesses would then pay Jackson to make the trouble go away, and to chase away other potential troublemakers.

In return for his efforts, Jackson would typically receive hundreds of thousands in annual donations from the company, plus jobs and minority contracts that would go through his network, and finally other goodies such as free flights on the corporate airplane, supposedly for his "charitable work." Later Jackson would go national with this blackmail approach. In New York, for example, Jackson opened an office on Wall Street where he extracted millions of dollars in money and patronage from several leading investment houses, including Goldman Sachs, Citigroup, Credit Suisse, First Boston, Morgan Stanley, Paine Webber, and Prudential Securities.

On the national stage, Jackson was joined by another race hustler, Al Sharpton. For two decades these shakedown men in clerical garb successfully prosecuted their hustles. Jackson was the leader at first, but eventually Sharpton proved more successful than Jackson. While Jackson's star has faded, Sharpton is currently President Obama's chief adviser on race issues.

While Jackson used the blackmail threat of alleging racism or backing race discrimination suits to extract money from corporations, Alinsky had his own distinctive strategy. "One of the largest stores in the city and in the country," Alinsky recounts, "refused to alter its hiring practices and wouldn't even meet with us." So Alinsky figured out how to teach them a lesson. He lined up several hundred blacks from the inner city to swamp the store. "Every Saturday, the biggest shopping day of the week we decided to charter buses and bring approximately 3,000 blacks from Woodlawn to this downtown store. Now you put 3,000 blacks on the floor of a store, even a store this big, and the color of the store suddenly changes. Any white coming through the revolving doors will suddenly think he's in Africa. So they'd lose a lot of their white trade right then and there.

"But that is only the beginning. At every counter you'd have groups of blacks closely scrutinizing the merchandise and asking the salesgirl interminable questions. And needless to say, none of our people would buy a single item of merchandise. You'd have a situation where one group would tie up the shirt counter and move on to the underwear counter, while the group previously occupying the underwear counter would take over the shirt department. This procedure would be followed until one hour before closing time, when our people would begin buying everything in sight to be delivered COD. This would tie up delivery service for a minimum of two days, with additional heavy costs and administrative problems, since all the merchandise would be refused upon delivery."

Once Alinsky had his plan, he said, "We leaked it to one of the stool pigeons every radical organization needs and the result was immediate. The day after we paid the deposit for the chartered buses, the department store management called us and gave in to all our demands. We'd won completely." This was Alinsky transcending Don Fanucci and acting in true Godfather style. In the vocabulary of Don Corleone himself, Alinsky had made them an offer they couldn't refuse!

And when other retail establishments learned of his techniques, they surrendered in advance because they didn't want to risk the kind of mayhem that they knew Alinsky could cause. "We didn't win in Woodlawn because the establishment suddenly experienced a moral revelation," Alinsky said. "We won because we backed them into a corner and kept them there until they decided it would be less expensive and less dangerous to surrender to our demands than to continue the fight."

For Alinsky, this was not a matter of coercion. Rather, it was "popular pressure in the democratic tradition. People don't get opportunity or freedom or equality or dignity as an act of charity; they have to fight for it, force it out of the establishment. That's where you need organization—first to compel concessions and then to make sure the other side delivers. No issue can be negotiated unless you first have the clout to compel negotiation."[20] One can see here that for Alinsky, democratic politics is basically a mechanism of legal extortion, justified by appeals to justice and equality.

Alinsky profited handsomely from his rackets. Even Hillary Clinton notes in her thesis that while Alinsky spoke endlessly about poverty and disadvantage, he himself lived very comfortably, far removed from the people on whose behalf he allegedly fought.[21] It was part of Alinsky's shtick and they both knew it. Toward the end of his life, Alinsky moved to Carmel, California. By this time Alinsky was a millionaire. He enjoyed dining in Carmel's exclusive restaurants and taking walks on the white-sand beach. In fact, it was in ritzy Carmel that Alinsky died of a heart attack in 1972. His biographer Sanford Horwitt portrays this as a paradox. "This is not the way Saul would have preferred it, not the ending he would have written, not such a prosaic death. And in Carmel of all places! That postcard-perfect oasis where not a speck of the world's troubles was to be found on the soft, white beaches caressed each day by gentle Pacific waters."[22]

Actually, I agree that if Alinsky had his way he would have concocted some fantastic report about how he was gunned down by his dangerous enemies, while in the pursuit of social justice. But in reality Alinsky would have known that it was all a big lie. In reality there was nothing inappropriate about Alinsky dropping dead in affluent Carmel. That's the whole point of being a thief, to get rich.

Would Don Corleone have been in the least bit embarrassed to live in a mansion by the sea? Horwitt may have his own blinders on, but Alinsky had no illusions that at his core he was some social justice guy; he was a guy who used social justice as part of his business plan. Alinsky understood, as have mafia dons both in the movies and in real life, that crime is a business whose objective is to bring a life of cool winds and white beaches to the top criminal.

Personally, I wish Alinsky had ended up like Henry Hill. At the end of *Goodfellas*, Hill has lost the high life, and he is in the witness protection program. "Today everything is different," he says. "I have to wait around like everyone else." Hill, in other words, is forced to become a normal person again. Alinsky, however, lived like a racketeer and died like one.

Still, Alinsky's own take was comparatively small. The reason is that throughout his life, Alinsky remained, as he put it, an "outside agitator." He firmly believed that activists should not become part of the government. Yet ironically, Alinsky became the mentor to two fig-ures, Barack Obama and Hillary Clinton, who would learn from his techniques and then take them into the innermost corridors of power. Their expertise would not be as outside agitators but as inside power brokers. If Alinsky had survived, he could have taken justified pride for his role in being their guiding star, their Godfather. To a considerable degree, he was the one who taught them how to steal America.

Chapter 10

BARACK AND HILLARY:

The Education of Two Con Artists

All the criminals do their work on the screen, which people can see. Politicians work behind the screen, which the public can't see.[1]

—Gang leader Chotta Shakeel, in
Suketu Mehta, *Maximum City*

It's one thing to pull off a con from outside the government; it's quite another to turn the government itself into a con operation. Cons are not new to American government. At the local level, Tammany Hall was a racket. The Daley machine in Chicago was a racket. Other cities have had equivalent rackets. And even at the national level, we have seen how government cons its citizens through shakedown schemes that are sold through false advertising and false promises.

Social Security, for instance, is marketed as a program to enable people to save for their own retirement. People put money into the program while they work, and collect benefits when they retire. One might imagine that each American has a Social Security account in his name, in which his savings accumulate, and then he has access to that account at retirement age.

Sounds reasonable, right? It is reasonable. Yet this is not what Social Security is. This is not how it was designed. Rather, Social Security is a scheme in which working Americans put in money that is paid out now to older Americans, so that the system has no accumulated funds to provide for the retirement of the people who are currently paying into it. The government's obligation to future retirees is called an "unfunded liability." Between Social Security, Medicare, and federal pensions, our government has around $100 trillion in unfunded liabilities.

President Franklin Roosevelt designed Social Security in such a way—he boasted—that no future politician could undo it. In effect, the whole program is a Ponzi scheme. Charles Ponzi was an Italian who came to the United States in the early twentieth century. In 1920, he caused a sensation by starting a new type of investment company. He raised money from investors promising to pay them exorbitant returns. Some of his bonds pledged 50 percent interest payable every three months; others promised to double your money in six months. His promises attracted hordes of new investors, and he would pay the old investors their interest out of the funds put in by the new ones. But he had no money to pay those new investors. He simply accumulated his "unfunded liabilities." Ultimately the racket was exposed and Ponzi was arrested. He served prison time and was eventually deported back to Italy.[2]

Social Security is based on the Ponzi principle. It pays existing retirees out of the seed corn from existing workers. It does not have the money to pay those existing workers. When the time comes, it will figure out what to do with them. Millions of Americans are paying into a fund not because they want to but because they have to. They are doing so in the expectation that their government will eventually provide for them—that government has an obligation to look after them when they need it. Little do they realize that government has no such obligation. Promises, after all, are only promises.

Why design a program this way? The answer is that it advances the purpose of progressive government, which is to establish an empire of control over the lives of the citizens. Progressive government seeks to make citizens dependent on the state, and then to ensure that progressives are elected to run the state. Social Security advances both objectives.

Ponzi went to prison, but FDR is absurdly lionized. And FDR's prediction proved correct. Progressives run for office as the champions of Social Security. Progressives viciously attack any politician who exposes the financial irresponsibility or speaks out against the Ponzi scheme as being "against Social Security" and "against seniors." The Ponzi scheme becomes more precarious each year, but it's still going on.

Hillary Clinton attempted another con in the early 1990s, but it failed. Barack Obama finally pulled it off, in a slightly different form. The con is called Obamacare. As with Social Security, the health care law was offered in response to a genuine problem—actually two genuine problems. What were the genuine problems? They were, first, that health care costs too much in America, and second, that several million Americans who wanted health insurance could not afford it. Clearly these were two aspects of the same problem, because health insurance premiums were unaffordable to many because they had risen in tandem with rising health care costs.

So why does American health care cost so much? The main reason is that the person receiving the service is not the one paying for the service. Imagine if you could go to Safeway or Giant, fill your cart with food, and then have *someone else* pay for it. Obviously you would get all kinds of stuff you don't really need. Obviously the food chain would charge whatever it felt like, and you wouldn't care, because you would not be the one paying.

Now imagine further that the third party paying for the food was itself relatively indifferent to what it was charged. It raised its money through premiums paid for by millions of customers, and it could simply pass the cost to those customers in the form of higher premiums. This would be a scenario virtually set up to ensure runaway food costs. We don't have it for food, but we do have it for health care.

The good news is that this problem has an obvious solution. The solution is to redesign the system in such a way that the person who receives the service pays for the service. This would ensure that there is real bargaining and real competition. That alone would dramatically lower costs. Government could help those who still couldn't afford insurance—it could provide, for example, catastrophic insurance to people below the poverty line. Catastrophic coverage costs a lot less than full medical coverage because catastrophic events are relatively rare. So this would be a modest program with a relatively modest price tag, utterly different than what Hillary wanted and what Obama eventually got.

Obamacare is a program designed to shift control of the health care industry from the private sector to the public sector, from doctors, hospitals, and insurance companies to the federal government. The program was sold by Obama feigning outrage over insurance companies refusing to grant insurance to people with "preexisting conditions." But this is the same as an insurance company not granting fire insurance to a guy whose house has already burned down. The whole point of insurance is to share the risk before the catastrophe occurs, not to have a catastrophe and then get other people to pay for your losses.

Having castigated the insurance companies to gain public support, Obama then turned to the insurance companies to get their support for Obamacare. This might seem like an uphill, if not impossible, task. Yet Obama pulled it off. He managed to get many corporations and most insurance companies to support his health care plan and even to pay for ads promoting it.

Why would corporations and insurance companies do that? Why would they support the man who publicly excoriated them, and consent to a health care takeover scheme by the government? In the case of corporations, Obama assured them that the law would enable them to drop employees from their health care coverage so that those people would then be forced to sign up for the Obamacare health exchange.

Obama also informed the insurance companies that a big part of the law was to force Americans who didn't want to buy health insurance to do so. In other words, Obamacare guaranteed the insurance companies millions of new customers! Obama also assured the insurance industry that by giving millions of other people the right to free insurance, the federal government would be on the hook to pay for all those premiums. Insurance companies would give up some control to the state, but in exchange they would get bigger profits that would be, in effect, guaranteed by the state. Corporations could reduce their health care costs by dumping workers and turning over their health care problems to the state. It was a worthwhile deal for these profit-making entities. That's why they lined up behind Obamacare.

The insurance companies recognized, of course, that Obamacare was a rip-off. But they also knew the target of the rip-off wasn't them. It was the American taxpayer. Obamacare was a scheme to extract more money from the taxpayer through a combination of higher taxes and mandates. Basically the ordinary American would pay more for health care and get less in return.

This rip-off relied on a series of blatant lies. "If you like your health care plan, you can keep your plan." "If you like your doctor, you can keep your doctor." "The average family will save more than $2,400 per year." "Health care costs will decline." "Health care premiums will go down." "Everyone in this country will now have health insurance." Even though Obama kept saying these things, none of them was true. These statements were simply part of the con man's "pitch."

For progressives, Obamacare was a prize. The prize was control of the huge American health care system, representing virtually one-sixth of the whole economy. Obamacare put progressives in charge of more than 10 million doctors, dentists, pharmacists, nurses, and technicians and support staff. Obamacare gave progressives control of more than five thousand hospitals and almost a million hospital beds. The system included hospitals and also drug companies, insurance companies, and the producers of hospital equipment, not to mention research and educational institutions. Obamacare was a heist with a very big payoff.

A heist like this is not easy to pull off; it requires extensive theft education. This chapter is about the education of two Alinskyite con artists, both of whom studied the Godfather's techniques. The first one happens to be the president of the United States, and the second one an aspiring president of the United States. Is it possible we will have two thieves in a row as custodians of the U.S. Treasury? Unlikely though it seems, this may be the case, and the two, who despise each other, are nevertheless working together to achieve common goals. In other words, we have a situation of two Alinsky acolytes attempting to set up a con man's regime. Here we explore how they met their Godfather, what they learned from him, and what distinctive elements they themselves brought to the con man's trade.

Con men abound in my confinement center, and the younger ones quickly attach themselves to mentors. A young black guy, Flip, was undoubtedly the most charismatic guy in the confinement center. He was extremely tall, around six feet six inches, and usually dressed in sports attire, as if he was getting ready to play basketball. In a society where guys pull their pants down to reveal their underpants, Flip had his pants pulled almost down to his knees! He also wore legible underpants—underpants with all kinds of writing—and I found it interesting to try to read what messages they conveyed.

Flip went around telling everyone who would listen that he was a basketball star who averaged "twenty-eight baskets and fourteen rebounds." He showed little respect for the confinement center staff, frequently taunting them with lines like, "I got a thing for you, Miss Chavez" and "Hey, hurry up and check me in, homie, I gotta make a doo-doo." He complained relentlessly about the place, and on one occasion, in a fit of rage, he tried to rip a thermostat out of the wall because he wasn't able to adjust the temperature.

Flip hated the food in confinement, contrasting it unfavorably with what he ate in prison. "This food is like sh*t, man. At Taft, I ate better than I do at home. I had Stromboli. I had meat loaf. One time they had banana bread. I ate the best carrot cake I ever tasted. In the commissary they got carnitas, they got avocados, they got peaches." Flip insisted, "If I couldn't get out of this hellhole during the day, I'd ask to go back to prison." Flip portrayed himself as a real ladies' man, seducing women of all races and ages whenever he was let loose.

Flip was a young scammer who was into everything: petty burglary, car theft, growing and selling marijuana, even a little male prostitution. He developed a strange, fascinating relationship with the oldest guy in the confinement center, Hickey. While Flip was in his late teens or early twenties, Hickey was around seventy-five. He wore the same clothes every day—brown pants, brown shirt, very thin belt, black leather shoes—and walked with a limp. Hickey was almost bald and wore glasses with distinctive frames—the frames had mirrors along the sides, so that you could see yourself in them. Hickey was an institution man if there ever was one. He had been in prison most of his life. Hickey was an old con artist, a confidence man, who had done it all, from counterfeit money to real estate scams to selling "vitamins" that had no nutritional value.

The rumor was that Hickey had killed someone, way back in the early 1970s, and done a long sentence. I wasn't scared of him; no one was; clearly now he posed no threat to anyone. Indeed his sole mode of violence these days is his rhetoric. Hickey's specialty is to bark epithets at other guys from his bunk, when everyone is trying to sleep.

"You young bucks are making too much noise!" yells Hickey, making the most noise of all. "This isn't the jungle, remember? An old man is trying to sleep!"

From which a chorus of insults comes back at him—"Shut the f*ck up, old man!"—and he responds heartily, "I ain't shutting up, you m*therf*ckers!" I put on my earphones. Eventually the racket subsides and everyone dozes off.

Flip and Hickey, I noticed, became inseparable right away. They ate together, did weights together, and played dominoes every evening. Even so, the relationship between Flip and Hickey was not entirely harmonious. The following exchange, which I noted from a recent dominoes game, could be heard by the entire top-floor dormitory. It was punctuated by the crashing sound of dice being slammed on the table.

Flip: It's game time, sh*tface!

Hickey: Leave the winning to me. You just remember to wash your ugly ass every now and then.

Flip: F*ck you, old man! You are going to die soon! Good riddance, you stupid piece of sh*t!

Hickey: Goat-smelling ignorant m*therf*cker! Somebody raped your mama and got you! What a dumdum!

Flip: This ain't over, homie! I'm going to kick your ass so badly you won't be limping no more. You going to be in a wheelchair.

Hickey: Count my money, n*gger. And you can eat *this* while you at it.

Flip: Somebody bring a wheelchair for this old m*therf*cker.

Hickey: Lowlife African, even the monkeys climb the trees when they see you.

Certainly I found this dialogue of anthropological interest, both in terms of the vocabulary and the underlying concepts. But at first I didn't know its purpose. In the subsequent weeks, I realized: this is a surrogate father-son relationship. Through the peculiar argot of insults, Flip had found in Hickey an older guy who knew the system and could initiate him in its labyrinthine methods. Flip didn't just want to survive; he wanted to thrive, both on the inside and on the outside. He thought that maybe Hickey could help him do that.

Over time I saw that Hickey was actually Flip's hero. The young con artist was actually modeling himself on the old con artist, even to the extent of developing a slight limp himself. And while I doubted that Flip could actually write a book, if he could I would not be entirely surprised if he wrote one called *Dreams from My Father.*

At first glance, comparing the president of the United States, Barack Obama Jr., with a part-time prostitute and street hustler like Flip may seem, well, a bit flippant. How can I liken the relationship between Barack Jr. and his father, Barack Sr., to the relationship between two foul-mouthed cons?

A good deal of the scholarly writing on Obama might make this seem implausible. In fact, my own previous work on Obama makes the analogy seem strained. But during that research I missed an angle about Obama that is needed to complete our understanding. Once we fill in those blanks here, we'll see that the two Obamas are not so distant from Flip and Hickey.

In my two previous books on Obama, I stressed his affinity with his dad, how he absorbed the dreams of his father. This wasn't some bizarre theory I made up; I got it directly from Obama's own autobiography, *Dreams from My Father*, which conveys its main thesis in the title. I previously argued that while Obama saw that his dad was a failure, and refused to emulate his personality, he nevertheless embraced his Kenyan father's anticolonial ideology. Consequently Obama has sought to diminish America's wealth and power out of a moral commitment to global redistribution. My thesis was that Obama wants America to go down so that other countries can come up.

As an immigrant, I found this despicable, even abominable. I refused to believe that the American people, even Democrats, signed up for this. And over his two terms Obama has shown himself consistent in pursuing these objectives. My predictions about Obama have all come true.

Even so, I now see that I got an important part of my Obama story wrong. Obama's relationship to his dad was not one of ideological emulation; it was also one of the junior scam artist following the trail of the senior artist.

Obama came to admire his father from a very young age. At that point he was naïve: he aspired to become just like dad, a lion of a man, a figure of history. When Obama became a young adult, however, he discovered his father was no lion of a man, no figure of history. Rather, he was a petty con man. His cons involved an unending series of poses, impostures, and lies to make himself into something he was not, for the purpose of getting to America, or getting others to pay his bills, or seducing women, or advancing in his career, or attracting social admiration and prestige for things he had not done. While Barack Obama Sr. had some early successes in pulling off his scams, eventually they came crashing down on him, and he died a bitter, broken man.

Obama now realized that his father was a *failed* con man. Yet this did not cause Obama to give up on his childhood dreams. Obama still aspired to follow in his father's path. He decided to become a con man himself. And part of this involved embracing the con man's pitch, which was anticolonialism. This pitch was marketed as a "dream." In fact, it was less a dream than a scheme.

From the outset of his career, young Obama put that scheme to work. He knew, however, that he would have to redesign his father's con. He had no intention of being a petty con man. He wasn't going to do this for bigamy, social exhibitionism, or free drinks; he set his sights on the summits of wealth and power. Moreover, he was determined that while his father had failed, he would succeed. And one must admit that he has.

Obama was first exposed to the scams of his father when Barack Sr. visited his son in Hawaii. Obama was ten years old. Already he was quite the little con artist. "I explained to a group of boys that my father was a prince. 'My grandfather, see, he's a chief. It's sort of like the king of the tribe, you know . . . like the Indians. So that makes my father a prince. He'll take over when my grandfather dies.'" When the boys asked him if he were next in line, Obama Jr. responded, "'Well . . . if I want to, I could. It's sort of complicated, see, 'cause the tribe is full of warriors. Like Obama. . . . the name means Burning Spear. The men in our tribe all want to be chief, so my father has to settle these feuds before I can come.'"

But this was youthful braggadocio. Obama was actually worried that his father would embarrass him. He had images of poverty and primitivism and mud huts in his mind. So when his teacher invited his father to speak at school, Obama was filled with dread. "I spent that night and all of the next day trying to suppress thoughts of the inevitable: the faces of my classmates when they heard about mud huts, all my lies exposed, the painful jokes afterward. Each time I remembered, my body squirmed as if it had received a jolt to the nerves."

Yet Barack Sr. wowed the teacher and the class by arriving in spectacular African robes and regaling the group with fables of the Luo tribe, punctuated with a fantastic story of how as a young boy he had to kill a lion to prove his manhood. "When he finished," Obama Jr. wrote, "Miss Hefty was absolutely beaming with pride. All my classmates applauded heartily. . . . The bell rang for lunch, and Mr. Eldredge came up to me, 'You've got a pretty impressive father.' The ruddy faced boy who had asked about cannibalism said, 'Your dad is pretty cool.' " Young Obama was blown away, and right then, right there, he resolved to become like the great one. He had witnessed the lion slayer, and he wanted himself to learn the secret to Barack Sr.'s power.[3]

In fact, Barack Sr. was no lion slayer; he was actually a lion-size prevaricator. We see this pattern by briefly following his career. He said he came to America on the great airlift that brought promising African students to study here through an effort pioneered by President Kennedy. Proving himself to be his father's son, Obama Jr. repeated that fable when he was running for president. In fact, as the son knew, the father had taken the competitive examination for the airlift and failed. He needed a first-division score and he got only a third-division score.

Robert Stephens, the cultural affairs officer at the U.S. Information Service, interviewed Barack Sr. and remembers he tried to lie about his performance. "He really prevaricated about his school record," Stephens said. "He was a very good talker and tried to talk me out of it, but there was nothing I could do. He just did not have the grades."[4] Barack Sr. was rejected for the airlift.

Then Barack Sr. set about getting to America by an alternative route. He spent months charming two American missionary women, Helen Roberts and Elizabeth Mooney, to help him secure admission at an American university and to help him pay for his education. Mooney, who was unmarried at the time, was entranced by the young African, especially after he showed a personal interest in her and frequently took her dancing. She wrote him a letter of recommendation to several American colleges, and later, when he was admitted to the University of Hawaii, contributed a substantial fraction of her salary to cover Barack Sr.'s first-year expenses. Later Barack Sr. would try again to extract money out of her, but by this time she was married with stepchildren and was unable to help.

Barack Sr.'s own marital history was checkered, and also a testament to his con man skills. He had married a woman named Kezia in Kenya and left his family for America when she had borne him a child, with another on the way. Shortly after enrolling in school, Barack Sr. seduced a white teenage woman, Stanley Ann Dunham. He told her nothing about his family in Kenya. Soon he impregnated her, and Barack Jr. was conceived. At this point, Barack Sr. convinced Stanley Ann to marry him. His marriage to this American wife made Barack Sr. a bigamist, since he was now married to two women at the same time.

For him, however, it was no big deal. In fact, at one point he even conned Stanley Ann into believing that he was obligated under Luo tradition to take other wives in Kenya and have children by them, or else he would lose his position in the tribe. Only later, she found out that was untrue. Theirs was in any case an abbreviated courtship; indeed, Barack Sr. abandoned his wife even before Barack Jr. was born.

Then Barack Sr. got a scholarship to Harvard, where he told the authorities that he could manage financially because his wife had decided to put up their child, Barack Jr., for adoption. Once they bought his story, Barack Sr. settled in at Harvard and took up with yet another woman, Ruth Baker. By this time he was divorced from Stanley Ann but not from Kezia. He married Baker, and took her back with him to Africa, where he had a son by her, and where he also reunited with his first wife, Kezia, and had two more children with her.

Later in life Barack Sr.'s mobility was hampered because of his habit of drunk driving, which got him into several accidents, including one severe one in which both his legs had to be amputated and replaced by iron rods. This did not, however, undermine his courtship style, because he impregnated his fourth wife, Jael Otieno, in that condition, producing another child, named George. Altogether Barack Sr. had four wives—normally two at a time—and altogether he produced eight known children. Polygamy, he said, was customary for the Luo. But the Luo also customarily look after their wives and children. Barack Sr. did not. He mistreated all his wives and neglected all his children.

At Harvard, Barack Sr. got his nickname "Double Double" because he liked to order a double Scotch and tell the waiter, as soon as it was delivered, "Another double." He also became known for having others foot the bill, which they often did, because he was such a suave talker. Eventually, Harvard became suspicious of his falsifications and so did the U.S. Immigration and Naturalization Service. Harvard refused to renew his enrollment, and Barack Sr. was forced to return to Kenya.

Still, there as in America, he continued to tell his stories, which were amusing but utterly ridiculous. As one of his friends, Nyaringo Obure, later recalled, "One story he told over and over was about how when he was a boy he was looking after the family cattle. Suddenly a group of lions appeared and started to attack the cows. Barack pulls out a spear and kills the first lion by stabbing him in the chest. Then he goes for the rest, stab, stab, stab. Of course I knew it was a lie. Another time he said a buffalo attacked one of his relatives. Barack happened to be in the tree overhead and he dropped down on the buffalo's back and wrestled it to the ground. And so his stories went on and on."[5]

Barack Sr. frequently lied about his academic credentials not only to social acquaintances but also while applying for jobs. He said he was a Harvard graduate even though he had not completed his degree and had been effectively deported back to Kenya. He insisted on being called "Dr. Obama" even though he didn't have a Ph.D. He said he studied under Nobel laureate Kenneth Arrow even though Arrow did not arrive at Harvard until several years after Barack Sr. left there. In his work as an economist he would cite certain propositions as proved by his Ph.D. thesis, but when he was asked to substantiate his claims, he could not produce the document; he insisted that burglars had broken into his house and stolen it.

At first Barack Sr.'s lies paid off. He was given promising positions working as an economist in the government. During this time he cultivated a British accent and insisted that people call him "Bearick," not

"Barack." He also liked to correct other people's English and insisted that words be pronounced and spelled the British way. He expressed his dissatisfaction to hear bureaucrats speaking to each other in Swahili. He also wore silk suits, drove a green Mercedes, and employed house servants who bowed to him, Japanese-style, when he returned home. All of this may be considered the ego-satisfying rewards of scam artistry, comparable to how Henry Hill felt when he brought his girlfriend to the nightclub.

Alas for Barack Sr., the music soon died. Barack Sr. was eventually fired from every job he held, either due to his chronic drunkenness, irresponsibility in carrying out assignments, or pure deception. While his peers moved up in life, Barack Sr. moved down, being consigned eventually to make-work jobs. Even while his career was languishing and he held relatively low-level positions in government, Barack Sr. became known for impersonating important people so he could be treated as a celebrity. On one occasion, he attended a conference in Ghana where he pretended to be Z. T. Onyonka, the Kenyan minister for economic planning. When the real Onyonka showed up, the organizers thought *he* was the impostor. Needless to say, Onyonka was not amused and Barack Sr. was severely reprimanded.[6]

Eventually Obama found himself working for the Kenya Tourism Board, in a low-level post. Even there, he was discovered making unilateral decisions to award tourism contracts without getting proper approval, presumably to benefit people he knew or to get kickbacks. One board member, G. M. Matheka, said that before he joined the tourism board, when he worked in the tourism industry, he had met Obama, who was "posing as deputy general manager," a post that did not exist.[7] Once these deceptions piled up, the tourism board forced Obama to resign and, when he refused, fired him. In 1982, disgraced and virtually broke, Barack Sr. got drunk in a bar in Nairobi and drove his car into a tree, killing himself.

As a child Barack Jr. simply idolized his father, but in his midtwenties he visited Kenya and, through interactions with his relatives, realized that his father was not any of the things he had imagined him to be. This was a shocking revelation. "I felt as if my world had been turned on its head, as if I had woken up to find a blue sun in the yellow sky, or heard animals speaking like men," he wrote in *Dreams from My Father.* "To think that all my life I had been wrestling with nothing more than a ghost." [8]

But in Africa, Barack Jr. saw that Barack Sr.'s real talent had been as a poser and a fabricator, and that through a skein of lies and disguises he had managed to con various people over the years until the cons were finally exposed. Barack Jr. saw that lying and fakery were actually Barack Sr.'s talismanic secrets. He also figured out that these were precisely the skills he had inherited from his father.

Barack Sr. had huge con man aspirations. In an infamous article that he published in the *East Africa Journal* he proposed the idea of tax rates as high as 100 percent. "Theoretically," he said, "there is nothing that can stop the government from taxing 100 percent of income so long as the people get benefits from the government commensurate with their income which is taxed." [9] Barack Jr. seems to have resolved at that point to build on those skills, and also to attempt cons far beyond what his dad could have pulled off, or even imagined. Basically Obama Sr. envisioned confiscating the entire private earnings of the nation and putting it in the hands of the government, which would then be controlled by people like, well, him. Unfortunately this scheme came to nothing, but one can easily envision how it may have inspired his son. Perhaps where the father had failed, the son could succeed.

Back in America, Obama Jr. decided he needed high-level training to pull off his cons. The only place to get such training, he figured out, was Chicago. Obama had no ties to Chicago. He was raised in Hawaii and Indonesia and went to college in California, New York, and Massachusetts. Chicago, however, was the base of the political operative Saul Alinsky. By this time Alinsky was dead but his organization had built a formidable network in the city, with satellite operations in several other cities as well.

Obama visited Chicago several times during his college years before attending Harvard Law School. He didn't go to Harvard Law to learn how to practice law but rather because, in his words, "it was the perfect place to examine how the power structure works." [10] Upon graduating, he received numerous offers on account of his well-publicized presidency of the *Harvard Law Review*. Yet Obama turned them all down to return to Chicago. His first job was with an Alinsky community organizing outfit, and it paid $10,000 a year. It was a meager sum even then. Obama didn't care about the money; he cared about the training. The money, he knew, would come later.

Obama was hired by Jerry Kellman, one of Alinsky's top deputies. Kellman was delighted to see that Obama was smart, and equally delighted to see that he was black. The Alinsky shakedown operations worked closely with blacks, and Alinsky himself had written, "Native or indigenous leadership is of fundamental importance in the attempt to build a People's Organization, for without the support and cooperative efforts of native leaders, any such venture is doomed to failure from the very beginning." [11] Obama wasn't exactly "native" to Chicago, but Kellman was sure that he could form ties with local African American shakedown activists, and he was right.

According to Obama biographer David Remnick, "Kellman may well have played the most influential role in Obama's life outside of his family." Later Kellman introduced Obama to other professional Alinskyites, such as Greg Galluzzo and Mike Kruglik. All three were top extortion men who recognized in Obama the potential to equal, or even surpass, the master. From the beginning Kellman saw that Obama wasn't a slacker; indeed, he brought a certain work ethic to his apprenticeship in the shakedown business. Kellman said of Obama, "He was very disciplined in the way he lived. He wasn't dating. He was doing his interviews, doing his reports. . . . He was very focused, monkish not in the sense of being a celibate but of holing up and reading." [12]

Obama quickly taught himself Alinsky's shakedown techniques. So good was the student that he soon became a teacher. Obama began to instruct other aspiring community activists in the shakedown technique. We can find online from those days a picture of Obama standing before a blackboard, explaining to a group of attentive acolytes how to use power to extort money and concessions from businesses and government entities. Eventually Obama would become the first Alinskyite to take over the White House.

The first, but perhaps not the last. Hillary Clinton met Saul Alinsky while she was in high school. Hillary had been raised as a "Goldwater girl," a conservative, but in her teen years she became enamored of a left-leaning Methodist minister who convinced her that capitalism was a system based on theft and injustice. Hillary then became a liberal idealist seeking ways to fight the evil business establishment.

The Methodist minister introduced Hillary to Alinsky, and this is where Hillary's political education truly began. When Hillary went to Wellesley College she invited Alinsky to speak there. She wrote her senior thesis on him. This is an important document that has not been adequately analyzed. For many years Wellesley kept it under lock and key, hidden from public exposure. Only when sufficient pressure was applied by journalists and others insisting that the document should be made public did the college release the thesis. It is now available on the Web, and makes instructive reading.

Hillary admires Alinsky's martial rhetoric, quoting him saying, "How do you gain a victory before you have an army? The only method ever devised is guerilla warfare: to avoid a fixed battle where the forces are arrayed and where the new army's weakness would become visible, and to concentrate instead on hit-and-run tactics designed to gain small but measurable victories." For Hillary, as for Alinsky, politics is not a contest between friends who disagree about the direction of the country; it is a form of warfare and the other side is an enemy to be vanquished.

Hillary's thesis is titled "There Is Only the Fight." The title is a trademark Alinsky phrase that appeals to Hillary because it suggests a move from the politics of idealism to the politics of power. Alinsky convinced Hillary that idealism gets you nowhere; the only way to get somewhere is through power. Hillary recognizes, however, that politics requires a pretense of idealism, or at least an appeal to it. In her thesis she invokes labor leader John Lewis, who was asked to comment on spontaneous labor strikes involving trespassing and seizure of private property. Such lawlessness seemed indefensible, but Lewis declared, "A man's right to a job transcends the right to private property." Hillary notices how an appeal to the higher principles of social justice can be used to legitimize conduct that would otherwise be reprehensible.

Alinsky was so impressed by her that when she graduated from Wellesley he offered her a job as a community organizer in his Industrial Areas Foundation. Alinsky himself described this organization as providing "training for professional radicals."

Hillary, however, turned him down. The reason is that by this time the student had become smarter than the teacher. Hillary figured out two flaws in Alinsky's approach. "One of the primary problems with the Alinsky model," she writes, "is that the removal of Alinsky drastically alters the composition." Hillary sees that Alinsky is a unique character, particularly creative and gifted in the art of outsider shakedown techniques. The Alinsky method, to be most effective, requires Alinsky.

Hillary's second point is much more profound. She observes that Alinsky relies on neighborhood organization, and she comments that "the territorially-defined community is no longer a workable societal unit." In other words, people don't operate through their local aldermen and neighborhood reps anymore. "Accompanying the decline of the traditional neighborhood as a living unit," Hillary writes, is "the massive centralization of power on the federal level."[13] This, she sees, requires a different type of organization—what we may term the Hillary method.

How does the Hillary method differ from the Alinsky method? Alinsky had insisted that community activists be outsiders, that they use their pitch to recruit allies and threaten the establishment. From this point of view, the "take" would be whatever could be cajoled or extracted from that establishment. Hillary figured out that there was a way to do a bigger con. This con was built on a simple insight: the government has a legal monopoly on the use of physical force.

Hillary realized that if she could figure out a way to take over the government, she'd have all the powerful instruments of government, from the military to the FBI to the IRS, at her disposal. Today many agencies of government have become militarized, a process that began under George W. Bush but has expanded greatly under the Obama administration. We might expect the FBI, for example, to have its own SWAT teams. But now multiple federal agencies—including the Department of Agriculture, the Office of Personnel Management, the State Department, the Department of Education, the Department of Energy, the U.S. Fish and Wildlife Service, the Consumer Product Safety Commission, the Bureau of Land Management, the Railroad Retirement Board, and the National Park Service—all have SWAT teams.

These SWAT teams have access to military equipment, from bayonets and M-16 rifles to armored personnel carriers. They break into homes using battering rams and incendiary devices called flash grenades, which blind and deafen anyone in the vicinity. Journalist Radley Balko reports that they are frequently used against nonviolent citizens, in other words, as instruments of terror.[14]

This is the enforcement apparatus for the legalized thievery that is carried out by progressive government. If you don't do the state's bidding, the state is literally ready to *kill you*. If this seems like an exaggeration, consider a thought experiment. Imagine if I write a letter to the government, saying that I understand it has a scheme called Social Security to help me provide for my retirement. Being an emancipated American, however, I have decided I don't want it. I am perfectly happy to provide for my own retirement. If my efforts fail and I become dependent when I am old, I will rely on friends and family, or private charity. So I've decided to stop paying into Social Security.

If I did this, what would happen? The government would insist I pay, and send me notices with penalties. I would then ignore those notices. Eventually they would come to get me. Seeing armed people approaching my home, I would attempt to defend myself. And this would be no contest: the SWAT teams would take aim and I would be dead. This is the prospect facing every citizen who doesn't meekly conform to government coercion and pay up.

Here is Hillary's insight. If you control the militarized apparatus of government, then you have thousands—actually hundreds of
thousands—of killers with badges at your disposal. You are then the
biggest crime boss in the world. You can use this power to extract
money from citizens, against which they are virtually powerless. Imagine the shakedown possibilities! You can also use this force against
your enemies, to terrorize them into capitulation or silence. In other
words, Hillary transcended Alinsky by shifting the ground of community activism: why be a shakedown artist on the outside when you can
be a shakedown artist on the inside? Why try and shake down Fort
Knox when there might be a way to take over Fort Knox?

Hillary set her sights not on this retail store or that local government; she set her sights on the wealth of the nation. Her con would
be of a kind never previously imagined. To pull off this type of a con,
Hillary realized, the pitch would have to change; it would have to be a
pitch to *voters*. The con would be constructed within democratic politics; it would involve exploiting discontent to recruit political allies to
empower the con artist to pull off the biggest heist ever imagined: theft
of the accumulated wealth of America. Why try to extract money and
benefits from corporations and government when you can use government power—including the FBI, the police, and the IRS—to extract
money and benefits from the private sector and from the taxpayer?
Hillary, in other words, figured out a way to steal America.

But Hillary had a problem: she needed a pitchman. Obama didn't;
he was his own pitchman. Hillary, however, was not a gifted snake-
oil salesman like Obama. So she found Bill, a Rhodes scholar who
dodged the draft by skipping off to Oxford. Hillary met Bill at Yale,
where he was the fast-talking charmer. She saw that behind his in-
fectious charm Bill had a burning ambition, but it was nothing more
than a personal hunger to be popular. To summarize Bill's personality
I recall the self-absorbed devil Belial in Milton's *Paradise Lost*: "To vice
industrious, but to nobler deeds, timorous and slothful." [15]

Hillary saw that Bill also enjoyed the attention of the ladies. Satisfying these appetites seemed for Bill to be the height of his aspirations. In

exchange for tolerating his affairs, he would be her lifelong pitchman, and she could accompany him as his "roadie" until he made it big—really big. Then, perhaps, it would be her turn.

Hillary did have a pitch to make. She had to pitch Bill on this arrangement. And Bill was smart: he went for it. He married the plain girl with the heavy spectacles because he recognized that she could take him to places where he couldn't go himself. Once there, he would have all the power and all the money and all the chicks he wanted.

She, for her part, would have to put up with Bill's bimbos; ideally he would have the discipline to be discreet about them, but if they ever surfaced she would have to cooperate in discrediting them and shutting them up. If this became impossible she would have to stick by him and play the long-suffering wife. This would be her pitch to the American people, and if she played her role well, some of them might even feel sorry for her. So when Bill's bimbos started surfacing, Hillary knew she had to do her part. She did it unhesitatingly. This is what she signed up for; it was just part of the deal.

Hillary has never openly confessed to "the deal," although in a 1979 interview—granted while Bill was still governor of Arkansas—she came very close. Asked about strains in her marriage on account of Bill's reputation for womanizing, Hillary was remarkably nonchalant. "We have, for me, an excellent marriage," she said, conceding, however, that "I'm not sure that it would suit other people." Even so, she added, all marriages have their own strains "and each couple has to work out an accommodation for whatever reasons there may be." As for her and Bill, "We're worked out ours and we're very happy." Asked if she ever had anguish or second thoughts about Bill's conduct in the marriage, she responded emphatically, "No, no, never, never." [16]

Bill and Hillary both detest Obama. They regard him as a small-time hood. From Hillary's point of view, he is an Alinsky wannabe while she not only mastered Alinsky's techniques but also ultimately went beyond Alinsky. During the 2008 campaign, Bill remarked to Senator Ted Kennedy that Obama was such a nobody that only "a few years ago this guy would be getting us coffee." [17] Even so, when Hillary ran against Obama for the Democratic nomination, the small hood beat the big hood.

This happened in part because, in the politics of the Democratic Party, race trumps gender. Blacks are regarded as bigger victims than women, and therefore the imperative for a black president is stronger than that for a woman president. Obama exploited this advantage. But he also beat Hillary because he was slicker than she was, and had a better pitch than she did. Even Bill, the consummate pitchman, couldn't change this. Bill did his song-and-dance routine for Hillary, but even he couldn't stop Obama because people realized that the person on the ticket was Hillary, not Bill. So to the amusement and even delight of many conservatives, Obama beat Hillary for the Democratic nomination. He then carried that momentum by routing John McCain and winning the presidency. The Alinsky acolyte who started on the outside, like Alinsky himself, ended up on the inside.

Hillary must have been crushed. The big hood knew she would have to kowtow to the small hood for an excruciating eight years. Still, the situation was not hopeless. The insider plan could still work, but it would now have to be reformulated to promote Hillary's succession to the presidency after Obama. Around the time of Obama's race for reelection, Bill and Hillary decided to make a deal with Obama. Although Obama has no affection for either Clinton, this was a deal he wanted. His popularity was down in the months leading up to the election, and he knew Clinton could help shore up his chances. Basically the deal was that Bill would put aside his contempt and shamelessly campaign for Obama; in exchange, Obama would agree that Hillary would be his anointed successor four years later.[18]

On this basis of mutual interest, two rival operations—the Clinton gang and the Obama gang—met and made their peace. Both sides have lived up to the deal. Clinton campaigned tirelessly for Obama's reelection and helped rouse the faithful at the Democratic National Convention. In January 2013, Obama reciprocated by appearing alongside Hillary on the CBS show *60 Minutes*, where he just about endorsed her as his anointed successor.

Is it possible, one may ask, for the Bloods and the Crips to make a deal? Yes, it is; rival gangs do work together to pull off common heists. Indeed, I learned from one of its former members that the Mexican mafia, which used to hate blacks, now employs blacks. In one insurance scheme, the Mexican mafia recruited black gang members to sign up homeless African Americans for life insurance; then the Mexican mafia would kill them, and the two groups would share the payout. "Black and brown," this guy told me, "sometimes come together for the green."

I wanted to learn more about gang rivalry and gang cooperation so I raised the topic in the confinement center with a South Sider named Emiliano. "The Aryan Brotherhood," he told me, "works with the Mexican mafia." But the Mexican mafia, he elaborated, is rivals with the Mexican gang La Nuestra Familia. Apparently the mafia is mainly urban Mexicans while La Nuestra is mainly rural Mexicans. And because the Mexican mafia opposes La Nuestra, Emiliano said, its ally the Aryan Brotherhood also opposes La Nuestra Familia. Not surprisingly, he added, the white supremacists are known enemies of all the black gangs including the Bloods, the Crips, and the Black Guerilla Family. Meanwhile, "The black gangs sometimes work with other black gangs and also with La Nuestra Familia, which makes them an enemy of the Mexican mafia." Despite this complex web of alliances, Emiliano stressed that even rival gangs sometimes make temporary deals when they serve common interests.

The same is true, I suppose, with political gangs. They don't have to like each other; it's strictly business. The Obama gang and the Hillary gang have come together to share access to the U.S. Treasury. Hillary knows that, more than anything else, she wants to control that wealth and power. Obama knows he can't run again so someone has to succeed him; why not hand the baton, on his terms, to another Alinskyite con artist like himself?

The goal of the two hoods—the little hood and the big hood who wants to succeed the little hood—is not totalitarianism or communism. It's not any kind of "ism" at all. The mafia's goal is not to make a "new man" or to achieve some kind of utopia but rather to steal the labor and wealth of existing human beings. It's basically mob rule, by which I mean rule by the Obama mob followed by the Hillary mob. If this reads like a crime story, that's because it is. For me, it is a story that retains its interest and suspense even though I know that I—we—are the intended victims.

Chapter 11

THE ENVY TRIANGLE:

Shaking Down the Wealth Creators

He gave Clemenza and Tessio each the title of *Caporegime* or captain, and the men who worked beneath them the rank of soldier.[1]

—Mario Puzo, *The Godfather*

In order to steal a country, one needs a large team of accessories, or co-conspirators. The film remake of *Ocean's Eleven* begins with George Clooney recruiting a group of specialized thugs to help him pull off his casino heist. Clooney needs an experienced electronics man, a safecracker, an inside man to get a job in the casino, a fake high-roller, and a practiced getaway driver. Imagine what kind of a team would be required to steal a country! Where would Obama and Hillary find their collaborators to do this? Or, in the language of *The Godfather*, where can the don find his soldiers and his caporegimes?

The problem arises for our larcenous duo not merely because looting the wealth of America is a big project; it is also because this is a special kind of thievery. This is thievery that requires organization, and activism, and votes. Thieves like Obama and Hillary need something more than a hired band of accessories; they need whole *constituencies* to join in their unsavory enterprise. These constituencies cannot be paid, in the traditional sense, although they can be offered rewards of one kind or another.

Still, it's not easy to find hundreds of thousands—perhaps millions—of Americans who can be openly talked into a robbery scheme. Thus recruitment requires its own ingenuity. In fact, it requires tapping into a shared sensibility that will draw people from quite different walks of life into the progressive heist. This chapter is about the recruitment process, which has proved highly successful by drawing on a single but powerful emotion: envy.

Envy is the mother of all human vices. Part of its power arises from the fact that it is so basic, and its origin so ancient. "Envy is the drive which lies at the core of man's life as a social being," Helmut Schoeck writes in a study of the subject. Envy, according to Schoeck, "occurs as soon as two individuals become capable of mutual comparison." Schoeck points out that envy permeates all the other vices, fueling greed and lust, stimulating anger, providing the motive for covetousness and theft. "In all the cultures of mankind, in all proverbs and fairytales, the emotion of envy is condemned."[2]

Yet Schoeck points out that there is very little discussion of envy in modern culture, and virtually none in contemporary politics. In America today, there are lots of books on greed, but virtually none on envy. Professors are loath to raise the topic with their students. American high schools instruct students on how to avoid all kinds of unhealthy feelings and behaviors, but not envy. The envious villain is almost never depicted in today's art, not even in the art of caricature. Our newspapers sometimes deplore the envy aroused by advertising, but never the envy aroused by politicians. Hollywood villains are virtually never motivated by envy.

Envy, in other words, is a political and cultural taboo, and this is not because it is so rare. On the contrary; envy is taboo because it is pervasive among the very classes of people who don't want to have the topic raised.

I decided to investigate envy in my confined quarters. By now—more than six months into my sentence—I'm a veteran of the place. Most of the people who were there when I arrived are gone. That's because the typical duration of stay is thirty, sixty, or ninety days. I am one of the few guys condemned to be there for eight months. By this time I have no fear whatsoever. In fact I've long taken off my cheap watch and put on my Rolex. My friends urged me against it. "Don't wear the Rolex. You are among criminals, remember?" But by this time I was recalcitrant. "I'm wearing my Rolex. It's not going to leave my wrist."

No more dressing like a convict; I've decided to be me, and am pretty much back to my normal clothes. Each day I drive out and back into the parking lot in my Mercedes. I'm not afraid of carjacking; the whole place is under surveillance, so who would steal a car here when you can do it elsewhere without being observed? Inside I have the run of the place, and I notice with amusement that some of the new guys give me a nervous look. They want to make sure that I am not going to be the one who rapes them. It seems crazy, but perhaps I have unconsciously internalized the *loco* style of the seasoned criminal.

The magazine *Vanity Fair* commissioned a profile of me to run around the time I got out of confinement. The reporter, Evgenia Peretz, struck me as fair-minded but politically naïve. She asked questions like, "Who is Saul Alinsky?" and "How can you say that Alinsky influenced Obama?" She also expressed puzzlement at my social media style. When Eric Holder announced his retirement I tweeted, "Is there a crime syndicate looking for a boss with government experience?" She didn't get that one at all.

Even so, she popped into the confinement center and rushed out, clearly flustered. "Dinesh, I am so sorry." She realized that the atmosphere in there was very rough, and that I had been sleeping with that crowd for many months. When Evgenia's story was done, the magazine dispatched a team to San Diego for my photo shoot. I worked with celebrity photographer Patrick Ecclesine and his model-girlfriend, Donna Feldman, who did my makeup.

They took pictures and video of "a day in the life of Dinesh D'Souza." That day began with me in sweatpants and a hoodie walking down an alley just outside the confinement center. It continued with me, having shaved and put on a suit, doing media interviews by Skype from my La Jolla office. I had dinner that day with Texas lieutenant governor David Dewhurst; *Vanity Fair* took pictures of us in the paneled dining room of the La Valencia hotel. Then at sunset the magazine shot me casually walking along the beach.

The article, which appeared in May 2015, ran for seven pages with a lavish photo spread. (Clearly going for brains instead of looks, the magazine chose to feature model and actress Sofia Vergara instead of me on the cover.) The title, "The Reeducation of Dinesh D'Souza," was an appropriate one, not only because I was re-educating myself, learning what I could from this new environment, but also because the judge continued his heavy-handed and increasingly absurd efforts to re-educate me.

With my confinement drawing to its end, my counselor wrote Judge Berman to say that I had made very good progress over the past several months. I had a very good understanding of what I did wrong, and why I did it, and there was no chance I would do it again. She recommended that my counseling be terminated, because I had no further need of it.

So at this point we had my trained counselor, who had examined me on a weekly basis for eight months, together with two medical psychiatrists, operating on the basis of a battery of tests, who had all pronounced me perfectly normal. Yet in a review hearing, Judge Berman dismissed these assessments. He said that as a psych major in college, he believed that I was in need of further counseling.

Speaking with his trademark monotone, the judge said that he was not doing this to punish me, but to help me. I thought of how dissenters are routinely declared mentally disturbed or insane in authoritarian countries, and forced to undergo medical treatment until they are cured of their recalcitrance. I also thought about Judge Berman's fictional counterpart, Nurse Ratched in *One Flew Over the Cuckoo's Nest*. She too was trying to help Billy, before she drove him to suicide. And when Jack Nicholson, playing R. P. McMurphy, resisted the system they strapped him down and lobotomized him. That too was for his own benefit. I thought of poor McMurphy, lying in his bed, glassy-eyed, mouth open. From Nurse Ratched's point of view, there lay another crazy man, finally cured.

Leftists were super-annoyed to see that my status as an imprisoned felon did not seem to have diminished my reputation and may even have enhanced it. They railed against *Vanity Fair* for giving me so much importance, and when I posted a picture of me and my girlfriend, Debbie Fancher, they railed against her with undisguised fury. I couldn't help notice that many of these social media trolls had virtually no following on Facebook or Twitter. They tweeted every five minutes, raising the question of whether they even had jobs. Perhaps they were employees of Media Matters or some other leftist group and their job was to stalk and torment people like me.

At bottom, I recognized, their hostility didn't just spring from hatred and frustration, although there was plenty of that; it also sprang from envy. Many of these people are losers and self-styled victims who detest others who are not—particularly if those others do not commiserate with them and affirm their victim status. The left taps into these low and degraded emotions for its political benefit, to facilitate its rip-off schemes.

I didn't expect to see much envy in the confinement center, however, for the reason given by Milton in *Paradise Lost*. Milton says of the fallen angels that they are all in the dungeon of hell, and their shared experience is one of pain, so that there is none who are so dissatisfied with their share of suffering that they covet more. Consequently, says Milton, there is no envy in hell, even though envy of God's perfection was what motivated the rebellion of the apostate angels in the first place.[3]

If hell were bereft of envy, surely it would be just as scarce in prison or in a confinement center. Yet a guy from Tijuana, Paredes, told me of his experience, which seems to belie Milton's contention. This guy was a very dangerous dude, who had apparently killed a number of people. Because stabbing and murdering are accomplishments, from the gang's point of view, Paredes had been granted several letters and numbers. "I had Cell 66 tattoos across my body," he boasted, "and each letter, each number had to be earned, either by stabbing or by murder." As a consequence, the man was now considered a respected member of the gang's inner circle, a "marked man."

In prison, however, Paredes discovered that another gang member was spreading rumors about him. He was telling people Paredes had snitched him out to the government. "He went around telling everybody that I was responsible for him being in prison, and for me this was the kiss of death. There is no forgiveness for snitches, man. I literally had to sleep with one eye open."

So when Paredes got out he went straight to the gang leadership, and the accuser was summoned to a kind of hearing, in front of senior gang members. There Paredes confronted him. "I went up to him and said, what the f*ck? And he began to talk sh*t, and say how I had ratted him out, and how he was going to smoke me, and all this stuff, and I simply said to him, where are the papers?"

"Papers?" I asked.

"Yes, I asked him where were his papers that proved that I had ratted him out? And he didn't have any papers."

So the gang leadership concluded that the charge was baseless, but they did not impose any sanctions on the accuser. Paredes said he went straight home "to get my knives. I decided I was going right back to kill that guy."

When he returned, however, the gang leader told Paredes, "I have no objection if you want to kill him, but I think you should spare his life. He's just jealous of you."

Paredes was incredulous. "Jealous?"

"Yes. He knows you're a marked man. He knows you've done all these stabbings and killings. I told him, you're not going to move up in the gang by pulling other homies down. Go out and earn your own stripes, dog. He's an ambitious m*therf*cker, but I told him that he was going about it the wrong way."

Paredes decided to let the matter pass. But listening to his story, I found it interesting that even something so gruesome as a reputation for murder could become an object of envy. And true to form, envy involves not building a reputation for yourself but trying to lower the other guy's.

By comparison with Paredes's story, Earl's story is more conventional, and involves envy of a more familiar sort. Earl was a serial entrepreneur who met a woman from Canada and moved up there. In Winnipeg, Manitoba, he noticed that prescription drugs were much cheaper to buy than in the United States. So he started an Internet business to purchase cheap drugs in Canada and supply them through the mail to customers in the United States.

He was doing pretty well, until one day in 2011 when his house in Florida was swamped with cop cars and he was arrested on more than twenty-five counts of conspiracy, racketeering, wire fraud, mail fraud, you name it. Collectively, he told me, "The charges carried a hundred and thirty-one years in prison."

Earl, who had never been in trouble with the law, stood before a Florida judge who solemnly read the charges and the prison time he was facing for each. "I was shaking the whole time he was speaking," Earl recalled. "When he got to fifty years, I just broke down. I knew my life was over."

The government put out a press release, dutifully reported in the media, which suggested that Earl was cheating old people of their retirement savings by supplying them with counterfeit drugs. "Actually," Earl said, "I was selling them the same drugs that they were getting in America, but at a fraction of the price. There was nothing counterfeit about the medications. My crime was that the drugs bore a serial number that designated them to be sold abroad. I was not authorized to sell those drugs here. This gives the big pharmaceutical companies the ability to charge higher prices, by restricting the supply and preventing Americans from getting it from foreign countries."

So it was the pharmaceutical companies that had discovered what Earl was doing. "They were envious of my success," he said. "Everywhere their distributors told them they had encountered customers who were buying from abroad, and one name kept coming up: mine. So Big Pharma decided that something had to be done about me."

According to Earl, the pharmaceutical companies notified the U.S. Food and Drug Administration (FDA), which brought in the cops and the SWAT team. "The cops acted like I was Al Capone or Don Corleone," Earl said. "They kept asking me, where is the money? Where are the guns? I told them, this is not *Godfather: Part 2*. I am just trying to sell people the medications they need at a cheaper price."

Although Earl was a partner in the business with his Canadian girlfriend, nothing happened to her. "The Americans kept calling her, and each time she told them to f*ck off. She hadn't done anything wrong. The Canadians had no problem with anything she had done. She was just running an online business, for God's sake. Finally she went to the authorities there, and they told the Americans to stop bothering a Canadian citizen. That's when they stopped calling."

When Earl got to California, where he was to be tried, he found out that, without explanation, most of the charges against him had been dropped—except for a mail fraud charge and a charge of conspiracy to import unauthorized drugs. "One day I was facing a hundred and thirty-one years and the next day I was not facing a hundred and thirty-one years. Go figure!" And then, Earl says, "I sat down with my attorney, and we got into the game."

The game, as he called it, was that the government threatened him with a mail fraud charge carrying twenty years in prison, but said it would drop that charge if he would plead guilty to the conspiracy charge, carrying just twenty-four months in prison. "I didn't have a choice," Earl said. "I pleaded to the lesser charge. I didn't care if I was guilty or innocent. My lawyer said I had a defense, with a seventy-five percent chance of getting off. But I didn't want to take a twenty-five percent chance on getting twenty years. This is a rigged game. They knew it, and I knew it. So that's why I'm here. I am a product of the envy of the drug companies, and the American system of justice."

So envy is indeed pervasive among criminals, as indeed it is among human beings generally. How, then, does envy work as the engine of recruitment for the progressive heist?

Imagine a fellow in San Francisco, Houston, or Boston who works in an office building adding up numbers or cleaning floors. He is struggling financially, with his house underwater, his credit card bills piling up, and very little leftover each month to spend. As he makes his way home he happens to look through the glass windows of a restaurant, and inside he sees people eating heartily, sipping wine, talking and laughing. He knows it's a terrific steak house, and he would love to be there himself, arriving in a Mercedes 550 in a silk shirt and Armani suit.

It dawns on him that that is a fantasy—it will never happen; it is not his life. And at this point he begins to feel that ancient and consuming human emotion of envy. Now, envy is perhaps the most destructive and vile of all human emotions. It is vile because it has no trace of goodness in it. In a book on the seven deadly sins, Henry Fairlie points out that with other vices, such as anger, greed, and lust, we at least get some pleasure out of the emotion. But envy involves ill will toward another with no corresponding satisfaction for oneself. Envy is self-torment, and the only pleasure the envious person feels is the pleasure that some harm might come to someone else.[4]

Envy is not emulation. Let's say the man looking into the restaurant says, "Wow, look at those successful, happy people. I would like to be like them. I need to go back to school and improve my skills. Or I should start a profitable business." This is positive thinking, and it's not envy. The envious man is the one who says: "I would like to lift myself up, but since I don't know how to do that, I'd just as well see those guys pulled down." Envy seeks leveling, but its method is not to level the envious person up; rather, it's to level the target of his envy down. Envy, noted Immanuel Kant, is "intent on the destruction of the happiness of others."[5]

A classic example of envy comes from the ancient Greeks. The Greeks had a practice called ostracism, which allowed the elector- ate composed of at least six thousand citizens to vote every year and impose a ten-year exile for any reason on one public figure. Perhaps the most tragic case involved the Greek statesman Aristides. Plutarch reports that Aristides, who set the dues for the Delian League, the al- liance of subordinate Greek states under the leadership of Athens, had a reputation for incorruptibility and outstanding virtue. Consequently he came to be known as Aristides the Just. Even so, the Greeks voted to dispatch him.

Aristides himself was nonplused by the verdict. Without disclos- ing his identity, he approached a man from the countryside who had voted for his ostracism and asked him, "Tell me, why do you want to ostracize Aristides? What has he done to you?" The man replied, "Oh, nothing. I don't even know the fellow. I'm just sick and tired of hearing everyone refer to him as 'The Just.' "[6]

Envy is often confused with jealousy, because both involve a loss of self-esteem that arises out of coveting something, but actually the two emotions are quite different. Jealousy can sometimes be noble, while envy is always despicable. Consider Shakespeare's Othello and Iago. Othello is jealous because he believes that his wife, Desdemona, is cheating on him. He's wrong about that, but if he weren't, he'd be right to be angry. Jealousy refers to the frustration we feel at being deprived of something that does belong to us, or to which we have a legitimate right. Even though Othello is a flawed man, he remains the hero of this play. Othello is a champion of justice; at the end of the play, he recog- nizes that he has killed his innocent wife and so he kills himself.

Contrast Othello's jealousy with the envy of the play's villain, Iago. While Othello's jealousy has a motive, Iago's envy seems to have none. It is portrayed utterly without cause, and also utterly illegitimate. Even at the end, when Iago is exposed, he remains a paragon of injustice; he doesn't repent or even seek to justify his actions. The only time Iago gives any kind of explanation is when he says of Cassio, "He hath a daily beauty in his life which makes me ugly."[7] Cassio owes Iago nothing, yet Iago hates him. He hates him purely because Cassio has something that he doesn't; Cassio is a better man. While jealousy covets something that is ours by right, envy covets something to which we have no right whatsoever. Unlike the jealous man, the envious man is a thief because he seeks, without deserving it, what someone else legitimately possesses.

Envy is also the most secretive of all human vices. Other vices, like greed and lust, are out in the open; it is in the nature of envy to hide. The envious man conceals his feelings so well that he does not admit them even to himself. What person ever declared, either in public or in private, "I am envious of what others have that I don't"? Yet what no one can deny is the resentment that inevitably accompanies envy. Our man at the restaurant window may not acknowledge his envy, but he recognizes full force the gale of antagonism that he directs toward those seemingly happy people inside. The one thing he can be sure of is that he hates them, and he would actually feel pleasure if they could be made to suffer. He seeks, in other words, schadenfreude—a joy in the misery of others. He wants them to be at least as miserable as he is.

Frequently this resentment, generated by envy, grows into hatred. And when money and success are involved, hatred often becomes, strangely enough, self-hatred. This requires some explanation. Why would the envious person who covets someone else's money or success hate himself? The reason is that envy is an intellectual vice. Envy itself springs from a conundrum: why them and not me? Envy demands an exploration, and self-hatred is the result of that exploration.

This self-hatred, however, only arises in certain types of societies, open societies where success is largely the result of one's own actions. In his remarkable book *The Rise of the Meritocracy*, the British sociologist Michael Young points out that in hierarchical and aristocratic societies, envy did not typically lead to low self-esteem. Nor, I might add, does it today in places that retain the hierarchical code. I think of servant girls in India who live in affluent households but feel no envy or resentment toward their memsahibs, whose lives are just too remote from their own. (They are much more likely to envy and detest the neighbor's servant, who is paid a little better or enjoys more recreational privileges than they do.)

Sure, the medieval serf at the bottom might envy the lord of the manor his great house and lands. But there was no question of the serf blaming himself. The top guy obviously lucked out; the serf just got the short end of the stick. The serf can regret this fact, but he has no need to consider the other guy as better than he, in the sense of deserving his affluence or success. Were he born into those favorable circumstances, the serf knows, then he would be enjoying those luxuries.

Young observes that in a merit-based society, however, such excuses are not available to the ones who fall behind. In a society where the laws protect everyone equally, and where anyone can start a business, or apply for a position, it seems pretty obvious that where people end up is largely the result of the talents they have and the choices they make. It cannot escape the realization of the envious man that he could have studied more, or worked harder, or thought of that innovation or app that made his high school buddy so successful.

He could have, but he didn't. He cannot avoid feeling envy toward the other guys; he also cannot avoid the nagging suspicion of his own inferiority. His low self-esteem arises from the recognition that he didn't lose because the rules were rigged against him; he lost because he is a loser. Now he begins to despise not only the object of his envy, but also himself. Young's book makes the point that meritocratic societies—even more than their hierarchical predecessors—produce discontented loser constituencies and thus generate a potent political situation. "For the first time in history," Young writes, "the inferior man has no ready buttress for his self-regard."[8]

In this potent situation, who should show up but the professional progressive con artist, the Obama or Hillary type. Of the two, I'm going to focus on Obama because he's been at this for a while; Hillary at this point is merely an aspiring Obama. Now, Obama, we must recognize, is the most resentful person of all. Why? Not because he lacks talent, but because his talents are not the ones that are important in an entrepreneurial society. As we saw in an earlier chapter, America is, from its origin, an entrepreneurial society—a capitalist society—in which the businessman and the entrepreneur, not the politician or the community organizer, are at the top of the ladder. Entrepreneurs do most to change the lives of people, and they reap the greatest rewards. Moreover, the best of them can do things that inspire wonder. In a sense, they are the miracle workers of modern society. Consider Steve Jobs and his iPhone: it's hard to think of anything that has changed contemporary life more than that little device.

Obama, of course, couldn't possibly build an iPhone; he can't even put up a website. Obama's only connection with phones was to label them Obamaphones and hand them out for free through his community organizer network. Now millions of Americans and illegal immigrants have cell phones paid for by the U.S. government and funded through one of those obscure charges that appear on your phone bill, the "lifeline" tax. Obama undoubtedly hopes you never notice the charge, or ask about it. It's so much better to rip people off when they don't even know they are being ripped off.

Obama has no experience in starting a business or running a business; the only business he has ever run—the U.S. government—is $18 trillion in debt, a full one-half of that accumulated during Obama's two terms. Any CEO with that record would certainly be fired; any private enterprise losing money at that pace would long have gone out of business. Obama didn't discover his lack of entrepreneurial talent at the White House; he's known it for most of his life. That's why he decided, at a young age, to go a completely different route. Envious of the entrepreneur, he would become the anti-entrepreneur. He would put his talents to use in taking from the entrepreneurs and getting away with it.

So Obama's lack of entrepreneurial talent doesn't mean that he is untalented. He is talented, but his talent lies in other areas. Driven by envy and resentment toward entrepreneurs, Obama specializes in fostering and mobilizing the resentment of others. He's not a community organizer; he's a resentment organizer.

And his technique can only inspire admiration. In a political sense, he approaches the envious, resentful guy who is stewing in rage and self-pity. Obama in effect says to him: "My friend, you are not envious; you are righteously indignant. You feel low, you feel used, and you feel like a victim. That's because you are being victimized. You are a victim of theft. See those guys in the restaurant. They have actually been stealing from you. They are actually in possession of your stolen goods. That's why they have so much and you have so little. They are enjoying their life at your expense. But don't worry. You don't have to do much at this point. All you have to do is to vote for me. Then I will go and take away their stuff, and I will give some of it to you."

Now, Obama doesn't actually put it this way. He's too smart a pitchman for that. Not for nothing did he spend all those years with the Alinsky operation, learning how to camouflage larceny schemes in moral language. What he does, therefore, is to publicly demand justice and equality. More equality in education! More equality in income! More equality in wealth! More equality in power! This equality is presented as the sine qua non of justice. Fair share! Fair share! Fair share!

In fact, there is nothing just or fair about it. Aristotle says that justice is equality but not for everyone, only for those who are equal.[9] What Aristotle means is that justice is giving people their due. Obama, however, inverts this Aristotelian principle. Obama's position is that justice requires that the unequal be treated *as though* they were equal. This is the progressive definition of "fairness."

In demanding this, Obama is articulating the envious man's most secret desire: that the inequalities due to merit be erased and that those who have produced little or nothing be given the same resources and respect as those who have produced most or everything. In order to achieve what might otherwise seem impossible, Obama promises his envious disciples that he will demonize and diminish the status of the productive classes while he seeks to elevate the status of his unproductive followers. He will castigate those who are pulling the wagon even as he celebrates those who sit in the wagon. In Obama's America, the wealth creators are greedy, selfish, and materialistic while the wealth stealers are the most morally wonderful people in the country.

Obama's assault on the wealth creators does not appeal merely to hardworking guys who are falling behind in the competitive race. It also appeals to a whole host of others, including academics, major-media journalists, Hollywood types, some mainline clergy, and professional activists. This is the progressive coalition that makes up our homegrown Fagin's army of pickpockets. They are all, in one way or another, motivated by a deep and abiding envy. Yet they do not all benefit financially from the progressive heist. Obama doesn't offer them material rewards, and they don't demand any.

So how does this alliance work? Let's examine this coalition a bit more closely, to see what role they perform, and how each group benefits from being part of the team.

Let's begin by exploring why academics, media and journalism types, and Hollywood people are so envious. Their envy comes from the fact that they consider themselves devalued. They are sometimes well compensated, but even so, their product—mainly words and images—do not command the same level of success as the products of the wealth creators.

Here is a typical example: while Apple works on generating new products, Elizabeth Warren works on researching her Cherokee roots. This is not unproductive effort on her part; she knows that if she can plausibly claim to be one-sixteenth Native American, it would pay huge dividends for her academic career and also for her political credibility in the progressive menagerie. Similarly, Amartya Sen writes big books on how to distribute a flute. Sen knows that this kind of lengthy cogitation, accompanied by the appropriate flimflam, will win him progressive acclaim and perhaps even respectable book sales.

Entrepreneurs cannot fathom this. An entrepreneur who invested his efforts in proving he was one-sixteenth Native American would be laughed out of the boardroom. His only hope would be to apply for an affirmative action loan from some government agency. Entrepreneurs don't write books about how to distribute a flute; rather, they make flutes. In an entrepreneur's world, all those children that Sen frets about would be able to afford flutes, because flutes, which were once rare and expensive, can now be ordered on Amazon or eBay for just pennies.

One might expect that intellectuals would love this, because it solves their academic conundrums, but in reality they hate it. They hate it because it moves the fulcrum of power toward entrepreneurs and away from themselves. Most entrepreneurs respect academia in the abstract but they don't give academics much thought. All of this intensifies the envy and increases the determination of academics to bring the entrepreneurs down and appropriate their resources.

One has to remember that intellectuals, for the most part, regard themselves as the smartest members of society. Henry Rosovsky, Harvard's longtime dean, expressed this sentiment when he said that Harvard intended to keep its A students for itself—turning them into academics—while it dispatched its B and C students to run the institutions of society. This arrogance is endemic in academia. For this reason, academics cannot understand why they don't get the biggest rewards. For them it is a matter of injured merit.

Not that intellectuals are poorly paid. That used to be the case, but today professors often earn six-figure salaries and even schoolteachers earn a pretty decent living. Yet many intellectuals find this unsatisfactory because, in their own eyes, they are the most brilliant, capable figures they have ever encountered. From their point of view, entrepreneurs are, well, boobs and yahoos.

Intellectuals of course know that most people would rather place their dollar bets on entrepreneurs than on them. This irritates them to no end. Intellectuals by and large reject the idea that value is in the eye of the beholder. They are repulsed that people prefer to spend their money doing their nails or texting on their phone rather than attending academic lectures or purchasing academic books. For intellectuals it is nothing short of scandalous that a professor of romance languages at Bowdoin earns a mere $150,000 a year (this is three times the income of the average American!) while some entrepreneur makes $2 million a year selling pest control or term life insurance.

Still, it may be argued, the progressives cannot actually increase the take-home pay of academics. Actually they do, through various government grants for dubious or useless purposes that keep the university system fat and prosperous. Still, I want to argue, the greatest benefit progressives offer academics is not money. It is enhanced power and self-esteem.

Let's recall what the ultimate goal is for these people. Progressive thieves seek to change the balance of power in society so that wealth creators are diminished and a new progressive ruling class is enhanced. Intellectuals get to be respected members of this ruling class and that is what they cherish above all else. I'm not saying that they are indifferent to money; on the contrary, I recall with amusement one leftist professor who has published many books denouncing the rich for selfishness and greed. Even though the latest one has been out for a while now, he regularly calls his publisher to find out how it's selling. When he gets the dismal sales figures, his response is inevitably to curse and say, "Next time I'm really going to slam those greedy bastards."

So money matters to this group, but their position in the social pecking order matters even more. Even when they don't get much money out of it, they fight against business for the same reason that poor white guys in the South fought on the Confederate side in the Civil War. These poor white guys didn't own slaves, but they enjoyed the prestige of living in a racial caste society where the lowest, most ignorant white guy still had a higher place on the social ladder than the most cultivated, intelligent black man.

In the same vein, envious academics and journalists are eager to fight for a social order in which power and prestige accrue to wordsmiths like themselves, not to some guy selling widgets. No wonder that these envious, resentful social climbers have become willing recruits for the progressive con.

What is the job of academics within the larcenous coalition? It is to come up with academic-sounding justifications for the government confiscating the resources of the successful and handing them to the progressives. These arguments may be ultimately ridiculous, but they should be sufficiently ingenious that they are hard to refute, at least on the part of the entrepreneurs themselves.

This task is perfectly suited to the sort of idiot savants who abound in academia. These are people who cannot balance their checkbooks and even have trouble getting dressed in the morning, but they can tell you a surprising amount about stuff that you've never heard of and that has no effect on your life. They also have a very high opinion of themselves. When the envy of these people is sufficiently activated, they become an army of malevolent Iagos. Like Iago, they specialize in setting up an *alternative reality* in which the real world disappears. This magic trick is performed so skillfully that the gullible, and even some of the not-so-gullible, are bamboozled by the stage effects. Also like Iago, they rig the evidence while insisting on their scrupulous honesty. "Hey, don't question my motives. I got my Ph.D. in sociology from Yale."

Consequently one academic purports to show that rich people don't get much happiness from their money, which would be enjoyed far more by other people if it were transferred to them. This is called the utilitarian argument. Another academic purports to prove that society is just like a family: from each according to their ability, to each according to their needs. Yet this same guy would be outraged if a neighbor came over and had sex with his wife, or disciplined his kid, or helped himself to the contents of his refrigerator. He knows, as we all do, that a neighborhood, a community, and a country are not the same as a family, and our rights and obligations within each of those institutions are quite different. So this academic work is mostly BS, but it is routinely acclaimed as brilliant, usually by other academics or journalists, for the sole reason that it advances the progressive pitch.

Journalists who make up the mainstream media are also part of the progressive coalition. What motivates someone to go into journalism? For the most part, it isn't money. Indeed journalism, which has never paid well, pays even more poorly today. Most people get their information for free, which is basically the market's way of telling a journalist that he or she is worth nothing.

Some journalists, of course, are pretty well paid. A TV anchor, for example, or the executive editor of the *New York Times*, receives a six-figure salary. But even they don't make nearly as much as some franchisee who owns twelve Denny's restaurants in Tyler, Texas. That guy, whose product is the highly popular Denny's breakfast—three eggs, bacon, sausage, hash browns and toast, all for $3.99—seems to be providing more satisfaction to his customers and reaping a correspondingly handsome reward. If forced to choose, the journalist who had just five dollars would himself rather spend it on a Denny's breakfast than on the Sunday edition of the *New York Times*. Still, this same fellow wonders: does that business guy really deserve to make more money than I do? He arrives at the emphatic conclusion: no, the SOB does not.

Despite its relatively meager financial rewards, journalism remains an appealing profession for a certain type of person. Typically this is because journalists have a lot of power. This is not the power to build people up, but the power to take people down. Journalism is most successful when it humiliates, and the power to humiliate is what draws people to the field.

Anyone who has spent time with journalists—and is not one himself—can see that they are often cruel people who take a fairly unconcealed pleasure in inflicting emotional pain. I see this type in the confinement center; only here they are called sociopaths. In journalism, envy and resentment become job assets because they fuel the journalist's ambition and drive. So journalists, like community organizers, have their own set of talents. They too are part of the resentment industry.

In a sense there is nothing wrong with this, because the founders wanted a press that keeps a skeptical eye on the government. The press, for this reason, has been called the "fourth estate." It is intended to be part of our system of checks and balances. The problem is that mainstream journalism today has become one-eyed. In fact, it scarcely checks the government at all. Mostly it attacks private individuals and private business. Our "adversary" press is adverse to the private sector, not to the public sector. Consequently, the effect of the media is not to expose or undermine the progressive larceny scheme. Rather, it is to enable it.

How? The mainstream press tells "stories," but where do these stories come from? What is the basis of deciding what is a story, how to cover it, what is the headline, what pictures to use, and so on? The short answer is that these stories all derive from "meta-stories," and these meta-stories are the mainstream media's ideological perspective on how the world ought to be. Basically the governing meta-story is the progressive pitch.

Consequently, the mainstream media covers the world as if private business and successful people were the real thieves, and government were the instrument of correcting this theft. The real theft—which is the progressive attempt to use government to transfer wealth and power from the wealth creators to the progressives themselves—goes unnoticed. The mainstream media covers thievery as if it were theft prevention, and the victims of theft as if they were the perpetrators of it. Thus the real progressive theft is made possible by the media routinely praising the actual perpetrators and blaming the actual victims.

Hollywood too has a meta-story and it is basically the cartoon version of the meta-story one finds in the mainstream media. Notice who the typical bad guys are in Hollywood films: white businessmen in suits! Think of Michael Douglas as Gordon Gekko in *Wall Street* or Leonardo DiCaprio in *The Wolf of Wall Street*. One Hollywood guy told me that this is because when Hollywood screenwriters think of villains, they imagine the studio producers that they routinely deal with. Even whodunits are usually boring because you can be sure it's the middle-aged white guy in the suit who did it. Occasionally Hollywood seeks a bit of variety, and finds its villains among pastors and small-town sheriffs—preferably with a southern accent.

Meanwhile, Hollywood's heroes are typically progressive types, and sometimes shows are devised to advance the prospects of a favored candidate from the left. The TV show *Madame Secretary* seems to be nothing less than an extended promotion for the candidacy of

Hillary Clinton. In the show, the secretary of state is portrayed as the true mover and shaker, often working behind or around the president, getting things done while everyone else dawdles or is completely clueless. Occasionally the show lapses into heavy-handed absurdity, but in general it's effectively done and for anyone with a brain, the message is clear: we sure could use that kind of a woman in the White House.

This is a propaganda pattern that can be traced back for a quarter of a century. When Hollywood isn't explicitly promoting progressive Democratic candidates, it is hyping up the image of blacks, leftist women, and gays. Think Meryl Streep in *Silkwood* or Julia Roberts in *Erin Brockovich*. Blacks in the movies are less likely to be inner-city criminals and more likely to be God, or brilliant engineers and physicians, or unbelievably capable people who solve problems that baffle everyone else. Ultimately and inevitably the evil businessman, who is in league with the evil pastor and sheriff, is foiled by the brilliant machinations of the black guy in league with the cool gay guy. And that's Hollywood for you! It's a giant engine for selling the progressive pitch.

In Hollywood, Michael Moore is considered to be a highly intelligent guy who makes "deep" movies. I went back and watched Moore's most highly regarded film, *Roger & Me* (1989). The basic premise is that General Motors is an evil capitalist corporation that threw Michael Moore's dad out of work when it closed its plant in Flint, Michigan. Moore gallantly goes in search of Roger Smith, the head of GM, to ask him to explain. The film has amusing exploits along the way, but it's a pity Moore never finds Smith. If he did, Smith could have told him that the reason GM closed its Flint plant was that the plant was losing money, and the reason it was losing money was because of people like Moore's dad.

In other words, the autoworkers unions had pressured GM to raise hourly worker pay and benefits so high that it was now a lot cheaper to make those same cars for less in North Carolina, or for someone else to make a better and cheaper car abroad. One might expect

Moore to examine this argument and attempt to refute it in the film, but he never raises it. Moore's films are relentlessly inane and relentlessly anticapitalist; he too is an instrument of selling the progressive pitch.

What is the effect of all this? It is precisely the effect that Obama and Hillary seek. They seek to enlist a professional cadre of envious and resentful people to promote their pitch, and in academia, the media, and Hollywood, they have assembled it. They seek to recruit envious, resentful losers in the marketplace and convince them that they are being robbed and that they should feel good about participating in a political effort to transfer resources from more successful people to themselves. In other words, they want to remove people's shame from being part of a theft and make them feel entitled to the fruits of it. These are the voters who sustain the progressive, Democratic coalition.

In the case of Obamacare, leading members of the intellectual class produced the appropriately rigged studies to promote the racket. Then members of the Obama administration and liberal Democrats in Congress took up these studies as an irrefutable demonstration of the wonders of Obamacare. Finally anchorpeople and reporters lined up to amplify the falsehoods and complete the sale to the American people. Despite all this, the American people remained unconvinced. Even so, the con men generated enough support that Democratic legislators, on a straight-party vote, got Obamacare through.

Imagine the horror of Obama and his aides, therefore, when one of the leading academic champions of Obamacare, economist Jonathan Gruber of the Massachusetts Institute of Technology, decided to reveal the con, even to the point of confessing it was a con. Gruber himself received $2 million in consulting fees related to Obamacare. Approximately $400,000 of that came from the Department of Health and Human Services. Regarding him as the administration's designated expert on Obamacare, eight states hired Gruber to help design their health care exchanges. Gruber's advocacy of Obamacare also resulted in enhanced visibility and higher speaking fees. So we can see at the outset that his academic pimping for Obamacare was hardly disinterested. Gruber was a stooge.

Why, then, did the stooge become a snitch? He was one of them, so why did he rat them out? Sometimes a snitch has simply had it with the crime scheme and decides to blow the whistle on it. That was the case with Edward Snowden. Sometimes snitches get themselves into a compromised position, as when they confess to a lover or get drunk and start talking too much. Typically, however, snitches do it for gain. In *The Godfather*, the bodyguard Fabrizio snitches on Michael Corleone because he is paid off by Michael's enemies. In real life, Sammy "the Bull" Gravano told the feds about the Gotti crime operation because he was facing life in prison and wanted to work out a deal with them.

Gruber had none of these motives. Gruber's candor about Obamacare was not caused by the desire to be a whistle-blower nor by a drinking spree nor by the prospect of gain. Rather, it was caused by Gruber's arrogance. The man is a smug self-promoter who wanted to take credit for his participation in a clever racket. Speaking to fellow academics and liberal political activists, Gruber apparently thought he was in a room of thieves cackling about the latest heist they had pulled off. He thought he was swapping notes with others who were "in" on the con.

Gruber said that Obamacare was sold based on lies. He said the lies only worked because of the stupidity of the American people. Of one key Obamacare provision, Gruber said it was a "very clever exploitation of the lack of economic understanding of the American voter." He said that while the administration promised transparency, lack of transparency was the key to getting the legislation through. Basically Gruber's message to his fellow con men was, we fooled the rubes, and we got away with it.

Gruber is a good example of a smart guy who has no political sense. This is hardly uncommon among academics. They are good at one thing but somehow convince themselves that they are experts on everything. This is an inherent danger of involving intellectuals in any practical theft enterprise like Obamacare. One may say that Gruber, in trying to be a "Goodfella," turned out to be a "Dumbfella." At first the left tried to dismiss Gruber by saying he wasn't an important architect of Obamacare. But earlier this same Gruber had been hailed by Harry Reid, Nancy Pelosi, and others as the Oracle of Obamacare.

Gruber's confession came too late to stop Obamacare, but it has permanently damaged its reputation. Now the left hates Gruber, not because he lied, but because he told the truth. Telling the truth is a cardinal sin among thieves. For the mafia, it has a special name: *omertà*. Omertà is the vow of silence that mafiosi take; even death is considered preferable to breaking the vow. John Gotti used to say, "If there was a church robbed and I had the steeple stickin' outta my ass I wouldn't tell them I did it."[10] This is an expression of omertà.

Obama is pretty good at omertà. Even though his Obamacare claims—you can keep your doctor, your premiums will go down, the scheme will reduce health care costs—have all been proven to be lies, Obama refuses to admit it. He raises his head and sticks out his jaw and pushes forward, like the toy soldier who walks into the wall but keeps going. I can understand how mad Obama must be at Gruber. I suspect Obama will make sure that Gruber pays for his sin—the sin of "singing" about the crime, and thus endangering the other criminals. Snitches are very unpopular with progressives, as they are with criminals in my confinement center. Snitches violate a basic rule of progressive thievery: never, ever give up the con.

Obama may be pretty good, but no one beats Bill and Hillary Clinton when it comes to omertà. Bill has to be literally caught with his pants down before he will confess that he got it on with Monica. To get a straight answer under oath from Bill, you need extreme linguistic precision, even to the point of having to define the word *is*. We are now getting the same evasions regarding inquiries about conflicts of interest involving Hillary and the Clinton Foundation. And to this day the Clintons maintain that their foundation is purely philanthropic and that they have not received millions of dollars of personal benefit out of it. The Clintons are experts at covering up the con.

In sum, progressives have set up a triangular alliance of envy—made up of academics, media types, and community and political activists—all seeking to broker the envy of ordinary citizens into economic and power gains for themselves. This coalition isn't perfect—as the Gruber example shows—but for the most part, it works. It works because the left controls the education sector as well as the megaphones that transmit political information to the American people. The con men, one may say, have taken over the mainstream organs of society. The danger to the ordinary citizen is grave and immediate. Too bad there is hardly anyone who is not in on the con, who has the guts to take on the con, and who has the reach to be heard, to alert him to it.

Chapter 12

CRACKING THE CON:

Restoring the Productive Society

Resistance to usurpation is possible provided the citizens understand their rights and are disposed to defend them.[1]

—Alexander Hamilton, *The Federalist*

Just after midnight on March 18, 1990, two thieves dressed as police officers showed up at Boston's Isabella Stewart Gardner Museum. They said they were responding to a report of someone attempting to break into the museum. The guards let them in, and the policemen promptly tied them up. Then they spent an hour going through the museum, surveying its treasures with the appreciation of art connoisseurs. They took thirteen priceless paintings, including Rembrandt's *The Storm on the Sea of Galilee*, five drawings by Degas, and Vermeer's *The Concert*, which is now regarded as the most valuable stolen painting in the world. The thieves also took an ancient Chinese bronze dating back to the Shang Dynasty. The FBI says the thieves were part of a national crime network. They seem to have had inside knowledge of the museum's surveillance system, and when they left they took the surveillance tape with them. This crime has never been solved.[2]

The two criminals disguised as policemen were both white males, so I cannot identify them as Barack Obama and Hillary Clinton. Moreover, Obama and Clinton aren't trying to steal art; they are trying to steal America itself. Still, there is a resemblance in that Obama and Clinton are highly skilled burglars who have presented themselves to us as police officers. They portray themselves as exposers of theft, custodians of our "fair share," and restorers of the wealth that has been taken from us. Just like the Boston burglars, they are the leaders of a criminal operation who are trying to make us believe they are our protectors.

It is time to consider the seriousness of our situation. America has been governed by a highly skilled con artist for the past seven years. Another con artist, perhaps even more adept, is waiting to take his place. This is truly historic. We think we made history by electing the first African American president, and we're going to hear a lot about making history by electing the first woman. Despite all the hoopla, those are relative trivialities. What really matters is that never before in history has America had a con artist as its chief executive and commander in chief. And we may be getting ready to anoint another in immediate succession. One is bad enough; two con artists in a row may be our undoing.

These con artists are, just like their Boston counterparts, part of a crime network. This crime network is the Democratic Party, and its leaders are the progressives. For decades now the progressives have assailed theft in America, blaming it on the greedy capitalists. They have claimed a virtual monopoly on political virtue, declaring themselves the champions of justice and equality.

Not only is that wrong, but the truth is the very opposite. The progressives are the real thieves, masquerading as opponents of theft. They are the criminals posing as the Justice Department. And they have, for the past seven years, actually controlled the Justice Department, turning it into an accessory of their crimes and an agency for going after whistle-blowers and crime fighters.

Harry Reid, Nancy Pelosi, Eric Holder, and Lois Lerner are all part of this crime organization, but so are hundreds of thousands of ordinary people, the envious, the resentful, the hateful, the entitled. These are the people who still have the Obama-Biden signs on their vehicles and are now eagerly anticipating Hillary. Together, they are "the criminals next door."

It's time to wake up, open our eyes, get on our feet, and shut down this con. That means halting the Obama con and repudiating the Hillary con, but it also means closing down the whole operation that goes by the name of progressivism or, alternatively, the Democratic Party. Is it possible for an entire party and political movement to become crooked in this way? Yes, it is. In this chapter I draw on the philosopher Nietzsche to show the genealogy or psychological root of this criminal enterprise.

Is it possible to shut it down? Yes, it is. Here I also suggest the four steps we must take to thwart this criminal operation and bring the malefactors to justice. I conclude on a note of impatience—there is no time to waste—and with an appeal to the necessary virtue of courage. Why? Because, to cite a line I frequently hear in the confinement center, "This sh*t has got to stop."

Every con has its time. Cons, like prison sentences, sometimes last a while, but in every con there's a time to get out and a way to get out. For me, I was done with my eight-month sentence on May 31. I was allowed to get out as early as 4 a.m. By this time I had largely completed my research into this criminal culture in which I found myself. Still, there were new guys coming in all the time. This meant new experiences, new stories. I wondered if I should write the judge and ask for a one-month extension of my sentence. "Wow," my fellow inmate Earl remarked, "would that put a look on the face of that m*therf*cker!" But I decided against it. Being locked up for more than eight months may be more fun than I can handle.

On May 31, 2015, I woke up at 3:15 a.m. I brushed my teeth and got dressed. I had been emptying my locker the previous week, taking home my books and the few articles of clothing I had stored at the confinement center. All that was left in my locker was my toilet kit. I stripped the sheets off my bed and rolled them into a ball, together with my pillowcase. By 3:55 I was at the front desk. The guy behind the counter—not someone I knew—looked quizzically at me. I said, "It's time to say goodbye." Without a word, he reached for my file to make sure my papers were in order. He handed me a garbage bag, and I placed the sheets and pillowcase in it. Then I went upstairs, got my mattress, and returned it. Then, without a word, I walked out of confinement for the last time. I was done.

I called Debbie. She could hear the excitement in my voice. I laughed. She cried. The full weight of what we had been through together suddenly hit her. I knew I had finally found a woman who would go the distance with me. She had proved it over the past several months. Now that I was done with the criminals, I could get on with my life with Debbie. Together, we would take on the bigger criminals who are in charge of our political system.

I walked toward my car to drive out of the parking lot for the last time. As I breathed the early-morning air—admittedly slightly fetid, on account of the waste disposal plant across the street—I thought to myself, I've learned a lot in this place. I now know the going rate— seven grand—for an illegal to pay a coyote to get him across the border. (The rate is nearly double if you're Muslim, or Chinese.) In the past I knew absolutely nothing about cocaine, crack, meth, spice, and marijuana. Now I do; and I'm even familiar with a lot of drug terms: a crack pipe, for example, is a "glass dick" and a woman who will give sex for drugs is a "head hunter."

My criminal vocabulary has expanded—mention the term *jewelry* to me and I know right away you're referring to handcuffed wrists— and my racial vocabulary is also more diverse. I didn't previously know that rural whites are called "Peckerwoods" by blacks and Latinos, and rural white women are called "Featherwoods." Whites have embraced these labels, so if you see Woody Woodpecker on some con's T-shirt, you can be sure you've encountered a proud Peckerwood. In such a situation it's okay to greet him, "Hey Pecker" or "Hey Wood." If I were planning to stay in that world, all of this would be very useful information. But I'm not, so I'm sharing it with you in case you ever find yourself in confinement.

On my last night in captivity, I ran into Ricardo.

"I hear you're leaving us, homie."

"All good things must come to an end."

He punched me on the shoulder—his way of wishing me well—and said, "I admire you, man."

"Why?" I asked. I felt strangely pleased to be admired by this longtime gang member.

"Because you went up against the Big Kahuna," he said. "You pissed off Obama! That's huge, dog. That's like telling Don Corleone to f*ck off."

Then he added, "We'll miss you."

I said, "I learned a lot from this place."

He said, "Don't get caught again. You're a smart guy. Do what they all do—figure out a way to play the system."

"No. I'm not joining the system. I'm going to blow the whistle on it."

"Oh man," he sighed. "That makes you one dangerous m*therf*cker."

"Yes," I said. "That's my goal."

We touched fists and said goodbye.

For my fellow inmate Cojones, the time to get out came several months earlier, even before he got to the confinement center. Cojones quit his con when he had a born-again experience in prison. "I accepted Jesus," he said, "and Jesus, not the gang, became my new master."

It was one thing to want to get out of the gang, however, and another to actually do it. "Normally," Cojones explained, "there is no way to leave a gang. Once you join, you become a soldier, and a soldier who leaves is considered a deserter."

How, I asked him, did he leave?

"I once did a favor for a man who was a contract killer for the Mexican mafia," Cojones said. "He needed money, and I loaned him the money. He never forgot that."

Soon after that, Cojones said, he and the contract killer went fishing. "I told him about my family, and he told me I should get out of the gang and look after my wife and kids. But I told him no, I don't want to leave. He said he understood, but if I ever changed my mind I should use his name."

Cojones was eighteen years old at the time. Four years later, he told me, "I sat crying in my cell, and repenting for my sins, and wishing I could get out of my old life, and then I remembered what that man told me."

So he approached the fellow in prison who was the highest-ranking member of his gang. "I told him I wanted to leave, and he said no way. I told him why, and he could see the conviction in my eyes. He knew I was done."

"Why," I asked, "did he say no?"

"I think it's partly because he knew that he himself could never get out. He's in it for life.

"Then I used the name of the man in the Mexican mafia, and that got his attention. But still he said he could not decide by himself. He said he would send a kite and let me know."

A kite? "A kite is a note to a guy higher up."

Cojones said the request went all the way to the top level of the gang, and even the Mexican mafia was consulted because he had done some work for them.

"I must have got the green light, because they told me I was free to leave."

I asked, "Are those your gang tattoos that you have been trying to laser off?"

"Yes," Cojones said with a smile. "My former life."

And now Cojones is a soldier for Christ, and he is completely fearless. One morning he saw me sipping coffee and sat across from me. "God used me yesterday," he said. "I felt the Lord's message on me."

Cojones was riding the trolley back from work to the confinement center, and he just got the urge to stand up and preach.

"I was really scared," he told me. "Maybe more scared than I have ever been. But I just stood up and addressed the people and I said: 'My name is Cojones and I just need three minutes of your time.' And then I gave my testimony. I told them what Jesus has done in my life. Then I went to the next trolley car and did the same thing. I did it three times."

"I have to say," I said to him, "that took a lot of cojones."

He smiled. "I didn't do nothing," he said. "It was the courage of the Lord working through me."

Cojones now works two jobs and he is also taking classes at a junior college. He cannot afford any textbooks, so he goes to the library to read there or attempts to find the material online. I wrote down the name of his math book and ordered a copy. Then, after confirming with the staff that it was okay for me to present it to him, I did. He hugged me. Seldom have I felt so good about doing a small favor for someone. Cojones, I think, is going to be all right.

Cojones's story is not typical. More typical perhaps is the case of Bones, a black guy who came into the confinement center insisting that he was a billionaire. Bones's bunk mate, another black guy, tried to shake his hand but Bones wouldn't. "I just don't shake hands," he said.

The first weekend, he got out on a hygiene pass, supposedly to pick up a toothbrush, deodorant, and some soap. He returned a few hours later saying that the hygiene thing was all BS, that he actually had a meeting with a real estate broker downtown. "I'm trying to buy the penthouse at the Harbor Club." Asking price: $7 million. He also claims to have stopped by the La Jolla Bugatti dealership. "You should have seen the look on that m*therf*cker's face," he said, "when I told him I want five."

Bones dressed like your typical bum but warned that this was no indication of his financial capacity. In fact, he said, rappers like Jay-Z and Birdman also dressed like him but were much richer than Bill Gates. "See, Gates has money but if Microsoft goes down, then that n*gger's broke. But that's not the case with Jay-Z. That n*gger's loaded, and he got his money in cash. Of course Jay-Z ain't got as much as Birdman.

I'm telling you, Birdman is the richest man in America. Birdman gives n*ggers money just to show that n*ggers got money."

I wish Bones well, but I worry that he lives in a fantasy world that does not correspond with the real one. He may do better in a confined setting where his gets free meals and where he can remain one of America's most secret billionaires.

Another guy who seems more typical than Cojones is Shaw, a white guy in his mid-thirties who came to the confinement center with a long rap sheet. Shaw told me he had been in prison "since the age of fourteen." I met Shaw when he approached me to do a favor for him. "Can you google my name?" he asked me. "I am going to be out on the street and applying for jobs. I want to see what people can find out about me."

"Why don't you do the Google search yourself?"

"I'd have to do it in here," he said, "and these m*therf*ckers would know what I'm doing."

"What's on your rap sheet?"

"Domestic violence," he said, "drug charges, theft, assault with a deadly weapon, kidnapping, armed robbery." He paused and added, "I also have an attempted murder charge, but they couldn't prove nothing.

"I didn't do it," he added. "I was just watching. Some white guys in the maximum-security ward of Pelican Bay prison killed a black guy. They said I was guarding the door, but I was just standing in front of the door."

He spoke matter-of-factly, but something in his eyes—a glint, perhaps—told me he wasn't telling the truth. Even if he was, I wondered how a guy could be so cavalier about *watching* a murder.

I didn't do any Google searching for Shaw. I wasn't sure I wanted to see this guy on the street.

I didn't see Shaw for a few days. Then one evening I saw the security guys pulling the sheets off his bed, clearing out his locker, and dumping all his stuff into garbage bags. I asked them what happened to Shaw.

"He took off," one of them said. "He hasn't showed up. We've informed the marshals. He's facing an escape charge."

The word in the center is that Shaw got high and didn't want to get caught for using drugs. Using drugs or alcohol can get a guy kicked out of the halfway house and sent back to prison. Still, it's better to risk that than to be apprehended after an attempted escape, which can get you an additional year or more in prison.

"I don't understand that mentality," I said to Shaw's former bunk mate. "How stupid can a guy be?"

"You *don't* understand his mentality," the bunk mate said. "That m*therf*cker *wants* to go back to prison. Prison is all he knows. He's more afraid of life on the outside than he is of going back to prison."

I remember Shaw talking about his life in prison. At times he was positively enthusiastic. He liked the fact that his prison showed movies once a week that had been newly released into the theater. He had apparently won ten dollars in the prison's Ultimate Frisbee league. In his last facility, he said, there was an "activities director" who organized bingo, tennis, and aerobics classes.

But on multiple occasions Shaw had also found himself in the prison's special facilities—the "prison within the prison." One time after a big fight he was placed in a solitary cell for three months. On another occasion, following some other infraction, he was cooped up with three other guys for five months in what he called "the cage." The cage had no windows, and the four of them were in there for twenty-two hours a day. They were let out into the yard for two hours a day. But that was so early in the morning it was "before the sun came out, so we never saw the sun." Why anyone would risk returning to that sort of life is unfathomable to me.

Of course the Mexicans who live across the border operate by a different set of rules. During my time in confinement several of those guys took off, and no one expects to see them again. "They just go through the front door. We don't stop them. Then they walk across the border and they are back home in Mexico. We notify the marshals but what good does that do?" one staffer told me. "When I worked in Taft prison we lost one or two of them every day."

But there are other guys in here who I think have a chance to make it. Cojones is not the only one. Another inmate, a South Sider who served a five-year prison sentence, has also decided to go straight. "I'm just tired of screwing up my life," he said. "I've used up all my nine lives. I don't have any more energy for this." He's been working construction part-time but they like him and he thinks they'll offer him a full-time job. "I've been preparing for this for five f*cking years, man, and now I'm ready."

Even Sam, the white guy who's been in prison off and on since the 1970s, seems to have decided he's had enough. "I'm sixty-f*cking-two," he says. "And I've never worked so hard in my life. Do you see me dragging my ass in here every night? That's because I'm carrying a belt with heavy equipment and installing air-conditioning units on the seventeenth floor of an office building. It's hard labor. But it's real work and I get real money for it, and I'm getting used to earning money instead of stealing it."

Even one of the guards, Alex, is quitting. "Don't say anything," he whispers to me as he pats me down and runs his wand across my body. "But I'm trying to get myself outta here. Too much bullsh*t, you know what I'm saying? This place is for losers, and I'm talking about the people who work here, not you guys. My IQ isn't low enough, you know what I'm saying? I came here to help people, and this place helps no one. I'm going to be looking for a new job. Hey, I don't know if you have security, but if you need someone, let's talk, you know what I'm saying? I can even be your driver and provide security at the same time. Think about it." I said I would.

It would be good if Democrats and progressives would, like Alex, come to the sober conclusion that enough is enough, and that it's time for them to get out. This, however, is not likely. The reason is not merely that they benefit materially from the con. Some of them do, but others don't, or they benefit only marginally. Even so, it's hard to convince thieves that they should stop being thieves when they have convinced themselves they are crusaders for justice.

How can thieves be so self-deluded?

The philosopher Nietzsche helps us to answer that question. In one of his books, *On the Genealogy of Morals*, Nietzsche attempts to account for the origins of morality. Specifically, he seeks to explain the rise of Judeo-Christian morality. His explanation is both brilliant and controversial, and ultimately I find it unconvincing. I don't want to get into that issue here. Nietzsche remains, however, the great diagnostician of the psychological roots of morality. If Nietzsche is read politically—which is not how he is normally read—he supplies us with an illuminating way of understanding the larcenous con that is modern progressivism.

Morality, Nietzsche shows, is not merely an application of conscience or values to a given situation. Rather, morality sometimes grows out of a deep psychological desire to escape a given situation, to invert it, to provide a justification and a rationalization for changing things for one's own benefit. Using Nietzsche's framework, I will show that progressive morality, through its bogus invocation of "fairness" and "justice," attempts a transvaluation of values. Upon examination, we can see that it is a cheap and transparent cover for systematic theft and for what Nietzsche terms the will to power.

Let's begin with the settlers and entrepreneurs in America, the ones who built this country in its first 150 years, from the founding through the early part of the twentieth century. These were hardy, frugal, industrious people who came to this country with nothing and owed nothing to anyone. They recognized that this was a country set up to encourage wealth creation, and they seized on that project with a vengeance. They became successful by growing things or making things that other people wanted. These other people benefited from what they made, and consequently their success was a measure of the degree to which they had served the wants and needs of their fellow man.

Obviously there was nothing to apologize for in this form of productive activity; on the contrary, it was considered unambiguously good. America's entrepreneurs and builders were doers and visionaries. I think of the greatest of them in Nietzschean terms. They raise life itself to higher pillars, recognizing that to do this they must struggle, they must create, and they must compete. Entrepreneurs are not exclusively cooperative and they are not exclusively competitive; in fact, finding the right combination of these two rival qualities defines the successful entrepreneur.

Historically entrepreneurs have regarded success as a reflection of the good of enterprise. They have defined the ingredients of entrepreneurship—hard work, thrift, creativity, courage, competitiveness, and honest earning—as positive values, and their opposites—laziness, profligacy, vacuity, timidity, do-nothingness, and dishonest taking—as negative values. The capitalists affirmed the virtue of prosperity.

This is not to deny that this society, like every other, had thieves who sought to deprive citizens of their hard-earned wealth. Thievery is the way of the world, and it was certainly the way of the societies from which the American people originally came. What Americans appreciated, however, was that this country was founded as an anti-theft society with a constitutional framework that protected your property and your right to keep the wealth you create. Of course, not everyone's wealth creation efforts paid off. Not everyone was either successful or happy, but the American story was that everyone aspired to be. This is the "pursuit of happiness" that the Declaration of Independence speaks about.

There is one group, however, that will always be unhappy to live in an anti-theft society. That group is called thieves. The thieves in this case are not the workers who are employed by the capitalists and entrepreneurs. Never in history has the working class of its own accord revolted against the capitalists who employ them. Indeed, since workers are salesmen of their labor, the capitalists are their best, indeed their only, customers. Nor are thieves to be found among the general public that benefits from the products that the entrepreneurs and workers jointly produce. Most people, in their role as consumers, are quite content to pay for the products that they purchase, and the thieves among this group have a special name: shoplifters.

The thieves I speak of are neither workers nor consumers; rather, they are recruited from the classes that are ignored or left behind by capitalism: the avaricious politicians and community activists, the envious intellectuals and pseudo-intellectuals, the resentful journalists and media types. Nietzsche has a term for them: the avengers. He says that these people are dangerous, but they are also very clever. Thieves they may be, but of a particular sort; Nietzsche even says they know how to make crime *interesting*. Ultimately, Nietzsche says, their goal is to avenge themselves on the good and the successful, and extract wealth and power for themselves. "They are people of a low sort and stock," Nietzsche says. "The hangman and the bloodhound look out of their faces."

The avengers know that, at one time, they used to be the ones in charge. That period was for them the glorious age of exploitation, in which they created aristocratic and caste hierarchies and installed themselves conveniently at the top. Then they ordained that their superior status was part of the natural, eternal order of things. They set up systems so that they could, through tributes and confiscation, seize the wealth of merchants and entrepreneurs.

They could also, through feudal arrangements of one sort or another, appropriate the earnings, meager though those might be, of workers and laborers below them. It was an age of deprivation, but the thieves enjoyed it, because they were not the ones being deprived. For them, the ancien régime was wonderful while it lasted, and it lasted for many, many centuries. Until America came along.

In America, the thieves seethed with hatred and envy, aching to seize the abundance that the wealth creators were generating all around them. They could not understand how that abundance was generated; what they understood was that they wanted access to it; actually, they wanted to be in control of it. In a sense, they pined for a restoration of the ancien régime. But only in a sense, because they had no intention of returning to the age of deprivation. Rather, they wanted capitalist abundance, but with progressives in charge of the distribution of the rewards.

Their project, however, seemed hopeless. Capitalists paid no attention to their nonsense and were not about to turn over control to these malcontents and losers. The thieves tried to stir up worker revolts—essentially organized forms of thievery—but usually these did not materialize, and the police were more than sufficient to suppress the few that did. That's the problem with living in an anti-theft society: large-scale thefts become harder to pull off.

Then, starting in the twentieth century, the avengers got their act together. They came together in a progressive movement that soon found its natural home in the Democratic Party. The progressives were, from the point of view of wealth creation, a useless lot. They were, however, highly skilled in the art of a new type of thievery. This was political thievery, thievery that operated through the democratic process itself. Community organizing, voting, political wheeling and dealing, legislation, and regulation would be some of the instruments of this type of organized crime.

It also was incremental thievery, in that it began small and then grew bigger. The thievery of the New Deal was modest, almost symbolic. FDR knew that his Social Security program was a Ponzi scheme, and his rhetoric about people setting aside money for their own retirement completely dishonest; even so, he regarded forcing working people to pay for older people's retirement as a necessary response to an emergency situation, the Great Depression. The thievery of Lyndon Johnson and the Great Society was more scandalous and had no legitimate crisis to warrant it, but still it was modest in terms of the overall economy. Jimmy Carter was too inept to be much of a thief, and Bill Clinton was more interested in his personal ego and appetites to attempt a systematic heist. With Obama and Hillary, however, progressive thievery has come into its element. These thieves have their sights on the wealth of the whole country, and the process of stealing it is well under way.

Progressive thievery is thievery of a special sort, thievery that marches behind the banner of justice. In one of his other books, *Thus Spoke Zarathustra*, Nietzsche writes that for the avengers, justice is a camouflage for envy and revenge; these are "tyrants who shroud themselves in words of virtue."[3] This seems odd: thieves don't normally attempt to wear a halo. In *The Godfather*, criminals like Luca Brasi never tried to pose as pillars of society.

Yet today's thieves do have historical precedent: for centuries, kings and aristocrats sought to justify their larceny through corrupt, self-serving invocations of God and the natural order of things. They claimed a right and an entitlement to other people's money on grounds of their own alleged superiority.

Progressives may privately consider themselves superior, but they know they cannot include that claim in their pitch. Consequently they claim superiority by default. In a society where government controls things and distributes wealth, the power of the bureaucrat becomes predominant. Here's how that works. First, progressives develop their pitch. They take all the virtues of the wealth creators, such as creativity, frugality, hard work, self-discipline, self-reliance, innovation, and the aspiration to success, and redefine them as vices. Creativity and frugality, for instance, become greed. Hard work and self-discipline become materialism. Self-reliance becomes arrogance. Innovation and the aspiration to success become proof of a lack of compassion as well as engines of inequality. In sum, the capitalists are now the exploiters, the expropriators, the bad guys. In the progressive view, their wealth is not earned but rather stolen.

Conversely, progressives take all the losers under capitalism—the failed businessmen, the displaced workers, the ne'er-do-well intellectuals, the useless activists—and redefine them as victims. This takes the frustration and envy of the losers and gives it meaning. In Nietzsche's terms, resentment becomes creative and gives rise to new values. The avengers are creative in the sense that they have come up with these new values. They know how to turn grief into grievance. Their purpose is to convert impotent frustration, on the part of useless and displaced classes of people, into useful mobilization. The progressives have a new task for these people. They want them to become burglars. But first they have to convince them that burglary is good.

The progressive pretense is that these people, who have created virtually nothing, are actually the real creators of the nation's wealth. In avenger talk, businesses and workers don't create wealth; wealth is created by people outside the business. Since those people are not in possession of the wealth, though, that wealth has clearly been stolen from them. It has been stolen by those who have it, namely the capitalists and the productive employees.

So naturally the victims are angry. Suddenly their vices of envy, resentment, and rage become signs of justified indignation. Their covetousness becomes a measure of their legitimate entitlement. A moral inversion is under way here: what was previously defined as good now becomes bad; what had previously been considered bad now becomes good. Now we understand why Obama glorifies the people sitting in the bandwagon and castigates those who pull the wagon. Obama wants to mobilize the people in the bandwagon, not to get jobs, but to get involved with his theft scheme.

This moral inversion—what Nietzsche terms the transvaluation of values—is necessary to justify theft. Theft is not easy to justify, but justifying it is a progressive specialty. It's not easy to convince hundreds of thousands, perhaps millions, of people to become thieves or participate in a theft scheme. If you asked them to go into a department store and loot stuff, they would emphatically refuse. The idea is too offensive to their image of themselves. Consequently, progressives recognize that you have to convince thieves that they are not really thieves. Rather, they are restorers of stolen goods. The capitalists are the real thieves.

This is the point of the transvaluation of values. It is to recruit thieves to the progressive cause and give them a high self-esteem over the crimes in which they participate. It is also to convince at least some of the targets of theft—the gullible ones—to feel guilty about their success and concede moral superiority to the avengers that want to forcibly take their money.

The progressives are the ones who are the organizers and administrators of theft. This is not an easy job. Nietzsche emphasizes the dual challenge. First you must activate and mobilize a mob of people, rousing them out of their sluggish stupor. Nietzsche insightfully notes that drawing on the frustration and resentment of people is not enough;

the avenger must work to *create more of it*. Speaking of the avenger, Nietzsche writes, "Before he can play the physician he must first wound; so while he soothes the pain which the wound makes, he at the same time poisons the wound."

Once this has been accomplished, however, once the mob has been mobilized, Nietzsche says the avenger then has to tame that mob, to prevent it from getting out of control and simply smashing things. Once the activator of resentment, the avenger now becomes what Nietzsche calls "the diverter of resentment."[4] While despairing of the capitalist system, the mob must learn to trust the avenger to handle things on its behalf. Progressive avengers don't want random disorder or violence; they want controlled rage that they can direct politically so that the result is an organized transfer of power and wealth.

Theft, you see, is like a business; it requires entrepreneurship, although of a political sort. Progressives may not be talented in making airplanes fly or coming up with medical treatments, but they are talented in putting together systematic political larceny schemes. Here, then, is the avenger's proof of superiority. And avengers demand to be elevated to the top of society so that they can oversee the institutional rip-off. This, in Nietzsche's terms, is their will to power. Nietzsche emphasizes that the will to power is not just about money; it is also about control. More than anything else, Obama and Hillary want to lord it over the wealth creators, and over the rest of us.

But they also want money. And, given their leadership position in the crime scheme, they believe they deserve a more-than-equal share of the take. No wonder that Obama, Hillary, and other progressive crime bosses have no compunction about living high on the hog while continuing their dishonest pitches about fair shares, injustice, and inequality. It never crosses their mind that any of their rhetoric applies in the least to them. Nor do they expect their progressive underlings to complain as long as some of the benefits, both in terms of political control and financial rewards, are disbursed down the ladder. Even while it deplores the concept, progressivism is based on "trickle-down economics." The ordinary gang member had better understand that he's not going to get the same as the mob boss.

What, then, is the solution to this organized thievery? It is fourfold. First, we have to recognize the con. This book is an effort toward that. It seeks to turn a flashlight onto the robbery scheme that is modern progressivism. I'm so glad I had the opportunity, in confinement, to learn about how gangs and crime schemes work; otherwise I may never have had a full understanding of modern progressivism and the Democratic Party. We need to lose our illusions about these guys. We need to cut back on debating progressives about whether their redistribution schemes will or will not undermine greed and produce social equality. We need to recognize that these are simply pitches aimed at taking our money. Holding on to our wallets is far more important than convincing or appeasing the avengers.

Second, we have to publicize the con. Nothing frustrates a con so much as exposure to the light. I'm doing what I can. I'm making a big film for next year and I hope its message will reach not only conservatives but also moderates and independents. I am also expanding my efforts to influence the culture. I'm going into feature films, in order to give Hollywood a run for its money, and I'm creating a new type of online education. The conservative project to infiltrate the campus, in the manner the left did in the late 1960s, is a quixotic one. It's not going to happen. Our best hope is to create new forms of education and make the existing university system—which is outdated and costs way too much—obsolete. I'm not even trying to create "conservative education," just liberal education in the original sense of the term. Free Market University will open its doors soon.

That's me; what about you? Many times people ask me, "What can I do?" Use your networks and your influence to help get the word out. The more people who know that there is a con under way, the less cover the con men have to keep doing it to us. If you're young, think about new ways of applying conservative principles to the world as it is now. Look for new opportunities to publicize and implement your ideas.

Don't ask, What existing institution can I work for? Rather, ask, What institutions need to be created that don't exist now?

This is the entrepreneurial approach. Our goal is to become a progressive nightmare. When progressives see that glimmer of recognition in people's eyes as they approach them, they will know that we know what they are up to, and they will slink away, and look for some other sucker to steal from. Ultimately our goal is to reduce the population of suckers, so that the only people the thieves can steal from is other thieves like themselves.

Third, we have to get the con out of the Capitol and the White House. This can be done piecemeal, by blocking this or that political larceny scheme. But ultimately the progressives will continue to come up with new schemes unless we get rid of the progressives. There's a perfect way to do that: the 2016 election. We must vote out the con artists and remove their party from power. America has painfully endured one con man, Obama; we certainly don't need another in Hillary. After the 2016 election, Obama, Bill, and Hillary can all be private-sector thieves where they will continue their cons, but at least their tentacles will not be in the public Treasury.

Finally, we have to reaffirm America as an anti-theft society. This requires teaching our young people a new story about America. It's not just a matter of restoring the curriculum circa 1950. The new story must take into account the progressive assault of recent decades. It should incorporate a refutation of progressivism into its affirmation of America's founding principles. This restoration of America also has a judicial element: it means holding the most egregious con artists accountable for their misdeeds.

The GOP has to wake up from its chronic slumber. It should use its power in Congress in the manner that the Democrats did when Nixon and Reagan were president. It shouldn't just hold hearings; hearings should be the prelude to prosecutions. Yes, it's time to send some people to prison—and I for one am looking forward to that. I've vacated my bunk in the confinement center, creating a spot for Obama.

And there's a female confinement center down the street that I'm sure would accommodate Hillary. I want the big cons in the political realm to make friends with the little cons who are already in prisons and confinement centers; I'd be happy to introduce them to some of my former fellow inmates.

Conservatives are the true liberals. Why? Because we are conserving the spirit of the American Revolution, which was a liberal revolution in the classical meaning of the term. Progressive Democrats are not liberals; they are the descendants of the thieves of old. They are the ghosts of corrupt aristocrats, self-serving Brahmins, and extortionist mafia dons. They are also the modern-day American equivalents of despots, autocrats, and bureaucrats in third-world countries who use their offices to gain power and accumulate money. In short, they are the criminals and we are the crime fighters. I am a criminal—a very small criminal—who is now ready to be a frontline crime fighter.

I'm not saying it will be easy. We are tempted to keep doing things the old way, the way that is proven not to work. Many of us are also tempted to resignation. So often on social media I see people say, in effect, that oppression and double standards are now hallmarks of our society; that they are just the way things are. I am reminded of Joseph K. in Kafka's *The Trial*. This poor man is subject to a nightmare of oppression. He has been brought up on capital charges, but he cannot figure out by whom, and for what.

Yet as the novel develops we discover something strange: Joseph K. begins to act as if he were guilty and collaborates with his oppressors. He is interrogated on a Sunday and when it's over they tell him they will contact him for the next interrogation. The following Sunday, even though he hasn't heard from them, he shows up at court for his interrogation. Later he tells his landlady that he has been arrested. She asks him what he has done, and he says that the prosecutors will inform him in due time. In fact he hasn't done anything wrong, but slowly, chillingly, he comes to believe the lie that he is guilty. At the end of the story, when two executioners are passing the knife between each other, he considers grabbing it and plunging it into his chest. Incredibly, he blames his failure to do so on his own weakness. So eventually they stab him to death, a tragic and tragically also a willing victim.[5]

I mentioned the fate of Joseph K. to a friend who said, "That sounds like the Republican Party." I pray he is wrong about this. We do not want to be Joseph K. It is our passivity that encourages the abuses of power by the other side. As Cassius says of Caesar, "He would not be a wolf, but that he sees the Romans are but sheep."[6] We Americans now need fresh thinking, and new types of action, and most of all the political virtue of courage. Courage is the necessary antidote to envy. If envy is the mother of all vices, courage is the mother of all virtues. That's because it takes courage to be honest, it takes courage to be self-controlled, it takes courage to put ideas into action. It also takes courage to be patriotic, to go beyond loving America and do what is necessary to restore America.

Many years ago a college professor told me the story about the lion tamer and the lion. So here's the clever lion tamer, with his little twirl-ing stick, and there is the lion, prancing obediently to the machina-tions of the lion tamer. Clearly the lion tamer is in charge. But, asked my professor, who is actually more powerful, the lion tamer or the lion? Obviously it is the lion. Why then does the lion do the bidding of the lion tamer? Because the lion doesn't know its own power. We, the American people, have been exploited and stolen from and we have put up with it at least in part because we are awed by the power of the pro-gressive lion tamers. I admit they do have power, but I am also saying we do not appreciate our own strength. Let's put that strength to work, right here, right now.

ACKNOWLEDGMENTS

A book is a hard thing to write. A good book is even harder. This, I hope you agree, is a good book. The following people helped a lot.

Bruce Schooley, my best friend and longtime co-conspirator

Ed McVaney, mentor, supporter, longtime friend

Danielle D'Souza, my daughter, whiz kid, and confidante

Debbie Fancher, my heartthrob, collaborator, and happiness consultant

Aaron and Sonia Brubaker, whom I adore and rely on

Kimberly Dvorak, researcher par excellence

Adam Bellow, my editor and friend of twenty-five years

The Texas women who prayed for me throughout my confinement

Hey, I'm not done yet. Without the following people, this book would not be possible.

My fellow convicts, who shared their lives and stories

Obama, the original con man

Holder, the henchman

Preet, Carrie, and the gang, the enforcement goons

Judge Richard Berman, who taught me more lessons than he intended

NOTES

Chapter 1: Crime and Punishment

1   John of the Cross, *Dark Night of the Soul* (Mineola, NY: 2003), p. 85–86.

2   Jonathan Capehart, "Dinesh D'Souza Is So 'Ghetto,' " *Washington Post*, February 18, 2015, washingtonpost.com.

3   The subsequent report of the sentencing is based on my recollection, aided by the court transcript, *United States v. Dinesh D'Souza*, U.S. Southern District of New York (14 CR 34), September 23, 2014.

4   Paul Bond, "President Obama's Campaign Trashes *2016: Obama's America*," *Hollywood Reporter*, September 11, 2012, hollywoodreporter.com.

5   Associated Press, "US Prosecutor Defends Arrest and Strip-Search of Indian Diplomat," *Guardian*, December 19, 2013, theguardian.com.

6   Natalie Villacorta, "Senators Write FBI Over Dinesh D'Souza Case," *Politico*, February 21, 2014, politico.com.

7   Harvey Silverglate, *Three Felonies a Day* (New York: Encounter Books, 2011), p. l.

8   Stephanie Clifford and Russ Buettner, "Clinton Backer Pleads Guilty in a Straw Donor Scheme," *New York Times*, April 17, 2014, nytimes.com; Stephanie Clifford, "Hotelier Avoids Prison for Violating Campaign Finance Laws," *New York Times*, December 18, 2014, nytimes.com.

Chapter 2: The World as It Is

1   Niccolò Machiavelli, *The Prince* (New York: Penguin, 1981), p. 90.

2   Alexander Solzhenitsyn, *One Day in the Life of Ivan Denisovich* (New York: New American Library, 2009), p. 80.

3   Machiavelli, *The Prince*, pp. 90–91.

4   Sari Horwit and Carol Leonnig, "Report: DEA Agents Had 'Sex Parties' With Prostitutes Hired by Drug Cartels," *Washington Post*, March 26, 2015, washington post.com.

5   Augustine, *City of God* (New York: Penguin, 1984), p. 139.

6   Franz Kafka, *The Trial* (New York: Schocken Classics, 1984), p. 86.

Chapter 3: How to Steal a Country

1   Suketu Mehta, *Maximum City* (New York: Vintage, 2004), pp. 198–99.

2   Romans 7:19.

3   Cited by David Brion Davis, *The Problem of Slavery in Western Culture* (New York: Oxford University Press, 1988), p. 26.

4   Arthur Brooks, *Who Really Cares* (New York: Basic Books, 2006).

Chapter 4: Creating New Wealth

1   Ayn Rand, *Capitalism: The Unknown Ideal* (New York: Signet, 1967), p. 45.

2   Ibn Khaldun, *The Muqaddimah* (Princeton, NJ: Princeton University Press, 1967), pp. 118, 210.

3   Thucydides, *The Peloponnesian War* (New York: Penguin, 1985), pp. 400–408.

4   Edwin Mora, "Mexican Cartels Increasingly Corrupting DHS Employees to Smuggle Aliens from Countries Likely to Export Terrorism," August 22, 2012, cnsnews.com.

5   Ian Urbina, "Using Jailed Migrants as a Pool of Cheap Labor," *New York Times*, May 24, 2014, nytimes.com.

6   Alex Anderson, "After the Government Takes His Life Savings, This 22-Year-Old Fights for Justice," *Daily Signal*, June 9, 2015, dailysignal.com; Michael Sallah, Robert O'Harrow Jr., and Steven Rich, "Stop and Seize," *Washington Post*, September 6, 2014, washingtonpost.com; Jared Meyer, "How to Restore Innocent Until Proven Guilty," December 19, 2012, townhall.com.

7   Senator Tom Coburn, *Wastebook 2014*, October 10, 2014, showmethespend ing.com; Romina Boccia, "Federal Spending by the Numbers, 2014," report by the Heritage Foundation, 2014, heritage.org; Shane Goldmacher, "Nearly One in Five Members of Congress Gets Paid Twice," *National Journal*, June 27, 2013, national journal.org; Government Accountability Office, "Farm Programs," Appendix IV, Report to the Ranking Member, Committee on the Judiciary, U.S. Senate, September 2013.

8   Katherine Boo, *Behind the Beautiful Forevers* (New York: Random House, 2012). The quotation from Abdul appears on p. 242.

9   Alexander Hamilton, James Madison, and John Jay, *The Federalist* (New York: Barnes & Noble Classics, 2006), No. 1, p. 9.

10   Cited by Forrest McDonald, *Novus Ordo Seclorum* (Lawrenceville: University Press of Kansas, 1985), p. 3; Hamilton, Madison, and Jay, *The Federalist*, No. 12, p. 65.

11   Hamilton, Madison, and Jay, *The Federalist*, No. 10, p. 53.

12   Harry V. Jaffa, *A New Birth of Freedom* (Lanham, MD: Rowman & Littlefield, 2000), p. 3.

13   Thomas Jefferson, *Notes on the State of Virginia* (New York: Norton, 1982), p. 120.

14   Hamilton, Madison, and Jay, *The Federalist*, No. 84, p. 474.

15   Abraham Lincoln, speech at Kalamazoo, Michigan, August 27, 1856, in *Selected Speeches and Writings* (New York: Vintage Books, 1992), p. 111.

16   Lincoln, speech at Jacksonville, Illinois, February 11, 1859, in ibid., p. 208.

Chapter 5: History for Profit

1   Mark Twain, *The Adventures of Huckleberry Finn* (New York: Pocket Books, 1973), p. 159.

2   Flannery O'Connor, *A Good Man Is Hard to Find and Other Stories* (San Diego: Harvest, 1983), p. 194.

3   Sharon LaFraniere, "U.S. Opens Spigot After Farmers Claim Discrimination," *New York Times*, April 25, 2013, nytimes.com.

4   Robert Doar, "The U.S. Economy Is Still on Food Stamps," American Enterprise Institute, October 16, 2014, aei.org; James Bovard, "The Food Stamp Crime Wave," *Wall Street Journal*, June 23, 2011, wsj.com; Congressional Budget Office, "The Supplemental Nutrition Assistance Program," April 2012.

5   Michael Tanner and Charles Hughes, "The Work vs. Welfare Tradeoff: 2013," Cato Institute, Washington, D.C., 2013; Eric Boehm, "In Many States, Welfare Can Pay Better than an Honest Day's Work," August 21, 2013, watchdog.org.

6   Allen Guelzo, *Lincoln and Douglas: The Debates That Defined America* (New York: Simon & Schuster, 2014), p. 14.

7   Abraham Lincoln, *Speeches and Writings* (New York: Library of America, 1989), pp. 685–86; Abraham Lincoln, *Selected Speeches and Writings* (New York: Vintage Books, 1992), p. 149.

8   Lincoln, *Selected Speeches and Writings*, pp. 146, 176.

9   Philip S. Foner, *The Life and Writings of Frederick Douglass* (New York: International, 1950), pp. 188–90; Zora Neale Hurston, *Dust Tracks on a Road* (New York: HarperPerennial, 1991), pp. 206–8.

Chapter 6: The Things That Keep Progressives Awake at Night

1   Giovanni Boccaccio, *The Decameron* (New York: Vintage, 2008), p. 180.

2   Ibid., pp. 178–82.

3   Amartya Sen, "What Should Keep Us Awake at Night," *Little Magazine* 8, nos. 1 and 2 (2009).

4   Amartya Sen, *The Idea of Justice* (Cambridge, MA: Harvard University Press, 2009), pp. 13–14.

5   "Debt Clock," "Recent US Federal Deficit Numbers," usgovernmentdebt.us.

6   Karoun Demirjian, "Harry Reid Returns Campaign Money Paid to Granddaughter for 'Holiday Gifts,' " *Las Vegas Sun*, March 25, 2014, lasvegassun.com; Geoff Earle, "Reid Campaign Cash Paid to Granddaughter Hits $31,000," *New York Post*, March 28, 2014, nypost.com.

7   Peter Schweizer, *Clinton Cash* (New York: HarperCollins, 2015), p. 180.

8   Seth Cline, "Obama Campaign Fined Big for Hiding Donors, Keeping Illegal Donations," *U.S. News & World Report*, January 7, 2013, usnews.com.

9   Adam Smith, *The Wealth of Nations* (New York: Penguin, 1999), pp. 441, 443.

10   Adam Smith, *A Theory of Moral Sentiments* (New York: Gutenberg, 2011), p. 20.

11   Smith, *The Wealth of Nations*, p. 119.

12   "Obama to Wall Street: 'I Do Think at a Certain Point You've Made Enough Money,' " RealClearPolitics, April 28, 2010, realclearpolitics.com.

13   Thorstein Veblen, *The Theory of the Leisure Class* (New York: Penguin, 1994), p. 204.

Chapter 7: You Didn't Build That

1   Aaron Blake, "Obama's 'You Didn't Build That' Problem," *Washington Post*, July 18, 2012, washingtonpost.com.

2   Suketu Mehta, *Maximum City* (New York: Vintage Books, 2004), p. 211.

3   Blake, "Obama's 'You Didn't Build That' Problem"; "Elizabeth Warren: 'There is nobody in this country who got rich on his own,' " CBS News, September 22, 2011, cbsnews.com; Paul Singer, "Hillary Clinton: It's Not Businesses That Create Jobs," *USA Today*, October 25, 2014, onpolitics.usatoday.com.

4   Ravi Bhatra, "The Cost of Trickle-Down Government Job Creation: $1.5 Million Per Worker," January 8, 2012, truth-out.org; James Pethokoukis, "CBO: Obama Stimulus May Have Cost As Much As $4.1 Million a Job," American Enterprise Institute, May 30, 2012, aei.org.

5   See, e.g., Vicki Smith, "Pork or Progress: Either Way, Robert Byrd Changed West Virginia," *Washington Post*, June 28, 2010, washingtonpost.com; Adam Clymer, "Robert Byrd, a Pillar of the Senate, Dies at 92," *New York Times*, July 3, 2010, nytimes.com; Staff Reports, "Byrd's Name is Everywhere You Look in W. Va.," *Charleston Gazette*, July 1, 2010.

6   "Richard Wolff on Curing Capitalism," March 22, 2013, billmoyers.com.

7   Karl Marx, *The Portable Karl Marx* (New York: Penguin, 1983), pp. 407–9, 412–16.

8   Joseph Schumpeter, *The Entrepreneur* (Stanford, CA: Stanford Business Books, 2011), pp. 68, 70–71, 85, 92, 101, 115, 134, 140, 201, 242, 245, 265, 267, 301–2.

9   Cited by Walter Isaacson, *Steve Jobs* (New York: Simon & Schuster, 2011), p. 567.

10   Schumpeter, *The Entrepreneur*, p. 208.

11   Ibid., pp. 263–64.

Chapter 8: Silver Spoons and Genetic Lotteries

1   John Rawls, *A Theory of Justice* (Cambridge, MA: Harvard University Press, 1999), p. 274.

2   Peter Schweizer, *Clinton Cash* (New York: HarperCollins, 2015), pp. 77, 101–4, 112–13, 128–30, 133–34; see also Kyle Smith, "Hill and Bill Can't Hide from Shady Deals Exposed in 'Clinton Cash,' " *New York Post*, May 3, 2015, nypost.com; Rosalind Heiderman, "For Clintons, Speech Income Shows How Their Wealth Is Intertwined with Charity," *Washington Post*, April 22, 2015, washingtonpost.com; Nick Bryant, "Flight Logs Put Clinton, Dershowitz on Pedophile Billionaire's Sex Jet," Gawker, January 22, 2015, gawker.com; Michael Weisskopf, "Source: Ex-Wife of Pardoned Fugitive Gave $400,000 to Clinton Library," *Time*, February 9, 2001, time.com.

3   Boethius, *The Consolation of Philosophy* (New York: Penguin, 1969), p. 55.

4   Friedrich Hayek, *The Constitution of Liberty* (Chicago: University of Chicago Press, 2011), p. 157.

5   "The Bill and Warren Show," *Fortune*, July 20, 1998, p. 62.

6   Laurence Zuckerman, "Private Jets for (More of) the People," *New York Times*, June 27, 1999, p. C-2.

7   Niccolò Machiavelli, *The Prince* (New York: Penguin, 1981), pp. 130, 133.

8   "The Bill and Warren Show," pp. 62, 66.

9   Rawls, *A Theory of Justice*, pp. 7, 11, 13–14, 89.

10   Mark Twain, *The Adventures of Huckleberry Finn* (New York: Pocket Books, 1973), p. 160.

Chapter 9: The Godfather

1   Cited by Richard Poe, "Hillary, Obama and the Cult of Alinsky," January 13, 2008, rense.com.

2   Joseph Stiglitz, "In No One We Trust," *New York Times*, December 21, 2013, nytimes.com.

3   This story, on which the subsequent account relies, is told in Peter Schweizer, *Architects of Ruin* (New York: HarperCollins, 2009), see esp. pp. xi, 1–2, 10, 24–25, 47, 77–78, 92, 114, 177.

4   David Huntington, "Summary of Dodd-Frank Financial Regulation Legislation," July 7, 2010, blogs.law.harvard.edu.

5   Vikas Bajaj and Ron Nixon, "For Many Minorities, Signs of Trouble in Foreclosures," *New York Times*, February 22, 2006.

6   "Interview: Saul Alinsky," *Playboy*, March 1972.

7   Sanford Horwitt, *Let Them Call Me Rebel* (New York: Vintage Books, 1992), p. 24.

8   "Interview: Saul Alinsky."

9   Ibid.

10   Mario Puzo, *The Godfather* (New York: Signet Books, 1978), pp. 192–97.

11   "Interview: Saul Alinsky."

12   Ibid.

13   Saul Alinsky, *Rules for Radicals* (New York: Vintage Books, 1989), pp. 30–31, 36.

14   Saul Alinsky, *Reveille for Radicals* (New York: Vintage Books, 1974), p. 224.

15   "Interview: Saul Alinsky"; Alinsky, *Rules for Radicals*, p. ix.

16   Alinsky, *Rules for Radicals*, pp. xxi, 24–25.

17   Horwitt, *Let Them Call Me Rebel*, pp. xv–xvi.

18   Hillary Clinton, "There is Only the Fight: An Analysis of the Alinsky Model," Wellesley College, 1969, economicpolicyjournal.com.

19   Ibid.

20   "Interview: Saul Alinsky."

21   Clinton, "There Is Only the Fight."

22   Horwitt, *Let Them Call Me Rebel*, p. 539.

Chapter 10: Barack and Hillary

1   Suketu Mehta, *Maximum City* (New York: Vintage Books, 2004), p. 245.

2   Mitchell Zuckoff, *Ponzi's Scheme* (New York: Random House, 2006).

3   Barack Obama, *Dreams from My Father* (New York: Three Rivers Press, 2004), pp. 65–68.

4   Cited by Sally Jacobs, *The Other Barack* (New York: PublicAffairs, 2011), p. 86.

5   Ibid., pp. 209–10.

6   Ibid., p. 246.

7   David Maraniss, *Barack Obama: The Story* (New York: Simon & Schuster, 2012), p. 261.

8   Obama, *Dreams from My Father*, pp. 116, 220.

9   Barack H. Obama, "Problems Facing Our Socialism," *East Africa Journal*, July 1965.

10   Cited by Elise O'Shaughnessy, "Harvard Law Reviewed," *Vanity Fair*, June 1990.

11   Saul Alinsky, *Reveille for Radicals* (New York: Vintage Books, 1974), p. 64.

12   David Remnick, *The Bridge* (New York: Knopf, 2010), pp. 132, 137.

13   Hillary Clinton, "There Is Only the Fight: An Analysis of the Alinsky Model," Wellesley College, 1969, economicpolicyjournal.com.

14   Radley Balko, "Rise of the Warrior Cop," *Wall Street Journal*, August 7, 2013, wsj.com.

15   John Milton, *Paradise Lost* (New York: Barnes & Noble Classics, 2004), pp. 43–44.

16   Andrew Kaczynski and Dorsey Shaw, "Watch This Rare, Long-Forgotten Interview with Young Hillary Clinton," BuzzFeed, May 12, 2015, buzzfeed.com.

17   Cited by John Heilemann and Mark Halperin, *Game Change* (New York: Harper, 2010), pp. 218–19.

18   This deal between two feuding cabals is vividly, if somewhat sensationalistically, reported in Edward Klein, *Blood Feud* (Washington, DC: Regnery, 2014).

Chapter 11: The Envy Triangle

1   Mario Puzo, *The Godfather* (New York: Signet Books, 1973), p. 212.

2   Helmut Schoeck, *Envy* (Indianapolis: Liberty Fund, 1987), p. 3.

3   John Milton, *Paradise Lost* (New York: Barnes & Noble Classics, 2004), pp. 40–41.

4   Henry Fairlie, *The Seven Deadly Sins* (Notre Dame, IN: University of Notre Dame Press, 2010), p. 61.

5   Cited by Joseph Epstein, *Envy* (New York: Oxford University Press, 2003), p. 6.

6   Plutarch, "Aristides," reprinted at classics.mit.edu.

7   William Shakespeare, *Othello* (New York: Pocket Books, 1957), p. 109.

8   Michael Young, *The Rise of the Meritocracy* (New Brunswick, NJ: Transaction, 2008), p. 98.

9   Aristotle, *Politics* (New York: Barnes & Noble, 2005), p. 68.

10   Cited by George Anastasia, *Gotti's Rules* (New York: Dey Street, 2015), p. 235.

Chapter 12: Cracking the Con

1   Alexander Hamilton, James Madison, and John Jay, *The Federalist* (New York: Barnes & Noble Classics, 2006), No. 28, pp. 151–52.

2   Charlotte Alter, "The 5 Best Museum Heists in History," *Time*, May 18, 2014, time.com.

3   Friedrich Nietzsche, *Thus Spoke Zarathustra* (Mineola, NY: Dover Publications, 1999), pp. 123–26.

4   Friedrich Nietzsche, *On the Genealogy of Morals* (New York: Barnes & Noble, 2006), p. 94.

5   Franz Kafka, *The Trial* (New York: Schocken Books, 1984), pp. 49, 228–29.

6   William Shakespeare, *Julius Caesar*, Act 1, Scene 3, shakespeare.mit.edu.

INDEX

ABOUT THE AUTHOR

DINESH D'SOUZA is a number one *New York Times* bestselling author and the filmmaker behind the hit documentaries *2016: Obama's America* and *America*, which are respectively the second-highest- and the sixth-highest-grossing political documentaries of all time. In his thirty-year career as a writer, scholar, and public intellectual, D'Souza has been a policy analyst in the Reagan White House and a John M. Olin Fellow at the American Enterprise Institute. His bestselling books include *America*, *Obama's America*, *The Roots of Obama's Rage*, *What's So Great About Christianity*, and *Illiberal Education*.